LOCAL GOVERNMENT

LOCAL GOVERNMENT

By

P. W. JACKSON, M.A.

Lecturer in Government
Swansea College of Technology

SECOND EDITION

LONDON

BUTTERWORTHS

1970

ENGLAND:	BUTTERWORTH & CO. (PUBLISHERS) LTD. LONDON: 88 Kingsway, WC2B 6AB
AUSTRALIA:	BUTTERWORTH & CO. (AUSTRALIA) LTD. SYDNEY: 20 Loftus Street MELBOURNE: 343 Little Collins Street BRISBANE: 240 Queen Street
CANADA:	BUTTERWORTH & CO. (CANADA) LTD. TORONTO: 14 Curity Avenue, 374
NEW ZEALAND:	BUTTERWORTH & CO. (NEW ZEALAND) LTD. WELLINGTON: 49/51 Ballance Street AUCKLAND: 35 High Street
SOUTH AFRICA:	BUTTERWORTH & CO. (SOUTH AFRICA) LTD. DURBAN: 33/35 Beach Grove

ISBN—Casebound: 0 406 60451 7
Limp: 0 406 60452 5

Printed in Great Britain by
Spottiswoode, Ballantyne and Co. Ltd.
London and Colchester

To Audrey and Caroline

Preface to the Second Edition

My objective in this second edition has been to incorporate the main features of the many developments which have taken place in local government since 1967. At that time the reports of the Maud and Mallaby Committees had just been published, but the debate on their analyses and proposals had barely begun, while a Royal Commission had already spent a year on a comprehensive review of local government in England. Since then much new legislation has effected changes in local authority services, and experimental innovations in internal administration, stimulated by Maud, have been introduced; the Royal Commission on England has reported and its proposals, somewhat modified in a subsequent White Paper, have brought the nineteenth century structure to the threshold of a new system.

This edition provides the opportunity to chronicle these developments, to include new legislative provisions and to examine a number of aspects of our system of local government at one of its most interesting periods of change.

April 1970   P. W. JACKSON

Preface to the First Edition

Since the end of the Second World War, local government in England and Wales has undergone a period of critical appraisal. Its structure, constitution, personnel and functions have been examined by various commissions and committees; whilst some local authorities have themselves questioned the adequacy of traditional methods and attitudes in an effort to produce a more efficient service. This book provides an introductory guide to the present system of local government, describes the development of its main features and outlines the attempts which have been made since 1945 to adjust its structure, functions and organisation to contemporary needs.

It has been written with the examination requirements of students in mind, particularly those preparing for the Clerical Division and Diploma in Municipal Administration examinations of the Local Government Training Board, the Intermediate examinations of the Institute of Hospital Administrators and the Institute of Municipal Treasurers and Accountants, and for Advanced level and undergraduate students of the British Constitution. Its contents will also be relevant to Liberal Studies and Citizenship curricula in technical colleges and schools, and I hope that the general reader will also find the book of interest.

A number of people have willingly given their help and I wish to acknowledge my particular indebtedness to: Staffordshire County Council for permission to reproduce a map of their administrative county; Nottinghamshire County Council for the table of services provided; and Cheshire County Council for the diagram of their former committee structure; the Staff of Swansea Reference Library; my colleagues, Messrs. E. A. Hopkins, D. C. Ponsford, R. M. Jones and J. L. Bayliffe, for their advice; Mr. W. Combey, Chief Public Health Inspector of Oxford City Council and Mr. B. Huw Thomas, Senior Rent Officer, Glamorgan, for commenting upon certain sections; Mrs. Elizabeth Ellis for typing the manuscript; and my past and present students whose candid feedback has been so valuable a corrective.

I also wish to add my sincere thanks to my wife who has been a constant source of encouragement and help during the months when the manuscript was being prepared and subsequently during proof-reading.

However, I am wholly responsible for any factual inaccuracies, misinterpretations and exclusions. Regarding the latter, I have tried to include most of the recent developments and legislative provisions, but in an introductory study it is often more difficult to select what might be excluded than what should be included and doubtless my priorities will not satisfy everyone. If the book satisfies the students for whom it is intended my main aim will have been achieved.

Swansea   P. W. Jackson
March 1967

Contents

CHAPTER 1

The History of Local Government

1. Pre-Industrial Origins

The present structure of local government in England and Wales is the product of late nineteenth-century legislation, but its antecedent institutions originated in Saxon days. Self-governing municipalities existed even earlier in Roman Britain, but it was not until the second half of the fifth century, when the Anglo-Saxons infiltrated into east Britain and penetrated westwards along the river valleys, that we may discern the early beginnings of our local government structure.

The major territorial division, the *scir* or shire, developed from the ethnic settlements of Saxons in the middle, east, west and south parts of the country, and of the north and south folk in East Anglia, areas which later became Middlesex, Essex, Wessex, Sussex, Norfolk and Suffolk. Surrey appears to have been the "south region" of a larger territorial area, possibly of Middlesex, while Berkshire, Hampshire, Wiltshire, Somerset and Dorset apparently represented primitive subdivisions of Wessex, which had absorbed the Celtic Devonshire and much of Cornwall by the ninth century.

By the Danish invasion of 865–878 England was divided into several independent kingdoms which were not to be united under one king until the Danelaw was reconquered by the kings of Wessex in the tenth century. By that time, however, the shire system had developed in the midlands (Mercia) from the areas of the Danish boroughs, and certainly by the eleventh century all England with the exception of Northumbria was divided into shires.

"The affairs of the kingdom", remarked King Alfred (871–901), were "various and manifold",[1] and he entrusted responsibility for routine administration in each shire to an official called the *ealdorman* who, in addition, commanded the army within his district and presided at its judicial assembly. Later in the tenth century he came to exercise control over more than one shire, and when this occurred there emerged an official known as the *shire-reeve* or sheriff who presided

---

[1] D. Whitelock, *The Beginnings of English Society*, Pelican, 1952, pp. 72–80.

over the biennial shire moot as the king's representative when the ealdorman was absent.

The shire moot was an assembly of the shire's freemen for administrative, judicial and financial purposes, and much later came to play an important part in the electoral procedure for sending county members to Parliament. After the Norman Conquest, Henry I and Henry II curtailed the growing baronial threat to monopolise the office of sheriff by appointing lesser men who were supervised by itinerant justices. Nevertheless, the sheriff continued to act as the king's agent in the shire throughout the Norman period.

Shires were themselves further subdivided for fiscal, judicial and administrative purposes into *hundreds*. Their existence is first recorded about 950 and they continued until the nineteenth century. They possessed different names in different parts of the country: in Yorkshire, Lincolnshire, Nottinghamshire, Derbyshire, Rutland and Leicestershire they were known by the Danish word *wapentake* (a flourishing of weapons); in Northumberland, Durham and Cumberland they were called *wards*; and in Cornwall some were called shires. In some parts of the country another division existed between the shire and the hundred, known as the *trithing* or *riding* in Yorkshire, the *lathe* in Kent and the *rape* in Sussex.

There were approximately 700 hundreds of varying size, originating, according to one theory, from the area occupied by a hundred families, each family being supported by a *hide* of land. The royal agent in the hundred was the *reeve*, later a bailiff, and effectual control was maintained centrally by the Exchequer and locally by the sheriff. The hundred's main importance during the Middle Ages derived from its regularly held court, where customary law was administered, and as a unit for the collection of customary dues.

"The local and national affairs in early England were not relegated to a favoured few, but were settled in the councils by the people in their several 'moots', or meetings".[2] At the shire moot, each hundred would be represented by its reeve, four "best men" and the priest; at the hundred moot each village was represented; and at the lowest level, the *tun-scipe* (a hedge encircling the homesteads), or township, there was the town moot or folkmoot where every freeman participated in settling local matters. Where a township was fortified, it was named a *burh*, later a borough.

William the Conqueror removed many local powers to central government; the folkmoot was replaced by the *vill* or village, and the shiremoot by the manor court, controlled by the lord's bailiff. When

---

[2] J. J. Clarke, *A History of Local Government*, H. Jenkins, 1955, p. 6.

there was more than one bailiff, the superior bailiff became known as the "major" bailiff or major (mayor) who presided in towns over the meetings of burgesses. Ancient boroughs were often brought under the control of the manor, becoming manorial boroughs. Problems between landlord and tenants were settled at the manorial court which had two main forms—the *court baron* for agricultural problems, transfer of holdings, rights to service, and the *court leet*, dealing originally with criminal offences. Each court appointed officers for one year's compulsory service as haywards, hedge surveyors, pinders, ale-tasters, etc. Some boroughs secured independence of their lord by purchasing from him or the king charters which confirmed earlier privileges or granted various liberties, and many boroughs gained complete self-government in this way. The most important were the municipal corporations which represented the craftsmen of the guilds, the traders and the merchants.

The one institution which remained relatively unaffected by the Normans was the parish. It had developed from obscure origins as a district assigned to a bishop or priest, and in addition to its religious purpose came to possess social and deliberative functions. At its vestry meeting the parishioners discussed matters of common concern, and each year elected from among their number officers to manage parish affairs. The main offices were those of: (a) the *churchwarden*, the custodian of the parish and trustee of its common property; (b) the *constable*, responsible for supervising beggars and the poor; (c) the *surveyor of highways*, responsible for road maintenance; and (d) the *overseer of the poor*, who administered poor relief. Their duties were exacting and unpaid, and each parishioner was obligated to serve for one year when elected.

In Wales indigenous governmental divisions had developed in pre-Norman days. Each kingdom, or *gwlad*, was divided for administrative convenience into *cantrefi*, and each *cantref* comprised about a hundred townships or hamlets. For fiscal and judicial purposes each *cantref* was divided into two or more *cymydau* or commotes. After the Norman Conquest the border lords and marcher families moved into Wales, and their castles and subordinate fortresses became administrative centres for their localities. The lowland "Englishry" and the upland "Welshry" co-existed, with the latter retaining their customs and laws while recognising the overlordship of their alien masters. Where the land was cultivable, the manorial system was established on the feudal pattern of customary services, with agricultural and other matters being decided by bond tenants at the *halmote* or manorial court. Towns grew slowly and charters were bought, but the shire division did not appear until 1284 when the

Statute of Rhyddlan divided Wales into (a) the Principality, comprising the shires of Anglesey, Caernarvon, Merioneth, Cardigan and Carmarthen; (b) the shire of Flint; and (c) the Marcher Lordships, which continued to be ruled by English lords and loyal Welsh chiefs, each with their own courts, officials and laws. The shires were Crown lands and as such formed no part of the realm.

Not until the Act of Union of 1536 were the Marcher Lordships, whose disunity and legal licence had long troubled the monarchy, reorganised into Denbighshire, Montgomeryshire, Radnorshire, Breconshire, Glamorganshire, Monmouthshire and Pembrokeshire. From 1536 onwards the pattern of local government in Wales duplicated that of England.

The Justice of the Peace

The creation of the office of Justice of the Peace marks a new and important stage in the development of local government. Although the title *custos pacis* appears in 1264 to describe men appointed by the king to maintain law and order in each county, it was in 1361 that the office of Justice of the Peace is so named in Edward II's enactment that:

> "In every county of England there shall be assigned for the keeping of the peace one Lord and with him three or four of the most worthy of the counties, together with some learned in the law, and they shall have power to take all of them that be not of good Fame . . ."

They were generally members of the landed gentry entrusted with the preservation of the peace, the punishment of offenders and the control of the parish constables. By 1388 they were assembling on the quarters days at Quarter Sessions to exercise criminal jurisdiction and to deal with administrative matters appertaining to the county.

By Tudor days they had become the governors of the counties, the administrative maids of all work, and, in Maitland's phrase, "judicial beasts of burden". Being local gentry they had an intimate knowledge of their locality, and their status within rural society ensured obedience to their will. As they were unpaid and generally efficient, they were ideal functionaries as far as the Tudors were concerned, and their duties increased as need arose until they had become the main agents of royal power within the counties. They discharged the Elizabethan political and ecclesiastical policy, administered petty justice, and saw to it that all local government functions relating to roads, bridges, the maintenance of law and order were carried out, including the enforcement of the Poor Law, the Statute of Artificers and the regulation of wages and prices.

Thus, under the strict supervision of the Privy Council, the J.Ps. became the central figures in rural England in all judicial, political, economic and administrative matters, and frequently became the member of Parliament for their counties. As the population increased so did their duties, and after the weakening of the Privy Council's control in 1688, their powers grew to dominate almost every branch of social life, civil administration and judicial affairs in the counties. As Lord Coke observed: "The whole Christian world hath not the like office, if duly executed".

The system of local administration described above continued into the nineteenth century. The growth of population, the enclosure movement, the development of industries, and the growing concentrations of population threw burdens upon a local government system which was designed for the easier pace of rural life. The manorial court, the parish vestries, and voluntary service were no longer sufficient to meet the new challenges, nor were the closed oligarchies in towns prepared to relinquish their venal powers. In certain areas local acts had created such *ad hoc* bodies as Improvement Commissioners for paving, cleaning and lighting streets, Guardians of the Poor for poor-relief and Turnpike Trusts for road improvement, but their efforts were piecemeal and un-coordinated.

2. The Nineteenth Century

During the transition years from the eighteenth to the nineteenth centuries, society was consequently in flux, and the increasingly pressing problems of poverty and of community living demanded urgent attention. Leading the reform movement was Jeremy Bentham, the founder of the utilitarian school, who breathed a new life into English law reform and subjected every aspect of institutional life in Church and State to the blunt challenge of its usefulness. His incisive analysis of the utility of governmental institutions shaped not only a new philosophy, based upon the criterion of utility and the principle of the greatest happiness of the greatest number, but helped to create a new society unencumbered by the irrationalities of the past. He advocated a universal franchise, "the ascendancy of the democracy", the vesting of control over administration and expenditure to community representatives, and secret ballots by householders grouped in electoral divisions to elect an annual Parliament which was to be free from monarchic and aristocratic influence.

In local matters, he gave his attention to the main evil of the day, pauperism. His criticism of Pitt's Poor Law Bill of 1796 contributed greatly to its abandonment and he formulated the principle that the

2

able-bodied poor should be offered no alternative to the workhouse. His influence permeated the Poor Law Amendment Act 1834, and the Commissioners adopted his scientific approach in delineating districts and allocating an assistant commissioner to each to investigate conditions. The principle of "less eligibility" bears Bentham's imprint, as do the formation of a central controlling body over the locally-provided service, the demarcation of Poor Law areas according to criteria of convenience and natural features, the payment of officers, and the locally elected body in the Board of Guardians.

A. *The Poor Law Amendment Act* 1834

Meanwhile, the Whigs had forced the passing of the Reform Act 1832, which not only gave the middle class the vote but abolished about fifty rotten boroughs and removed the second member from ninety small towns. These seats would now be redistributed among the fast-growing industrialised urban areas. The Whigs then turned their attention to local matters, particularly the problem of poverty and the inadequate and debasing aspects of Speenhamland and like systems of poor-relief. In 1834 they passed the Poor Law Amendment Act, the main terms being:

1. Outdoor relief was to be abolished, except for the old and the sick.
2. Poor-relief was to be provided only inside the workhouses.
3. Conditions within the workhouses were to be "less eligible", that is, less desirable than those of the lowest-paid worker outside.
4. Parishes were to be grouped into unions, and each union was to maintain a workhouse.
5. Each workhouse was to be managed locally by a Board of Guardians, elected by the ratepayers.
6. The entire scheme was to be administered centrally from Somerset House, by the Poor-Law Commission, composed of three salaried members—the so-called "pinch-pauper triumvirate"—and a secretary, Edwin Chadwick, a disciple of Bentham.

The emphasis of the Act was upon deterring the poor from applying for relief, and the workhouse or, as it was commonly called, "the new Bastille", became reviled and feared by the poor for many succeeding generations.[3] Moreover, it resulted in a drastic reduction in the poor-rates from £27 million spent on poor-relief in 1831, to £5 million in 1851, despite a 29 per cent increase in the population, and was a main contributory cause of Chartism.

---

[3] See Crabbe's poem, *The Village*, for a horrifying description of the conditions within a workhouse, or M. Goodwin, *Nineteenth Century Opinion*, Pelican, 1951, pp. 50–56.

The act did, however, introduce three basic principles of administration in local government: (a) the principle of an *ad hoc* authority in the local Board of Guardians who were elected for the provision and control of a single service within a given area; (b) the principle of an area, the union of parishes, which was appropriate to the service to be provided; and (c) the principle of central control over a local service through the Poor Law Commission.

B. *The Municipal Corporations Act*, 1835

Having abolished corruption at parliamentary elections, the Whig government turned its attention to corruption in the government of towns, and set up a Royal Commission, composed mainly of young Whig lawyers to enquire into the defects in their administration. The majority of town corporations were ruled by self-perpetuating oligarchies of freemen whose status was defined by the charter which had constituted the particular borough. Their right to this status depended upon birth, purchase, gift or apprenticeship to a freeman, and generally they possessed exclusive rights of trading within the borough, of voting at elections and standing for election to the borough council. Charged with the administration of corporate property, the freemen could interpret their functions to include feasting and entertaining, payment of disproportionately large salaries to officials with few duties, and the promotion of self-interest. That they misused corporate property, legally, was indisputable, but as far as the Whigs were concerned, their main besetting sin was the fact that such corporations were controlled by Tories and Anglicans. As Professor Smellie has written:[4]

> "They were snug oases of privilege whose religious discrimination against dissenters, manipulation of markets, tolls and harbours for their more comfortable provision, and indifference to the provision of such urban necessities as competent police, firemen, or clean water and lighted streets, exasperated their under-privileged middle-class neighbours".

The result of the Royal Commission's quickly-drafted and condemnatory report was the passing, after compromises with vested interests in the House of Lords, of the Municipal Corporations Act 1835, which applied to 178 chartered boroughs but omitted London. Its provisions were:

1. Corporate property was to be put under the control of elected councils, who could also, if they wished, take over the duties of the

---

[4] K. B. Smellie, *A History of Local Government*, Allen & Unwin, 1968, p. 30.

Improvement Commissioners and statutory authorities which managed streets, paving, drains and lighting.

2. All ratepayers who had resided in an incorporated town for three years were to receive the vote.

3. One quarter of the council was to consist of aldermen elected by the council (a House of Lords compromise).

4. The accounts of the town clerk were to be audited once a year.

5. Council meetings were to be open to the public.

6. The administration of justice was separated from municipal government by the provision that borough magistrates would in future be appointed by the Crown, as in the counties, and not as formerly, by the borough corporations.

7. Urban communities which were unchartered could adopt the constitution of a municipal corporation.

8. No new areas were created, the council governing either the old borough area or the area of the parliamentary borough.

9. Councils were authorised to appoint paid officials—at least, a Town Clerk and a Treasurer.

10. No new powers, apart from the permissive powers in paragraph 1 above, were conferred. The main difficulty here was the vast population range of boroughs from small and ancient market towns to populous industrial centres, which complicated the framing of provisions about the powers which could be vested in each of them. They were all, however, compelled to appoint Watch Committees to exercise control over the police, to make bye-laws and to control the collection of rates. If they already possessed the statutory power to light part of their area, this power was extended to cover the whole area.

11. Licences might be granted for the sale of drink. To extend such powers the Corporation had to resort to Parliamentary legislation either by general legislation or by local Acts.

The 1835 Act was of fundamental importance to the development of town government. It eradicated existing abuses and prevented their perpetuation in the emergent and fast-expanding communities of industrial England and Wales. Although the franchise appeared to be more democratic than that of 1832, it was, in fact, narrower, and it was still a public vote; but the way was now clear for many of the formerly excluded residents, particularly among the new middle-class industrialists and merchants, to participate in the administration of their towns, and to ensure a high degree of responsible self-govern-ment. Finally, in contrast with the strong central control imposed by the 1834 Poor Law Amendment Act, it is noteworthy that this Act imposed little central control upon the corporations, apart from Treasury approval being required for the floating of local loans and to the alienation of any of the corporate real estate.

A similar lack of centralised control was evident in the Highways Act of the same year, which provided that the vestry of a parish maintaining highways should elect, for one year's duration, one or more persons to fulfil the office of surveyor, or should appoint a salaried surveyor. A well-populated parish could nominate, through its vestry, a highway board; a more sparsely populated parish might apply to the J.Ps., for the formation of a highway district from its combination with a neighbouring parish or parishes, and served by a paid surveyor. The significance of this act lies mainly in its provision for the creation of an *ad hoc* body by the vestries and J.Ps., not its election. It was, moreover, devoid of direction from a central authority. The extension of this model in the proliferation of boards for health, burial, schools and school attendance was to complicate even further local administration later in the century, when a state of chaotic diversity prevailed. Redlich and Hirst cite an earlier writer who described the confused system of 1885 as "a chaos of areas, a chaos of franchises, a chaos of authorities and a chaos of rates".[5]

C. Public Health Legislation

The rapid increase in the population, and its concentration in industrial townships, where houses were quickly erected for the lower orders of society, without such basic amenities as adequate and clean water supplies, refuse disposal arrangements, main drainage or any form of sanitation, had a deleterious effect upon the health of the populace. Filth accumulated in the streets and in the narrow alleyways between the overcrowded dwellings; drinking-water from polluted wells or contaminated rivers was used for cooking and drinking purposes. Contemporary descriptions of the period conjure up an odoriferous nightmare and it is little wonder that disease flourished. Mortality, especially amongst children, was high, and the disposal of the dead created major problems for the living; dirt and disease were everywhere apparent, but the precise nature of the connection was not known until the microbe was discovered. Meanwhile, no machinery existed to alleviate the horrific conditions which promoted ill-health and which in turn helped to increase pauperism.

The extent of the problem had been made apparent to the Poor Law Commissioners when they investigated the causes of destitution, and from their data Edwin Chadwick was able to prepare a memorandum in 1838 which showed that if sickness were prevented, poverty would be reduced and the poor rates would consequently fall. Chadwick established the correlation between ill-health, poverty and

---

[5] J. Redlich and F. W. Hirst, *History of Local Government* (Ed. B. Keith-Lucas), Macmillan, 1958, p. 199.

the foetid sanitary conditions, and wrote about his conclusions in the three-volumed *Report on the Sanitary Conditions of the Labouring Population of Great Britain* in 1842. A Royal Commission was nominated and it reported in 1844 and 1845, confirming Chadwick's conclusions. Legislation was delayed by Corn Laws agitation, but fear of epidemics particularly typhus and cholera, and the visitation of the latter scourge in 1845, claiming 55,000 lives, stimulated the passing of the Public Health Act 1848.

The Act created a strong central authority in the General Board of Health, which had the power to set up boards of health for local health districts, either on petition of one-tenth of the local ratepayers or where the death rate exceeded 23 per 1,000, regardless of whether the inhabitants petitioned for a board. Where a municipal borough adopted the Act, the town council became the local sanitary authority under the control and inspection of the General Board of Health. Outside the boroughs, the urban parts of the unions, established for poor relief under the 1834 Act, were made separate boards of health and became urban sanitary districts. Both districts performed a number of duties which included sewerage, drainage, water-supply, street management, supervision and maintenance of cemeteries and the regulation of offensive trades.

In all, 670 local boards of health were established, but the provision was inadequate to mitigate the health problems of communal living and the powers granted were far too slender. The austere zeal of Chadwick and the coercive central control of the General Board of Health attracted so much criticism that it was reconstituted in 1854 and lingered on until 1858 when its powers were finally transferred to the Privy Council. A series of epidemics between 1858 and 1871 prompted further research into the causation of disease, and the Royal Sanitary Commission of 1868, reporting in 1871, proposed the consolidation of the existing "fragmentary and confused sanitary legislation". It added that "the administration of sanitary law should be made uniform, universal, and imperative throughout the Kingdom", and also that "all powers requisite for the health of towns and country should in every place be possessed by one responsible local authority, kept in action, and assisted by a superior authority".

The Government accepted the Royal Commission's report immediately and the Local Government Act 1871, was passed. It created the Local Government Board, to which the Privy Council transferred its public health functions as did the Home Office; also transferred were the functions of the Poor Law Board and those of the Registrar-General's office. A further Act of 1872 transferred the Home Office's functions under the Highway Acts and Turnpike

Acts to the Local Government Board, and local sanitary authorities were established throughout England and Wales, outside London.

Finally, all the laws relating to public health were consolidated by the important Public Health Act 1875, which divided England and Wales, outside London, into urban and rural sanitary districts, the former being the districts of boroughs, of improvement commissioners, and of local *ad hoc* boards, and the latter being the poor law unions minus those parts which were within the urban districts. The local boards of the urban sanitary authorities were to be elected, whilst the rural authorities were to be governed by the poor-law guardians. Exercising supervisory control over the entire system was the Local Government Board.

The structure which thus emerged from the 1875 Act presaged the future pattern of local government, embodying the twin principles of central control of local authorities through a government department and of local responsibility for the administration of services through elected representatives. The assumption of additional responsibilities e.g., by the 1875 Act urban sanitary authorities also became highway authorities for their areas, and by the Elementary Education Act of 1870 boroughs and conurbations of parishes became school districts, anticipated the emergence of omnibus authorities and foreshadowed a dwindling reliance on *ad hoc* bodies for the running of local services. Moreover, the Reform Act of 1867, which had extended the franchise to the urban workman in municipal as well as parliamentary elections, had infused a new and radical vigour into the municipal administration of the big towns and had predisposed their councils to welcome responsibility for additional community services.

D. *Reform of County Government*

In the counties numerous attempts had been made since Joseph Hume's County Board Bill in 1836, to substitute elected representatives for the bench of nominated magistrates, "who levy and direct the expenditure of rates", yet, "are independent of those who pay them". The J.Ps.' powers appeared unassailable and their functions increased during the first half of the nineteenth century, particularly in the rural areas. Their judicial powers in Petty Sessions had been widely extended and by legislation of 1835 and 1839 they had added functions relating to highways and the police. Moreover, they wielded great influence at county elections where, up to 1884, there was a more favourable representation, proportionate to population, than in the boroughs.

Hume wanted to transfer their administrative functions to a new authority, the County Board, elected by the county ratepayers, but the Bill got no further than the first reading on two occasions. In 1849, with county rates rising steadily, Hume introduced a moderate County Rates and Expenditure Bill, which proposed County Boards comprising an equal partnership of J.Ps. and representatives nominated by county Boards of Guardians. This was dropped, and in 1850 a second County Rates and Expenditure Bill was introduced by Milner Gibson, which recommended County Boards made up half of J.Ps. and half of directly elected representatives of the ratepayers. The Select Committee to which it was referred reported against it, and it too was unsuccessful. A like fate befell similar bills in 1851, 1852 and 1860. Three further attempts were made in 1868 and in that year a Select Committee of Inquiry was appointed.

It reported in July, and in February 1869 the Queen's speech included a reference that "a measure will be introduced for applying the principle of representation to the control of the county rate by the establishment of financial boards for the counties". The bill proposed to add members elected by the Board of Guardians to the County Bench for administrative matters. It was finally introduced in May, and withdrawn two months later.

Thus thirty-three years of effort and campaigning to give the counties representative government came to an abortive conclusion. Happily, county government was not in the same corrupt state as the boroughs had been, and the J.Ps. on the County Bench provided a generally efficient standard of administration which was acceptable to the landed gentry and merchants from whose numbers they were appointed and whose interests they safeguarded.

However, with the increasing unionisation of agricultural employees and the spirit of radicalism in the counties, legislation to extend the franchise to agricultural workers could not be postponed indefinitely, and was finally achieved by the Reform Act 1884.

E. *The Local Government Act* 1888

The Conservative Government of 1886 depended upon the support of Joseph Chamberlain's Liberal Unionists, and it was under their influence that the Local Government Bill was introduced in 1888. Previously Sir Charles Dilke, the president of the Local Government Board from 1882 to 1885, had drawn up a bill which had envisaged elected councillors, without aldermen, for the counties, a reform of the unions and the districts, the dissolution of school boards and the transfer of their functions to the borough and district councils, and the exclusion of boroughs with a population of 100,000 or more from control by the county.

Such a radical and wide-ranging measure would undoubtedly have stimulated much political controversy, and little further was heard of it until it was presented in a much-modified form by the Conservatives in 1888. According to Redlich and Hirst the Bill

"was much more than a party manoeuvre. It was a measure conceived in a statesmanlike spirit to get rid of anomalies, and to supply wants which could not be supplied by the existing organisation. In truth, the substance of 'administrative law' had so grown in bulk and variety during the past two decades, that it could not satisfactorily be dealt with by the old machinery".[6]

The main features of the Act were:

1. The administrative powers and duties of the J.Ps. were to be transferred to county councils composed of representatives directly elected by the ratepayers. Counties maintained their historic boundaries, and with certain exceptions each administrative county had one council. The exceptions were Yorkshire and Lincolnshire, each with three administrative counties, and Suffolk and Sussex, Cambridgeshire and Northamptonshire each with two.

2. Each county was to be divided into electoral districts of equal size, and each ratepayer was to have one vote.

3. All towns with a population of more than 50,000 (i.e. fifty-seven towns), together with Burton-on-Trent, Canterbury, Chester and Worcester, were excluded from the administrative county structure and granted the status of county boroughs. Their burgesses were to take no part in county council elections.

4. The major problem of London government was to be resolved by the creation of an administrative county for the metropolitan area, excluding the City and Corporation of London.

The 1888 Act was a major reform which established the dual system of local government in the autonomous county borough and the administrative county; bodies which still form the twin bases of local government in England and Wales. The diminution in the role of the J.P. was lamented by the landed and manufacturing classes in the counties, but lauded by others who saw the J.Ps. as embodiments of a regressive oligarchic control, and regretted that their judicial functions had not also been removed.

The Act did nothing, however, to simplify the structure of government in the districts, although the original bill had included proposals relating to district councils. These proposals had been excluded before the committee stage, partly because they appeared to be premature. The subordinate authorities needed to be reformed

---

[6] Redlich and Hirst, *op cit.*, p. 197

and integrated into the democratic structure which was coalescing.

The Liberal party hoped that the extension of the franchise to the agricultural workers would rebound to its advantage within the counties and particularly in the parishes which had long been the focus of their attention. Since Goschen's Bill of 1871 had highlighted the parish unit as the basis of a reconstituted local government system, the Liberals had campaigned to reform rural and parochial government. Their resolutions to extend representative government to the rural divisions to some extent re-echoed the earlier nostalgia of Toulmin Smith who, on the basis of a mistaken interpretation of history, advocated a return to village democracy as exemplified in the Greek city states. Throughout the 1880's Gladstone reaffirmed the belief of the National Liberal Federation that the inhabitants of rural divisions should receive the benefits of local government, and in 1889 he censured the government for not establishing district councils, adding that the government should "go still nearer to the door of the masses of the people".

F. *The Local Government Act* 1894

The pressure (for the establishment of elected councils in parishes and rural districts) continued unabated during the next four years, until, in March, 1893, the President of the Local Government Board in Gladstone's fourth administration introduced "the last of the great constructive measures which built up a democratic system of local government in England".[7] After much opposition, particularly from the Lords, the bill was enacted in March, 1894. The main provisions were:

1. Local self-government was introduced into rural parishes by providing for parish councils, elected by all the rate-paying inhabitants, in the larger parishes, and establishing parish meetings of all rate-paying inhabitants in the smaller parishes.

2. The urban and rural sanitary districts established by the Public Health Acts of 1848–75 were reconstituted as urban and rural district councils, elected by the same popular suffrage as the parish councils.

3. Boards of Guardians were reconstituted, and guardians were elected as above. In rural parishes, there was to be no special election of Guardians, and each rural district councillor would represent his parish on the Board of Guardians.

Thus within the span of sixty-two years from the first Reform Act, every part of England and Wales was administered at the local level by an elected council, and the pattern of organisation completed by

---

[7] Redlich and Hirst, *op cit.*, p. 216.

the Local Government Act of 1894 has remained in existence to the present day.

A high measure of corporate unity has been given to each type of local authority by the formation, generally soon after the 1888 and 1894 legislation, of Local Authority Associations. The County Councils Association represents all county councils; the Association of Municipal Corporations, formed in 1873, now represents all the eligible authorities; the Urban District Councils Association, formed in 1890 as the Local Boards Association and assuming its present title in 1895, represents most of the eligible authorities; and the Rural District Councils Association, founded in 1895, represents all R.D.Cs. The most recently formed in 1947 was the National Association of Parish Councils with a membership of over 6,000 parishes. Membership is voluntary and the fee is based on the population size of each local authority. Their objects are to protect the rights, interests and privileges of their member authorities as they might be affected by proposed or enacted legislation, or by orders or regulations made by government departments. They disseminate information on matters of importance to their members and take action on any matter which is of interest or concern to their members. The associations have stimulated the formation of a number of bodies for their mutual benefit. They are well represented on the Local Authorities' Conditions of Service Advisory Board; they hold half the membership of the employers' side of the Board of the National Joint Council; they instituted the Local Authorities Mutual Investment Trust in 1961, and the Local Government Information Office in 1963; they were jointly responsible with the G.L.C. and the London Boroughs Committee for the establishment of the Local Government Computer Committee in 1965 from which developed the Local Authorities Management Services and Computer Committee in 1967; they were responsible with the minister for the appointment of the Maud and Mallaby Committees in 1964; and they held ten of the twenty-four seats on the Local Government Examinations Board from 1946 and are similarly prominent on the Local Government Training Board, formed from the L.G.E.B. in 1967.

Despite the undoubted activity of the associations, of which there is ample evidence throughout this book, the Maud Report referred to the "separateness" of the associations which "does not lend itself easily to vigorous action in the interests of local government as a whole. Separately . . . (they) do not present a single focal point for local government whereas together they could present an indentifiable institution of great national importance". The committee therefore recommended that the associations should set up a Local

Government Central Office which would bring together such central institutions as already existed. The Redcliffe-Maud Report called for "a single, powerful association to look after the interests of local government and to speak for it", and expressed the hope that with reorganisation the new authorities would join one association.

3. Twentieth Century Developments

One of the problems which had remained unsolved by the end of the nineteenth century was the continued existence of the Poor Law Guardians. The absorption of the work of this *ad hoc* body by the existing local authorities had been contemplated during the last quarter of the nineteenth century, but little was done about the Poor Law until Balfour's appointment in 1905 of a Royal Commission on the Poor Law and the Relief of Distress through Unemployment.

The Poor Law was still that of the 1601 Act as amended by the principles and machinery of 1834. Studies such as those of General Booth, Charles Booth and B. Seebohm Rowntree showed the chronic state of poverty of the working class in the 1890's. The Commisson found that during 1906–7 nearly two million people, excluding casuals and inmates of lunatic asylums, were in receipt of poor relief. The Poor Law was not administered uniformly, with outdoor relief in the form of money or in kind still being given, and mixed workhouses had barely changed since 1834. In 1909 the commissioners produced a majority report and a minority report.

The former, signed by fifteen members, advocated the abolition of mixed workhouses and proposed that the children, the aged and the infirm should be housed in separate institutions, and that the Poor Law should be radically reformed. The Minority Report, signed by four members who included Beatrice Webb and George Lansbury, went much further. It showed that since 1834 such services as public education, public health regulations, workmen's compensation, unemployment legislation and old age pensions had developed to prevent poverty, not cure it, and they consequently proposed the repeal of the 1834 Act and the abolition of Poor Relief and the Boards of Guardians, with their punitive attitude towards poverty. The powers and duties of Destitution Authorities were to be transferred to county and county borough councils, and children, the infirm, the aged and the mentally defective were to be cared for by *ad hoc* committees of these councils.

No action was taken by the government, however, to carry out any of the proposals, and the Poor Law and its Guardians continued to carry out their functions. The number of Labour or Socialist Guardians had, however, increased after the early 1890's, particularly in the poor areas of London, and there followed a period of activity particularly under the leadership of Lansbury and Crooks on the Poplar board, when relief was provided freely, much to the chagrin of the ratepayers and the Local Government Board. Eventually, after the imprisonment of the Poplar mayor and twenty-nine council members, for refusal to pay the London County Council precept on the pretext of the high cost of the poor relief, the cost was spread to the richer London boroughs by the Local Authorities (Financial Provisions) Act 1921. This Act gave the Poplar Guardians the money they wanted and they continued to distribute it freely, undeterred by threats from the Ministry of Health.

Briefly, in 1923, and again from 1924, the Minister of Health was Neville Chamberlain. His antipathy to "Poplarism", where surcharges had amounted to £86,600, together with evidence of corruption and nepotism in other authorities, and the financial difficulties of some Boards during the General Strike, with some allegedly financing the strike out of rates, ultimately led to Chamberlain's resolve to reorganise the Poor Law and abolish the Guardians. This was eventually achieved with the Local Government Act 1929, which abolished the Boards of Guardians and transferred their functions to the county and county borough councils.

The same Act also reorganised local government finance. Some measure of rating reform had been achieved four years earlier by the Rating and Valuation Act 1925, which abolished the overseers and transferred their powers to the local authorities. In addition, the variety of rates, the poor rate, the district rate, etc., were replaced by a single consolidated General Rate. Chamberlain had wanted to rationalise the structure of the grants-in-aid by substituting block grants for health services and needy areas for most of the assigned revenues and some of the percentage grants.

However, Winston Churchill as Chancellor wished to integrate these ideas with his own to remit the major part of the rates paid by industrial hereditaments, and to reimburse local authorities with a bigger block grant. The arrangement which was finally written into the bill was for the relief of industrial hereditaments of three-quarters of their rates, and agricultural lands and buildings were wholly derated. Additionally, the majority of assigned revenues and the percentage grants for public health were abolished. To compensate for these and to help equalise the burden of local expenditure an annual exchequer grant was to be made, computed for each local authority for a five-year period and paid out on the basis of need.

Other provisions of the Act included the transfer of many minor roads from county districts to county councils, and the latter were also required to undertake ten-yearly reviews of county district boundaries, and submit their reorganisation plans to the Minister. As a result of the reviews undertaken between 1929 and 1938, urban districts were reduced in number by 255, and rural districts by 169.

The main achievement of Chamberlain's successor, Arthur Greenwood, was the codification of the law relating to local government. He appointed the Chelmsford Committee in 1930 and from it emerged three major consolidating acts—the Local Government Act 1933, the Public Health Act 1936, and the Food and Drugs Act 1938—which effectively clarified the intricacies and inconsistencies of a mass of prior legislation. Thus by 1939 there existed

> "both the beginning of a consistent code of local government law and a uniform hierarchy of local authorities constituted in accordance with uniform principles. At last, it was thought, local government had been rationalised, and a logically consistent picture of its principles could be drawn".[8]

Certain changes had been taking place in the scope of local authority functions. In 1929 responsibility for hospitals was transferred from the minor to the major authorities; in 1930 the licensing of passenger road services was removed from local authorities to Traffic Commissioners; and in 1936 the trunk roads in counties became the responsibility of the Traffic Commissioners. The 1939–45 war accelerated the changes and imposed new demands. The immediate need was for national defence and local authorities were required to build air-raid shelters, organise warden and reserve services, appoint an Air-Raid Precautions Controller, arrange for the evacuation of children from target areas and their billetting in the regions. Such extra duties had to be provided in addition to the usual range of services, and provided, moreover, with a depleted staff. The tendency towards centralisation of control was intensified and may be seen, for example, in the merging of local fire brigades into a National Fire Service which was to remain until 1947. At the same time, the threat of imminent invasion and the capture of London necessitated the decentralisation of certain ministries concerned with civil defence and other wartime services into twelve regions, each with its own regional headquarters.

Between 1934 and 1948 various enactments transferred functions from the minor to the major authorities, and from local government

---

[8] W. O. Hart, *Introduction to the Law of Local Government and Administration* (7th Edn.), Butterworths, p. 33.

to central departments and *ad hoc* bodies. The Education Act 1944, placed the responsibility for public education upon the counties and county boroughs. The National Health Service Act 1946, transferred all local authority hospitals and nursing homes to the control of Regional Hospital Boards and Hospital Management Committees, while county districts lost responsibility for their health and welfare services to the counties. By the Police Act 1946, county districts lost their police function to the counties. The Trunk Roads Act 1946, removed responsibility for certain highways in specified districts to the Minister of Transport. Under the Fire Services Act 1947, county district fire brigades were taken over by the counties, as were their town and country planning functions by the Town and Country Planning Act 1947. The Transport Act 1947, transferred canal and harbour undertakings to the British Transport Commission, and under the River Boards Act 1948, responsibility for the prevention of river pollution was transferred to the River Boards. Valuation for rating became an Inland Revenue function by the Local Government Act 1948.

Meantime, two of the main municipal undertakings were nationalised by the Electricity Act 1947, and the Gas Act 1948, both industries passing out of the control of municipal and private enterprise to the control of area boards. The Transport Act 1947, threatened local authorities with the loss of municipal passenger road transport services.

The gains by local authorities during this period were the powers to provide and administer civic restaurants, under the Civic Restaurants Act 1947, to provide and support entertainments and the arts, under the Local Government Act 1948, and certain extended powers were given to the major authorities by the Town and Country Planning Act 1947, and the Children Act 1948.

Thus within four years there was a considerable recasting of local authority functions, and an overall loss of power and responsibility by local government. Meanwhile, the control exercised by the central departments continued to increase and the functions remaining to local authorities became more intricate and specialised. One result was a questioning of the adequacy of local government as it was constituted to cope with the demands being made upon it and whether its structure should be reorganised. The twenty years following the 1945 White Paper, *Local Government in England and Wales during the Period of Reconstruction* (Cmd. 6579) are largely absorbed by attempts to effect changes which were desirable "in the interests of effective and convenient local government", and the next chapter considers the various machinery set up to achieve this purpose. At the same time, however, much publicity has been given to the supersession of the traditional structure by some form of regionalism.

Regionalism may be defined either as (a) administrative decentralisation from Whitehall and the establishment of regional offices for the better utilisation of an area's resources, or (b) the remodelling of the existing structure of local government into larger territorial units. The first meaning is unlikely to have a major structural repercussion upon local government, whereas the second heralds the death-knell to the structure and the form of representative government which have developed since the latter years of the nineteenth century.

The concept is not new. In 1921, G. D. H. Cole in *The Future of Local Government* proposed the division of England into nine regions, each having a directly elected council; and during the Second World War Britain was, in fact, divided for defensive purposes into twelve autonomous and viable areas each under the control of a regional commissioner. This structure was unpopular with the local authorities, but since the war, regional organisation structures have been adopted by the Ministries of Labour, Pensions and National Insurance, Housing and Local Government, Health and the Board of Trade. Similarly, such public services as gas, electricity, hospitals, the coal industry and the railways are organised on regional patterns, while for census and demographic statistics England is divided into nine distinct regions.

A notable contribution to the argument for regionalism was that of J. P. Mackintosh who proposed eleven regions, with nine regional councils in England and two regional assemblies for Wales and Scotland.[9] Each would have "considerable power in terms of population and resources", would discharge extensive functions and would engage staff comparable in quality with the Civil Service. The regional councils would be directly elected for three years and organised on a parliamentary pattern with a prime minister and a cabinet, the latter consisting of about eight ministers responsible for departments not committees. Second-tier authorities would be decided by the regional governments and would vary from region to region in accordance with need, opinion and tradition. Such a scheme, it was suggested, would make a degree of devolution of central powers possible, permit regional variations of policy and local control, and meet "the legitimate aspirations of the Welsh and Scots for a degree of self-government".

Local authorities are naturally reluctant to espouse the cause of regionalism in the form of far larger and far fewer representative

---

[9] J. P. Mackintosh, *The Devolution of Power*, Chatto and Windus, 1968.

"local" authorities; and apart from the Liberals who favour such a structure, neither of the two major parties appear to envisage such a drastic change.

Nevertheless, the pressure of population congestion in the South and the Midlands, the decline of traditional industries in the North, in Scotland and in Wales and the under-utilisation of the resources of these areas constitute the bases of regional imbalance and have caused successive governments since 1945 much concern. The employment problems in the North-East were studied in 1963 by Lord Hailsham and a White Paper was produced, designating the area as a "growth zone". Further studies in the South-East, the West Midlands, the North-West and Mid-Wales followed. The Queen's Speech on 3 November, 1964, referred to the preparation of: "Central and regional plans to promote economic development; with special reference to the needs of under-employed areas of the country . . ." The following day, Mr. George Brown, the then Secretary of State for Economic Affairs, announced that the government's regional plans would take place within a national framework, with regional and national planning inter-related. To ensure regional plans were based on local needs two bodies were to be established:

1. *Advisory Regional Councils* with small memberships representing both sides of industry, the local authorities, the universities and commerce; they would have no executive powers nor would they replace the local authorities but would help in the study and analysis of their region's problems, and give advice; and

2. *Regional Planning Boards* comprising representatives of the main economic and social departments (i.e. all civil servants), each with a chairman appointed by Mr. Brown and staff from the Department of Economic Affairs. They were to be based in a regional headquarters and would work with the advisory regional councils and collaborate with the local authorities who would be responsible for implementing regional plans.

On 10 December Mr. Brown developed the scheme further and stated that the purposes of the regional councils and boards were to provide effective machinery for a full and balanced development of the country's economic and social resources and to ensure the regional implications of growth were taken into account in the planning of land use, development and services. He named six regions (two more were added in August, 1965) and regional headquarters. *The Times* (11 December, 1964) commented that the proposals revealed

> "a clear spreading of the Whitehall machinery into the regions. The Department of Economic Affairs is about to spawn provincial tentacles. . . . This will make for better decisions in the

3

light of local conditions and will make co-ordination with the national plans all the easier".

The newspaper then went on to point out:

"The snags may arise when these new links with Whitehall have to be fitted alongside the existing relations of local authorities with individual ministries in London. The machinery for carrying out changes in land use, for example, will presumably remain unaffected, although overall strategy will now be worked out by the new boards".

Mr. Brown emphasised that the regional bodies "will not affect the existing powers of local authorities", but many councils were perturbed about the long-term effect of the regional bodies upon their functions, particularly town and country planning. They suspected further limitation of their powers and feared that the regional bodies would form an intrinsic new tier, intruding upon and crossing their direct line of communication with Whitehall. The *Municipal Journal* (18 December, 1964) referred to

"the feeling that there is a threat to eliminate democratic local government",

and the *Local Government Chronicle* (23 January, 1965) commenting on the "wide misgiving" stated that

"a Birmingham alderman said that the people of Birmingham were not going to be 'shoved around'. The principal objection of many Local Authorities seemed to be that they would prefer to be obstructed by a Minister than by a regional economic board".

Professor T. E. Chester and Mr. I. R. Gough[10] state that one way in which local authorities are responding to the challenge of regionalism is by their combination for joint action—in the North local authorities have combined for industrial development, airport provisions, tourism, sport and art; in the West Country a number of local authorities have commissioned an economic survey of their combined areas; in the North-East the London Standing Conference on Regional Planning has brought the planning authorities of the area together; and in South-East Lancashire and North-East Cheshire a Transportation Study has involved sixty-two local authorities. The authors conclude their article by referring to the uneasiness and suspicion of local authorities to the regional bodies:

---

[10] *District Bank Review*, March, 1966.

"In this climate of opinion will it be possible to convince local authorities that the introduction of Regionalism is exactly the opposite to centralisation? It should mean in part the exercise of authority by a body nearer 'to the ground' and therefore much more aware of their needs than the remote officials in London who at present have the final say".

The local authorities are likely to retain their hostility, however, while there exists even the remotest possibility that in the pursuance of economic and technical objectives the regional bodies may find it inexpedient to tolerate what they may perceive to be the administrative shortcomings of the local authorities. The Chairman of the North-West's regional council was quoted as saying that:

"At the moment we are no more than caretakers conducting psychological warfare. If, as a result, local authorities begin to think on a regional basis all could be well. If the authorities do not co-operate we will have to be given executive powers. This is the rock on which we shall split".[11]

It is in the context of such attitudes and resultant fears that we may study the present organisation of local government, and view the attempts which have been made since 1945 to reform its structure. Here too it will be apparent that with every proposal for reform, from the work of the Local Government Boundary Commission (1945–49) to the Report of the Royal Commission on Local Government in England (1966–69), the one persistent fear is that structural change involving larger and fewer authorities will sweep away many councils and their members, so weakening the allegedly democratic content of local government. It will be observed that the real problems associated with change are largely human and emotional, and it may be unrealistic to expect any vested interest to agree willingly to its own demise without some defensive resistance and a strongly emotive appeal to loyalty and tradition. It would appear, however, that the only alternative to change is the continuation of the faults and failings of local government as revealed by successive examinations since 1945 and the consequential withering of local government as an effective, representative institution. The next chapter traces the attempts which have been made in the last quarter century to produce the changes which are regarded as necessary if the quality of local government and its services are to be improved.

---

[11] *Sunday Times*, 6 February, 1966.

CHAPTER 2

Structure and Reorganisation

1. The Units of Local Government

"For the purposes of local government, England and Wales (exclusive of London) shall be divided into administrative counties and county boroughs, and administrative counties shall be divided into county districts, being either non-county boroughs, urban districts or rural districts, and county boroughs and county districts shall consist of one or more parishes".

Local Government Act 1933, *Part I, Section I*

The Local Government Acts of 1888 and 1894 established the dual system—one form of administration for county boroughs, which were in the main densely populated viable towns, and one for the more extensive counties. Both are organised separately, the former being a unitary system in which all powers are vested in one authority, while the latter is organised on a two- or three-tier pattern with a division of responsibility for services between its constituent parts.

A. County Boroughs

The Local Government Act 1888, created sixty-one county boroughs from the largest municipalities and empowered the Local Government Board (later the Minister of Health) to make Orders, subject to parliamentary confirmation, conferring county borough status on non-county boroughs with populations of not less than 50,000. A similar procedure was provided for extending county borough boundaries. Alternatively, a county borough could attempt to achieve either objective by promoting a Private Bill. By 1923, an additional twenty-one county boroughs had been created and many of the original sixty-one had been enlarged.

By the Local Government (County Boroughs and Adjustments) Act 1926, the minimum population requirement for county borough status was raised to 75,000 and by the Local Government (Boundary Commission) Act 1945 (repealed in 1949) and the Local Government

24

Act 1958, it was further raised to 100,000, although local authorities with smaller populations are not precluded from applying. Population is only one of the factors, the prime qualification for promotion being the local authority's fitness to discharge the functions of a county borough; other factors taken into account are resources, administrative record, and the likely effect of promotion upon the "parent" administrative county. On 1 April, 1968, there were eighty-three county boroughs in England and Wales, thirty-five of which each had population figures below 100,000.

The council of a county borough consists of a mayor, aldermen and councillors who exercise all the powers vested in the corporation. In addition to the City of London, twenty county boroughs have a Lord Mayor[1] and thirty county boroughs, fifteen Municipal Boroughs and one Urban District Council have the status and dignity of a City. Neither title has any local government significance, but both are honours conferred by the Crown by letters patent.

B. Administrative Counties

The Local Government Act 1888, established sixty-two administrative counties. With certain exceptions, they are co-extensive with the geographical county or shire (excluding the county boroughs), and are based upon the areas to which the commissions of the various county justices in Quarter Sessions applied and whose administrative duties they took over.

The need to take account of certain ancient franchises and liberties has resulted in twelve administrative counties whose boundaries do not coincide with geographical county boundaries. Their division into administrative counties is as follows:

> Lincolnshire—Holland, Kesteven and Lindsey
> Suffolk—East Suffolk and West Suffolk
> Sussex—East Sussex and West Sussex
> Yorkshire—East Riding, North Riding and West Riding
> Hampshire—Hampshire and the Isle of Wight.

When the London Government Act 1963, came into effect on 1 April, 1965, the Counties of London and Middlesex were abolished. Also on 1 April, 1965, two new administrative counties were created, one in Cambridgeshire and Isle of Ely (from the separate administrative counties of Cambridge and the Isle of Ely), and the other in Huntingdon and Peterborough (from the separate administrative counties of Huntingdonshire and the Soke of Peterborough). There

---

[1] *Municipal Year Book* 1967, pp. 927–928.

are thus fifty-eight administrative counties at present, forty-five in England and thirteen in Wales (if Monmouthshire is included).

County councils are bodies corporate each consisting of a chairman, aldermen and councillors. Elections are held triennially in April, and all councillors retire together. County aldermen are elected by the council from their own number or from people qualified to be councillors, for six years, one half retiring triennially.

Administrative counties are organised on a two- or three-tier basis, the county council being responsible for certain services and the county districts—non-county boroughs, urban and rural districts—discharging other services within their own areas. The county districts may also have certain functions delegated to them by the county council. A rural district may be divided into parish councils and parish meetings which perform certain functions and provide a third tier to the county hierarchy.

Provision is made in the Local Government Act 1933, for a county council to review the circumstances of its county districts and to consider the need for effecting changes by the alteration or definition of their boundaries, their division, the transfer of parts, the conversion of rural into urban districts, or vice versa, or the formation of new urban or rural districts or parishes. The procedure for effecting such changes by ministerial order is detailed in Section 146 of the Act.

C. *Non-County Boroughs*

Non-County Boroughs, or municipal boroughs, have the same constitution as county boroughs but their functions resemble more closely those of an urban district. They vary widely in population, resources, and antiquity, and although many are substantial towns they are generally smaller than the county boroughs whose autonomy they often envy from their position of subordination to the county council's control. On 1 April, 1968 there were 259 non-county boroughs.

Boroughs may now be created by an order under the Local Government Act 1958, but more often have historic charters of incorporation granted by former monarchs which bestow certain special rights and privileges such as the right of owning property, and of suing and being sued in their own name. A noteworthy legal nicety is that whereas all county, district and parish councils are bodies corporate, their inhabitants are not incorporated by law; in any borough, however, it is the inhabitants, i.e. the burgesses (who include the mayor and aldermen) and not the council who form the municipal corporation, but the corporation can act only through its council.

TABLE 1. THE ADMINISTRATIVE COUNTY OF STAFFORDSHIRE

KEY

County Boroughs

Urban Districts

Municipal Boroughs

Rural Districts

County Boroughs are not included
in the Administrative County

Parishes not included

Under the provisions of the Seventh Schedule to the Local Government Act 1958, the possibility exists for the creation of a new type of borough, the *rural borough*. In this case an ancient non-county borough which is small in size and unable to provide the services which are demanded by law merges with an adjacent rural district, but continues to preserve its traditional and ancient privileges although its powers are those of a parish council. Its corporation comprises a mayor, councillors and burgesses, but no aldermen. By 1969 seven rural boroughs had been created.

D. Urban and Rural Districts

These are based upon the urban and rural sanitary districts set up by the Public Health Acts of 1872 and 1875. Under the Local Government Act 1894, urban district councils were established to administer those urban sanitary districts which were still governed by improvement commissioners or local boards of health, and rural district councils replaced the rural sanitary areas governed by the poor law guardians.

The Local Government Act 1933, required that every urban or rural district should have an urban or rural district council, comprising a chairman and councillors. The chairman is elected annually from the councillors or persons qualified to be councillors of the district. Elections are held in May, either annually or triennially, and councillors hold office for three years. Over 400 councils hold annual elections at which one-third of the councillors are elected. Annual elections may be replaced by triennial elections if a district council passes a resolution to that effect by a two-thirds majority, and the county council approves and makes an order providing that all district councillors shall retire together and a new council shall be elected every third year.

On 1 April, 1968 there were 522 urban district councils and 469 rural district councils (including the Council of the Isles of Scilly). All district councils must hold at least four meetings in every year. They are bodies corporate and have the dignity of a common seal.

E. Parishes

Resurrected as local government units by the Local Government Act 1894, every rural parish is required to have a parish meeting at which every local government elector may participate. By the Local Government Act 1933, rural parishes with a population of 300 or more are required to have a parish council consisting of a chairman and councillors and if the population is between 200 and 300 the county council is required by order to create a parish council if the parish meeting asks for one. If the population is under 200 there is no requirement for the county council to create a parish council but may do so at the request of the parish meeting.

If there is a parish council the parish meeting must meet at least once a year, in March; if there is no parish council the parish meeting becomes the local government authority for the parish and must hold at least a second meeting in each year. A parish council must hold at least four meetings in every year. On 1 April, 1968, there were about 7,500 parish councils in England and Wales and each consisted of a chairman and between five and twenty-one councillors elected for three years and all retiring together; the actual number of councillors will be determined by the county council. The chairman of the parish council is entitled to preside at parish meetings, but if there is no parish council the parish meeting annually chooses its own chairman.

A parish council is incorporated, whereas a parish meeting is not. Where there is no parish council, property is held by "the Representative Body" consisting of the chairman of the parish meeting and the councillor or councillors of the R.D.C. elected by the parish, and together they form a body corporate with perpetual succession. Neither parish council nor parish meeting has been granted a common seal.

Should a rural district consist wholly of one parish, the R.D.C. will have the functions of the parish. Also, two or more parishes, whether in the same rural district or not, may be combined under a single parish council, providing the parish meetings have consented.

Urban parishes, i.e. civil parishes within the boundaries of boroughs or urban districts, have no local government significance, their functions, apart from those of an ecclesiastical or charitable nature, having been transferred to the borough or urban district councils by the Local Government Act 1933.

F. *Greater London Government*

The units of local government in Greater London differ from those which obtain throughout England and Wales and are considered in detail in Chapter 3. Under the provisions of the London Government Act 1963, the Greater London Council and thirty-two London Boroughs came into being on 1 April, 1965, while the City of London Corporation retained its unique position and added to its powers.

The structure of local government is customarily illustrated by the following diagram which conveniently summarises the foregoing description:

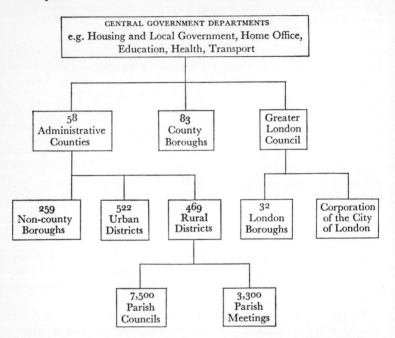

Unfortunately, the simplicity and order of such a diagram gives little indication of the weaknesses in the structure. Criticisms are directed at: the existence in all categories of too many small local authorities with inadequate resources, population and areas to provide and support adequate services; the difficulties of accommodating a number of services, each requiring different conditions for optimum efficiency and economy, in areas which are rigidly defined; the dual system of single-tier government in the county boroughs and the two or three tiers in the counties which is irrational, uneconomic, administratively wasteful and aggravated by mutual rivalry and suspicion; and the sometimes tense relationships which exist between counties and county districts. Moreover, the diagram gives no indication of the vast disparities in population, size and rateable value of local authorities of the same and different types, nor of the incompatibility between size and status of many local authorities. The following data from *The Municipal Year Book*, 1968 illustrate these points:

(a) *Population* at 30 June, 1967:

Councils	Largest	Smallest
Counties	Lancashire 2,396,000	Radnorshire 18,320
County Boroughs	Birmingham 1,101,990	Canterbury 32,910
Non-county Boroughs	Cambridge 100,340	Montgomery 1,000
Urban Districts	Thurrock 121,670	Llanwrtyd Wells 510
Rural Districts	Easington 86,230	Tintwistle 1,470

(b) *Area in acres:*

Councils	Largest	Smallest
Counties	Devon 1,649,401	Isle of Wight 94,146
County Boroughs	Birmingham 51,147	Smethwick 2,500
Non-county Boroughs	Rhondda 23,885	Cowbridge 84
Urban Districts	Lakes 49,905	Narberth 122
Rural Districts	Wing 361,502	Isles of Scilly 4,041

(c) *Rateable Value:* at 1 April, 1968:

Councils	Largest	Smallest
Counties	Lancashire £83,342,900	Radnorshire £558,317
County Boroughs	Birmingham £52,608,451	Merthyr Tydfil £1,371,987
Non-county Boroughs	Slough £7,654,329	Montgomery £16,182
Urban Districts	Thurrock £8,033,047	Llanwrtyd Wells £13,130
Rural Districts	Eton £4,760,575	Painscastle £26,075

2. Reorganisation of Local Government Structure

Many of the criticisms stem from the age of the structure. Since the structure was crystallised by the Local Government Acts of 1888 and 1894, Britain has experienced a complex of internal changes which have transformed its social, economic and political life.

The population of England and Wales increased by nearly 24 million between 1891 and 1951 and became overwhelmingly urbanised. Agriculture as a main source of employment declined seriously after 1880 and accelerated the movement of population from the country to the towns. Rural depopulation and migration to towns coupled with the peripheral growth of neighbouring towns into continuous built-up areas have resulted in an urban population of about 80 per cent in Britain, and has made nonsense of the dichotomy between town and country which is perpetuated in the dual system. Thus Victorian local government boundaries have to-day become irrelevant, and have helped to exacerbate relationships between rural and urban authorities, the former consistently opposing the extension of the latter or the creation of county boroughs, and the resultant conflict lessening the likelihood of willing inter-authority co-operation when the need arises.

Moreover, during this period, there has been a radical extension in the range and quality of the services provided by local authorities. Following the Education Act of 1902, a spate of social legislation has required local authorities to provide a wide array of personal and environmental services, far beyond the limited protective and public health functions of the late nineteenth century, and has greatly widened the functional role of local government units. An unprecedented scientific, technical and communications revolution, the evolution of the concept of a Welfare State, and the need for the provision of national standards, have formed the background to these changes, providing the tools and a philosophy for local government's assumption of increased responsibility for the welfare of the population.

Yet the dynamic aspect of these changes has not affected the basic structure of local government which has remained broadly unchanged since the 1888 and 1894 legislation, and the Minister's indictment of pre-1963 London Government as "ossified and anachronistic" might equally have been applied to the local government structure outside the metropolis. Moreover, there was no significant attempt to adapt areas to the requirements of the services which had been allocated to them, resulting in varying standards of service from authorities whose resources were too slender to fulfil their responsibilities.

By 1923 the number of county boroughs had increased from sixty-one to eighty-two and many of the original county boroughs had been enlarged. After the creation of Doncaster County Borough in 1926, no further application was made until 1949–53 when the boroughs of Ealing, Ilford and Luton introduced bills for the promotion of county borough status. The counties objected, and no bill reached the Statute Book. During the 1954–55 parliamentary session Ilford, Luton and Poole attempted to gain county borough status but withdrew their bills when the Minister of Housing and Local Government announced that proposals for local government reorganisation were being considered. Also between 1926 and 1939, substantial county borough extensions were made, and, following the Onslow Commission's Second Report and the Local Government Act, 1929, county council reviews between 1931 and 1937 resulted in the amalgamation of many urban and rural districts and their total number was reduced from 1,606 to 1,048.

3. Local Government Boundary Commission

The 1939–45 war brought an end to this piecemeal reorganisation of county districts and many claims for county borough status and the extension of county borough boundaries were held in abeyance. The Coalition Government and the Local Authority Associations, however, continued discussions and in January, 1945, a White Paper was published entitled, *Local Government in England and Wales during the Period of Reconstruction* (Cmd. 6579). It was, according to Professor Robson "mainly an escapist document . . . in many ways a highly misleading document", and its introductory statement indicates that the government was not convinced of the need for a root and branch reform of local government. The government had considered reform proposals put forward by the Associations and "other authoritative sources" and decided there was "no general desire to disrupt the existing structure", but that there was "need and scope for improvements" particularly in the amendment of the machinery for the adjustment of status, boundaries and areas. The White Paper did, however, create the Local Government Boundary Commission, not in the powerful form suggested by N.A.L.G.O. and the Labour Party, but with equivalent functions to those of the county councils and the Minister of Health in the case of county district reviews.

The Local Government (Boundary Commission) Act 1945, granted statutory powers to the Commission to review the boundaries, and, in certain cases, the status of local authorities. The Commission's highly experienced members[2] described their purpose briefly in their first report:

> "Our task is to make, so far as is practicable, all local government authorities, both individually and collectively, effective and convenient units. This is the language of our governing principle."[3]

Their task was immense, unprecedented and "the procedure is frankly experimental", but they began by reviewing the boundaries and status of the counties and county boroughs. There were 144 of these in England and Wales, and 117 (thirty-seven counties out of sixty-one and eighty county boroughs out of 83) had asked or indicated their intention to ask, for some boundary alteration which in the counties involved relatively small adjustments. Additionally, proposals were received from forty-four local authorities for the creation, either individually or in amalgamation, of thirty-three new county boroughs. The extent and significance of these creations would have had a radical effect upon the counties. As the Report said (at p. 11):

> "The proposals in the case of England would, if adopted in full, increase the area of the county boroughs by at least 2,160,000

---

[2] Sir Malcolm Trustram Eve (Chairman), Sir Evelyn John Maude (Deputy Chairman), Sir George Hammond Etherton (resigned January 1947 through ill-health), William Holmes, Sir James Frederick Rees, and Fred Webster (appointed January 1947).

[3] *Report of the Local Government Boundary Commission for the year* 1946, H.C.82, 1946–47, H.M.S.O., p. 3.

acres (266 per cent), and would reduce the population and rateable value of the administrative counties as a whole 26 and $25\frac{1}{2}$ per cent respectively, and, as an extreme example, those of Lancashire by at least 63 per cent in each case."

The counties would never have tolerated such losses which would undoubtedly have destroyed county government, but the county boroughs and those keen on achieving county borough status had nothing to lose from pressing home their respective claims. The many suggestions received by the Commission were classified under three heads:

(a) Limited extension of county boroughs, in accordance with past policy

(b) Large extensions of county boroughs, resulting in some areas in the creation of a solid block of county boroughs.

(c) The creation of new county areas within which all existing county boroughs would relinquish their county borough status.

It was the Commission's Report for 1947[4] which caused the greatest stir, however, and some 34,000 copies were sold. Having completed two years' work, the Commissioners diagnosed the weaknesses of local government and made specific proposals for remedying them. Their introductory section began:

". . . we may be asked why the Commission after two years of existence have made no single order altering the status or boundaries of any local authority. The answer is to be found in our Report as a whole . . .

"It would have been possible for us to have made some Orders . . . which would, in our view, have resulted . . . in 'effective and convenient units of local government administration' . . . But we have definitely reached the conclusion that in many areas—and these cover the bulk of the population—our present powers and instructions do not permit the formation of local government units as effective and convenient as in our opinion they should be. Thus the alternatives before us were to make Orders which would in many cases have resulted in second best arrangements or, taking the opportunity presented to us by our statutory duty to make an Annual Report, to set out our views. We have chosen the latter course, . . .

"We should add that much of our Report is devoted to the subject of functions of local authorities. Our experience amply confirms the statement made recently in Parliament by the Minister of Health. . . . 'Everyone who knows about local government feels that it is nonsense to talk about functions and

---

[4] *Report of the Local Government Boundary Commission for the year* 1947, H.C.86, 1947–48 H.M.S.O.

boundaries separately. They have to be taken together . . .'
We have no jurisdiction over functions."

Having underlined the fault in their terms of reference, the Report outlined the main defects in the system which impeded effective local government and gave rise to frustration:

1. The disparity in size and resources between individual counties, individual county boroughs and county districts, owing partly to historical causes but mainly to structural changes failing to keep pace with population and function changes.
2. The concentrations of population "living in neighbouring towns, which are closely knit as economic and industrial units but have little or no connection or cohesion as local government units", particularly in the five conurbations of the Black Country, Manchester and District, Merseyside, Tyneside and the West Riding, and in smaller degree in Tees-side, the Potteries and the areas in and near Brighton and Bournemouth.
3. Increased central control of local government "which, if carried much further, would cut at the root of local government".
4. Haphazard allocation of functions to authorities "without much reference to local government as a balanced organism".
5. Conflicts over boundaries between counties and county boroughs which have been a "constant feature" since 1888 "should cease". To do so: "We have sought a remedy which removes the causes of the battle rather than one which disables either combatant".

The major recommendations were:

(i) There would be three main types of local government units: counties (new counties), county boroughs (new county boroughs) and county districts.
(ii) The whole of England and Wales including the existing county boroughs would be divided into new counties. The bulk would be the existing counties, some being combined and some divided and arranged on a two-tier system; the remainder of the new counties would be large cities and towns, with suitable boundary changes and administration, as now, on a one-tier system. The former would have populations between 200,000 and 1,000,000 and the latter between 200,000 and 500,000.
(iii) The new county boroughs would consist broadly of the middle size towns—boroughs with populations between 60,000 and 200,000 and would include the cities of Liverpool and Manchester which would form the centres of two new counties. They would all be part of the administrative county and would look to the county for certain services but would control a number of important autonomous functions.
(iv) County districts would include all non-county boroughs except

those forming new county boroughs and the distinction between urban and rural districts would be abolished. All would have similar autonomous functions.

(v) Delegation of functions by county councils would be effected by "county schemes" taking into account the nature of the function to be delegated and the circumstances of the county and of each second tier authority.

In comparison with the 1947 Report's sixty-seven pages of detailed analysis and recommendations, the 1948 Report consists of eight pages, four of which review the first two Reports. It noted that neither Report had been discussed in the House of Commons, and as a result they had written to the Minister of Health, Mr. Aneurin Bevan, asking for "some idea of the Government's intentions in the matter of local government legislation" and whether their proposals were to be put before Parliament. Four months later, on 29 March, 1949, the reply included a copy of an answer to a Parliamentary question which stated that the Government had "decided that it will not be practicable to introduce comprehensive legislation on local government reconstruction in the near future". The Commissioners nevertheless reiterated in the concluding sentence to the 1948 Report their central belief that "neither we nor our successors can everywhere create effective and convenient units of local government without some amendment of local government legislation".

Very shortly afterwards, in the same year the Boundary Commission was abolished by the Local Government Boundary Commission (Dissolution) Act and the previous procedure for effecting boundary changes was reinstated with minor amendments.

It may well have been "impracticable to adopt the far-reaching changes in local authority areas, status and functions"[5] prescribed by the Commission, but it was also "a promising experiment which might have produced good results",[6] and its complete dissolution a regrettable decision in the light of the virtual standstill in structural reform over the next decade.

Discussions on reform continued at joint conferences between the four Local Authority Associations and the Government, with the Association of Municipal Corporations withdrawing in May, 1952, to prepare a separate statement. The National Association of Parish Councils subsequently joined in the discussions with the remaining three associations and in 1954 they jointly submitted a memorandum

---

[5] *Local Government in Britain*, C.O.I. Reference Pamphlet No. 1. 1963, p. 24
[6] W. A. Robson, *Local Government in Crisis*, Allen & Unwin, 1966, p. 91.

outlining their recommendations. The Association of Municipal Corporations submitted a separate memorandum which, not surprisingly, "showed a considerable divergence of opinion". The Joint Report of the four associations stated that "the existing framework of local government has proved to be not only satisfactory but also so flexible as to be capable of modification and evolution without the necessity of any alteration of structure". Its proposals were therefore confined to a preservation of the status quo, with the two-tier system in the conurbations (which were to be defined by the Minister) and administrative counties, and parish councils should be retained as a third tier in rural districts. One-tier government should continue elsewhere, but the nineteen county boroughs with populations under 75,000 should lose status and non-county boroughs outside conurbations were not to be permitted to apply for county borough status unless they had a population of 100,000 or more. This would have made only Luton Municipal Borough and the Rhondda Urban District eligible. The Minister was asked to conduct a general review of the boundaries of administrative counties and be authorised to change them by division, amalgamation, or extension if this were necessary to produce effective governmental units. The counties would undertake a similar review of the county districts. Finally, there was some disagreement between the associations on the distribution of services.

The memorandum of the Association of Municipal Corporations "favoured the one-tier system in all-purpose authorities and recommended its extension as far as circumstances allowed" (Cmd. 9831 p. 5). The Association was strongly critical of the proposals of the four associations, rejecting the suggestion that any county boroughs should lose status and moreover advocated 50,000 as a population minimum for county borough status.

At the end of 1954 the new Minister, Mr. Duncan Sandys, met the five associations and his attitude was that,

". . . it would not be fruitful to embark on any extensive reform unless there existed some broad measure of agreement among the local authorities themselves. Moreover he made it clear that he did not consider that the existing system of local administration had broken down, and that he would not be prepared to contemplate eliminating either the two-tier system in the counties or the one-tier system in the big towns" (Cmd. 9831 p. 5).

A fresh attempt to find a basis of agreement was thus made and a number of meetings followed culminating in an agreement by the associations' representatives "that this structure works well and that

4

it should be maintained" but that certain matters needed attention. These were: (a) the constitution of all local authorities so as to be effective and convenient local government units; (b) claims by county boroughs to extend their boundaries and by non-county boroughs and urban districts to become county boroughs; (c) the resultant effect upon counties of extensions and promotions claimed; (d) the wish of county districts to exercise "as of right" or by delegation some of the functions discharged by county councils; (e) the need to improve the organisation of local government in the conurbations; (f) the desirability after the necessary changes were made, to avoid further changes for a substantial period.

The policy proposals which catered for these issues and which were referred to the respective associations, stipulated that promotion to county borough status outside conurbations should be considered on the basis of ability to discharge the county borough's functions effectively and conveniently, the effect of the promotion on the county, and a minimum population, whether as a single or an amalgamated authority, of 100,000 unless it could "show exceedingly good reason to justify promotion". Inability by an existing county borough to discharge its functions effectively and conveniently could result in withdrawal of that status. The division, amalgamation, alteration and extension of counties might also be considered as part of any reorganisation. In conurbations the pattern of local government was to be looked at as a whole, with the aim of ensuring, throughout the conurbation, individually and collectively effective and convenient units of local government. The creation, or the boundary extension, of a county borough within a conurbation "should be looked at equally with the need for securing a proper organisation of local government on a two-tier basis in the parts of the conurbation outside county boroughs". Subject to this, applications for promotion to county borough status within conurbations should be treated in the same way as elsewhere *but* the minimum population should be 125,000. Middlesex should be preserved as a two-tier urban county. County councils should review county districts and make recommendations to the Minister for dividing, extending, altering or amalgamating their areas, having regard to such factors as community of interest, economic, and industrial characteristics, financial resources and population, but no non-county borough should lose status without the consent of the Minister and then only after he had held an enquiry to ascertain objections. The policy proposals concluded with a section concerning the extent of delegation of functions within counties, the allocation of responsibility for functions, and the preparation of a "county delegation scheme"; it also noted that the role of parish councils in focussing local opinion should if possible be strengthened.

The implementation of this policy was to be based on the creation of a Local Government Commission which would undertake reviews and, after consultation with all the local authorities concerned, make recommendations regarding, (a) promotion to county borough status; (b) extension of county borough boundaries; (c) withdrawal of county borough status; (d) division, amalgamation, alteration and extension of counties and of areas in conurbations. A separate Commission with similar terms of reference was proposed for Wales. Their reports would be presented to the Minister and their recommendations, subject to the Minister's amendments, would be embodied in orders which Parliament would approve or reject but not amend. After Parliament had made its decision no further changes should be made in the areas, or status of counties or county boroughs for fifteen years unless there were exceptional circumstances.

The Government accepted virtually all the recommendations and in July 1956 issued a White Paper, *Areas and Status of Local Authorities in England and Wales* (Cmd. 9831). It accepted the "far-reaching alterations" which had occurred since 1888 and 1894 but went on to state that "it does not necessarily follow that radical changes in organisation are needed". The structure had withstood the tests of the previous half century and "despite certain weaknesses, had on the whole shown itself capable of adaptation to changing conditions. . . . There is, therefore, no convincing case for radically reshaping the existing form of local government in England and Wales. What is needed is to overhaul it and make such improvements as are necessary to bring it up to date".

4. The Local Government Act 1958

This Act embodied the substance of three white papers, one being that mentioned above. Part II of the Act related to reviews of local government areas in England and Wales and proposed:

1. The establishment of two Local Government Commissions, one for England and one for Wales, to review the organisation of local government in:

(a) five "special review areas" (i.e. Tyneside, West Yorkshire, South East Lancashire, Merseyside and the West Midlands) and

(b) the remainder of England (excluding the metropolitan area) and Wales which were to be divided into "general review areas". The Commissions were to make proposals for changes which were desirable in the interests of effective and convenient local government.

2. The Commissions were bodies corporate with a common seal and each would comprise a chairman, a deputy chairman, and not more than five other members appointed by the Queen.

3. The changes which the Commissions might put forward in their proposals were to be produced by any one, or combination of, the following means:

(a) the alteration of the area of an administrative county or county borough (including the abolition of any county district in the course of the extension of a county borough);

(b) the constitution of a new administrative county by the amalgamation of two or more areas, whether counties or county boroughs, or by the aggregation of parts of such areas or the separation of a part of such an area;

(c) the constitution of a new county borough by the amalgamation of two or more boroughs (whether county or non-county), the conversion of a non-county borough or urban district into a county borough, or the division of an existing county borough into parts and the constitution of all or any of the parts of a county borough.

(d) the abolition of an administrative county or county borough and the distribution of its area among other areas, being counties or county boroughs;

(e) the conversion of a county borough into a non-county borough and its inclusion in an administrative county;

(f) the inclusion of the Isles of Scilly, as one or more county districts, in an administrative county.

4. In the special review areas, the Commission for England might, in addition to the changes in (a) to (f) above, make proposals for:

(a) the alteration of the area of a county district;

(b) the constitution of a new non-county borough by the amalgamation of a non-county borough with one or more other county district;

(c) the constitution of a new urban or rural district by the amalgamation of areas being urban or rural districts or by the aggregation of parts of county districts or the separation of a part of a county district;

(d) the abolition of an urban district or rural district.

(e) the conversion of a rural district into an urban district or of an urban district into a rural district.

Thus in the general review areas the Commissions were concerned mainly with administrative counties and county boroughs, whereas in the special review areas the Commission for England might also deal with county districts and put forward proposals, in certain cases, for the redistribution of functions between county and county district councils. In addition, in special review areas, a wholly new type of local authority was proposed, namely the "continuous county", i.e. a county within which there are no county boroughs.

5. The review procedure would take the following form:

(a) the intention to review an area had to be publicly advertised at least two months beforehand. The Commission would invite written observations from all the local authorities in the area and all public authorities and bodies of persons who appeared to be concerned.

(b) The Commission would investigate the circumstances of local government in the area holding consultations with local authorities and the forementioned bodies.

(c) the Commission would then prepare draft proposals if changes were deemed desirable, and these were to be made available for public inspection.

(d) Representations about the draft proposals might then be made by local authorities and other bodies and these would be discussed at Statutory Conferences called by the Commission.

(e) Following the Statutory Conferences, the Commission would submit their final proposals to the Minister of Housing and Local Government in the form of a Report.

(f) The Minister would publicise the Commission's Report and local authorities and other interested bodies would have a right of objection. If this right were exercised, the Minister would normally hold a public inquiry and he would be under a statutory duty to do so where a local authority objected to being downgraded or abolished.

(g) Having heard any objections, the Minister would embody his decisions in an Order which would be laid before Parliament with the Commission's Report for the approval of both Houses.

6. In each review area county councils must review the circumstances of the county districts and make such proposals for effecting changes which were desirable in the interests of effective and convenient local government. This duty was to be carried out as soon as the reviews by the Commission "have been carried to the point at which it is practicable" for the county. As with the Commission in the special review areas, the county councils might recommend the creation, amalgamation, alteration and abolition of county districts, parish councils and (excepting abolition) of non-county boroughs. In addition, they might recommend the conversion of rural into urban districts, or vice versa, and the inclusion of a borough in a rural district. In this last instance, if the borough wished it, a new type of authority, a rural borough, would be created. The amalgamation of a borough and an urban district would create a new borough.

In carrying out their reviews, the county councils had to consult county district representatives who would have the right of objection to the Minister. In such an instance, provision was made for the holding of a local inquiry. The Minister would give effect to district review proposals through orders tabled in Parliament and subject to annulment in pursuance of a resolution of either House. Each county review would have a separate order, and each review would be followed by a period of at least ten years when no claim for change might be presented.[7]

5. The Local Government Commissions for England and Wales

Both Commissions produced detailed analyses of what they considered to be the organisational defects of their review areas and proposed remedies. Nine reports were issued by the Commission for England and one report by the Commission for Wales and these are briefly summarised below in the order in which they were published.

A. *West Midlands Special Review Area*

The principal recommendation was the creation of five enlarged county boroughs in the Black Country based on the existing boroughs of Dudley, Smethwick (now Warley), West Bromwich, Walsall, and Wolverhampton. Despite a court action brought against the Ministry by certain authorities threatened with extinction, the Order was subsequently approved and the five county boroughs became operative on 1 April, 1966. Proposals in the *West Midlands General Review Area* to reduce Burton-on-Trent and Worcester to the status of non-county boroughs were not proceeded with, but Solihull gained county borough status in 1964 and approval was granted for boundary extensions to Coventry and Stoke-on-Trent.

B. *East Midlands General Review Area*

The draft proposals recommended (a) the abolition of Rutland as a county and its merger with Leicestershire; (b) the creation of a large new administrative county by merging Cambridgeshire, Huntingdonshire, the Soke of Peterborough, and the Isle of Ely; and (c) the granting of county borough status to Luton. The first proposal inaugurated a four-year fight by the small county against "the cloven hoof of Whitehall" to preserve its independence and status; the second proposal was also strongly opposed by the counties affected; but the third proposal was approved in 1964. Rutland finally retained its independent status, while the four counties were formed into the two new administrative counties of Huntingdon and Peterborough and of Cambridgeshire (incorporating the Isle of Ely) in 1965.

---

[7] Circular 35/62, issued on 2 October, 1962, gave further advice to county councils on carrying out the county reviews.

C. Wales

The report of the Local Government Commission for Wales was presented in May 1961 and recommended that the thirteen administrative counties of Wales (including Monmouthshire) be reduced by amalgamation to five. The final proposals which followed in December 1962 were: (a) the administrative counties should be reduced from thirteen to seven (Mid Wales, Anglesey, Gwynedd, Flint and Denbigh, West Wales, Glamorgan, and Gwent); (b) the county boroughs of Cardiff, Newport and Swansea should receive certain boundary changes, largely in their favour; (c) the county borough of Merthyr Tydfil should be reduced to non-county borough status and absorbed into Glamorgan; and (d) Rhondda and Wrexham non-county boroughs should not receive county borough status.

In February 1964 the Minister stated that the Government had decided not to implement these proposals because they would not "provide a fully satisfactory basis for an effective local government structure". He proposed that the pattern which reform should take should be reconsidered and that a White Paper would set out suggestions for discussion. This ultimately appeared in July, 1967 (Cmnd. 3340) and proposed a structure based on five counties (later six: Gwynedd, Clwyd, Powys, Dyfed, Glamorgan and Gwent), three county boroughs (as above, with Merthyr Tydfil losing its status), thirty-six (later thirty-five) new districts in place of the existing 164 county districts, and "common councils" at parish level. Legislation to implement the proposals was expected but the debate on the Queen's Speech in October 1969 indicated that there would have to be a new approach in the light of the Redcliffe-Maud proposals for England. The proposal to establish a Welsh Council of nominated members with advisory and promotional duties was, however, proceeded with and it first met in May 1968.

D. South Western General Review Area

The final report in 1963 recommended (a) the amalgamation of Torquay, Paignton and Brixham as a county borough to be called Torbay; (b) extensions to the boundaries of Bath, Bristol, Gloucester and Plymouth; (c) county borough status for Cheltenham; and (d) the transfer of Lyme Regis from Dorset to Devon. Ministerial approval was given to the creation of the new county borough of Torbay and it came into being in 1968. The boundary extensions in (b) were also approved, with modifications in respect of Bath, but the minister rejected proposals (c) and (d).

E. *Tyneside Special Review Area*

The Commission proposed that a continuous county, the Tyneside County Council be created consisting of four boroughs, with a population of 900,000 and replacing seventeen existing local authorities. The four boroughs were to be based on the existing county boroughs at Newcastle upon Tyne, Tynemouth, South Shields and Gateshead. The Minister, however, opposed the proposed two-tier structure and recommended that Tyneside should be reorganised as a single all-purpose borough. The reorganisation of the area was still under consideration when the work of the Commission was discontinued in 1965.

F. *North Eastern General Review Area*

The main recommendation was for the creation of a single county borough for the whole of Tees-side, replacing twelve existing local authorities. The Minister accepted the proposal with certain modifications and the new Tees-side C.B. came into being on 1 April, 1968. Ministerial approval was also given to the extension of Sunderland and to the proposed merger of the Hartlepools into a county borough (came into effect 1 April, 1967).

G. *West Yorkshire Special Review Area*

The final report recommended the creation of a new county borough based on Dewsbury with a population of about 165,000, and the reduction in status of Wakefield county borough whose population (about 60,000) was insufficient for the effective provision of services. No decision had been taken on these proposals, however, when the Commission was disbanded.

H. *York and North Midlands General Review Area*

The main recommendations were aimed at (a) considerably increasing the size and populations of Derby, Doncaster, Hull, Nottingham, Rotherham and Sheffield, and limited boundary extensions for York; (b) the reduction of Barnsley C.B. to non-county borough status; and (c) the transfer of Harrogate and Ripon from the West Riding to the North Riding, and of Scarborough from the North Riding to the East Riding. Proposals (b) and (c) were rejected by the Minister, and certain of the proposals under (a) were accepted with modification.

I. Lincolnshire and East Anglia General Review Area

The Commission's proposal to reduce Great Yarmouth C.B. to non-county borough status was rejected by the Minister, as was the proposal to amalgamate the two administrative counties of Holland and Kesteven into a single county. While agreeing to some extension in Lindsey of the city boundaries of Lincoln C.B., the Minister rejected proposals to transfer substantial areas from Kesteven to Lincoln. Certain of the boundary extensions proposed for Grimsby and Norwich were approved, but the amalgamation of Grimsby and Cleethorpes was rejected.

J. North Western General Review Area

The draft proposals recommended boundary extensions to Blackburn, Blackpool, Burnley, Carlisle, Chester, Preston, St. Helens, Southport, Warrington, and Wigan, and that Barrow-in-Furness should lose its county borough status. The review of the area was not, however, proceeded with owing to the dissolution of the Commission.

K. Merseyside Special Review Area

The main proposal was for a joint planning board to cover Liverpool, Birkenhead, Wallasey, Bootle and an outer area, with representatives from Lancashire and Cheshire county councils and the four Merseyside county boroughs. The board was intended to coordinate development and deal with all major planning decisions. The proposals were not proceeded with.

L. South East Lancashire Special Review Area

The creation of a new county of 500 square miles and a population of $2\frac{1}{2}$ million was proposed. There was to be a second tier of nine most purpose boroughs which would replace more than sixty existing local authorities. The proposals, if they had been proceeded with, would have entailed a loss by Lancashire and Cheshire of half their existing population.

M. County Reviews

Shropshire, Cornwall and Worcestershire undertook internal reviews and submitted reorganisation reports. The Shropshire plan included the merger of Britain's oldest borough, Bishop's Castle, whose charter dated from 1203, with an adjacent rural district to form a rural borough. In July 1966, the Ministry's circular 35/66 announced that county councils were to be relieved of their duty to carry out reviews.

The fifth and last stage was to have comprised the counties of Essex, Hertford and Kent, and the counties falling roughly within a triangle bounded by and including East Sussex, Buckinghamshire and Dorset. However, in December, 1965, the Local Government Commission suspended its operations on its own initiative, and in a letter sent with the Minister's knowledge, told local authorities affected by its reviews in southern and north-western England not to spend more time preparing evidence.

Since the summer of 1965 the Minister had expressed his feelings on a number of occasions about the limited terms of reference and inadequate tools of the Commission. At the annual conference of the Association of Municipal Corporations in September, 1965, he declared that he had seriously considered winding up the Commission, whose boundary review procedures, leading to long delays, had frequently been criticised by local government administrators. The results, however, had proved worthwhile and he had decided that it should continue. He said that the Commission's terms of reference prevented it from producing the reorganisation that local government desperately needed, and the best it could achieve was a patchwork; and when it did a good job of patching in one or two areas, the improvement showed up the threadbare fabric in other areas. He had considered establishing a new commission with clear terms of reference and instructions, but had come to the conclusion that any government would hardly be reckless enough to do so without first agreeing on the principles of reorganisation and analysing the main problems. These he saw as the relation of size and function in modern circumstances and the relation of local democracy and efficiency.

> "There are no accepted principles of reorganisation, no established doctrine according to which a commission could proceed to reshape the areas and the functions of local government so as to enable it to regain the public confidence that has been lost."

The government believed that only a committee which was sufficiently powerful and impartial to command the respect of the parties concerned in the conflict could produce such an analysis. Mr. Crossman stated that he was to discuss with the Local Authority Associations the precise form that the committee should take for he was anxious to get it working quickly as any results from its findings could take up to five years.[8]

In December Mr. Crossman rejected the commission's plan for two-tier government on Tyneside and a few days later the Commission after seven years of intensive and detailed work, voluntarily suspended its activities because of doubts about its future in the context of the Minister's expressed wish for something more radical.

On 10 February, 1966 the Prime Minister announced the appointment of Royal Commissions to undertake a comprehensive review of local government in England and Scotland respectively.[9] Wales was excluded because proposals for the reorganisation of its local government were in an advanced state of preparation and a White Paper was to be produced in due course. Mr. Crossman's statement followed and announced the discontinuation of the review of the Local Government Commission,[10] which had "produced some valuable results within the limits open to it . . . but its terms of reference did not enable it to propose the changes either in structure or in boundaries which fully meet present-day needs". He added that most of the work which it had completed would be "carried through", and where decisions had been made on its proposals the necessary orders would be presented before Parliament. "Other proposals on which decisions have not yet been taken will be considered on their merits. . . ." He went on to say that the Royal Commission could "do its work in not more than two years. . . . Then the legislation will immediately follow, I hope".

6. Royal Commission on Local Government in England, 1966–69

The terms of reference of the Royal Commission were announced in May, 1966:

> "To consider the structure of local government in England, outside Greater London, in relation to its existing functions; and to make recommendations for authorities and boundaries, and for functions and their division, having regard to the size and character of areas in which these can be most effectively exercised and the need to sustain a viable system of local democracy."

---

[8] *The Times*, 23 September, 1965.
[9] Commons Vol. 724, cols. 638–654.
[10] *Local Government (Termination of Reviews) Act* 1967.

The Royal Commission, under the chairmanship of Lord Redcliffe-Maud, extended an open invitation to anyone who wished to submit evidence on any matter within its terms of reference, and during its three years' existence evidence was taken from 2,156 witnesses. A variety of proposals was made.[11] Some favoured a regional system of elected councils, based roughly on the areas of the Economic Planning Boards and Councils, e.g. the Liberal Party suggested twelve regional authorities, each with a wide range of legislative and executive functions, while N.A.L.G.O. saw regional authorities as first-tier units with executive authority for a wide range of services and a strong second tier handling local matters. Another body of opinion recommended the establishment of a new two-tier structure based on the major authorities, these being variously described as "city regions"[12] or "continuous counties" or "provinces", and varying in size between the present counties and the economic planning regions. Some saw the top tier limited to a few functions and emphasized the services to be provided at the local level (e.g. the Association of Municipal Corporations and the Corporation of Secretaries); whereas other bodies (the Institute of Municipal Treasurers and Accountants, the Communist Party, the Confederation of British Industry and several Government Departments) saw the top tier with great operational and executive powers and little emphasis given to the second tier authorities. A third group of proposals centred on a two-tier structure comprising the existing counties with some mergers and the absorption of county boroughs and larger authorities at the local level. These views were largely those of the County Councils Association and the Rural District Councils Association. Another set of proposals suggested a single-tier system of all-purpose authorities only, based on the city region or the continuous county (evidence of the Royal Institute of British Architects, Institute of Local Government Administrators and "The Guardian"). Lastly, a few local authorities recommended the perpetuation of the *status quo*.

After assessing the voluminous evidence and detailed research

---

[11] I. Gowan and L. Gibson, "A survey of some of the written evidence to the Royal Commission on Local Government in England", *Public Administration*, Spring, 1968; and Chapter 10 of the first edition of this book.

[12] See D. Senior, "The City Region as an Administrative Unit", *Political Quarterly*, Vol. 36, No. 1, where he suggests that England and Wales could be conveniently divided into thirty city region units. The city region was later defined by the M.H. & L.G. as "a conurbation or one or more cities or big towns surrounded by a number of lesser towns and villages set in rural areas, the whole tied together by an intricate and closely meshed system of relationships and communications, and providing a wide range of employment and services".

findings the Commission concluded that: "We are unanimous in our conviction that local government in England needs a new structure and a new map". The Commission stated that English local government was "in a sense a random growth" which had "not been planned systematically in the light of what it has to do and the social and geographical conditions of each place". After commenting upon the "vast changes" with which local government had to deal, the four basic faults in the existing structure, which demanded "drastic change", were outlined: (a) the existing areas failed to fit the pattern of life and work in modern England; (b) the fragmentation implied by the dual system divided town from country, made the planning of development and transportation impossible, and stimulated hostility; (c) services were split between several authorities and so complicated the work of meeting personal needs; and (d) many authorities were too small in size and revenue, and consequently in qualified manpower and technical skill, to fulfil what was required of them. In addition, there were "serious failings in local government's relationships with the public and with national government".

The solution hinged on the "one fundamental question" of "size . . . or range of size, in terms of population and of area", for the "democratic and efficient provision of particular services and for local self-government as a whole". Each of the main services was therefore examined, and it was "decided that the answers to that question must be found by seeking to apply to each part of the country the following general principles":

1. The areas of local authorities "must be so defined" that citizens and councillors "have a sense of common purpose".
2. "The areas must be based upon the interdependence of town and country."
3. In each part of the country all "environmental" services—planning, transportation, and major development—must be run by one authority.
4. Similarly, all "personal" services such as education, personal social services, health and housing should be in the hands of one authority.
5. Both "environmental" and "personal" services should be controlled by a single authority in each area.
6. Authorities must be bigger than most county boroughs and all county districts.
7. The population of each authority should be a minimum of around 250,000.
8. For the personal services a population of 1 million should be the maximum.
9. Where the area required for planning and other environmental

services contained too large a population for personal services, responsibilities should be divided between two tiers and related services kept together.

10. Where practicable, the new pattern should stem from the existing one.

In considering the structure which would do most justice to these principles, the idea of the city region which had been advocated by the Ministry of Housing and Local Government and others was examined. It appeared feasible in the great urban concentrations and where a big town was the natural centre for a wide area, but it could not be applied uniformly because "in some parts . . . it did not seem to us to fit reality". Various alternatives were therefore examined, but there was now a growing conviction of the need for (i) "local councils" at the grass roots level "to promote and watch over the particular interests of communities", but not to provide services, and (ii) "provincial councils" to "handle the broader planning issues, work out provincial economic strategy in collaboration with central government and be able to act on behalf of the whole province".

Between the local and provincial councils, the operational authorities with responsibility for the provision of services would have to be areas which: (i) could properly be treated as units for carrying out the "environmental" services; (ii) have populations broadly within the range of 250,000 to not much more than 1 million, the size which would be appropriate for the efficient performance of the "personal" services; and (iii) could be looked after effectively and democratically by one council. Where there existed areas which met these three conditions, "the argument in favour of one authority for each of them would be decisive"; but elsewhere, where the planning problems of areas with large urban concentrations had to be dealt with, the single authority would be unwieldy and remote and there would be need for the division of responsibility between two tiers.

The structure which best gave effect to these considerations was as follows:

1. England (excluding London) should be divided into sixty-one new local government areas, each covering town and country.

2. In fifty-eight of them a single (unitary) authority should be responsible for all services.

3. In the remaining three—the metropolitan areas around Birmingham (West Midlands), Liverpool (Merseyside) and Manchester ("Selnec"[13])—responsibility for services should be divided between:

---

[13] The designation "Selnec" is an acronym derived from South-East Lancashire and North-East and Central Cheshire, the area covered.

THE PROPOSED NEW STRUCTURE IN ENGLAND

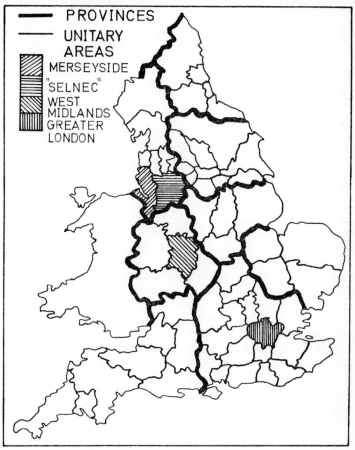

- (i) the three metropolitan authorities, whose key functions would be planning, transportation and major development; and
- (ii) a second tier of twenty metropolitan authorities[14], whose key functions would be education, the personal social services, health and housing.

---

[14] Seven in the Birmingham area, four in the Liverpool area and nine in the Manchester area.

4. The sixty-one new areas, together with Greater London, should be grouped in eight provinces, each with a provincial council. Its key functions would be to settle the provincial strategy and planning framework within which the main authorities would operate.

5. Provincial councils would be indirectly elected by the authorities for the unitary and metropolitan areas (including the Greater London authorities), but would also include a maximum of 25% and a minimum of 20% co-opted members. The provincial councils would replace the regional economic planning councils.

6. Within the 58 unitary authorities, and wherever they were wanted by the inhabitants within the three metropolitan areas, local councils should be elected for the area of each existing county borough, borough, urban district and parish council. The local council would serve as a link between the public and the main authority, and its most important function, and only duty, should be to make known the views of the local community on any matter affecting it.

In the opinion of the Royal Commission, the main gains resulting from the proposed changes would be: (i) greatly improved service to the public, both in providing a better environment and in taking care of the needs of individual people and families; (ii) more effective use of scarce resources of money and skilled manpower; (iii) increased ability of local governors to meet the challenges of technological and social change; (iv) more likelihood that people would recognise the relevance of local government to their own and to their neighbour's well-being; and (v) the revitalising of local self-government throughout the country, so that in England as a whole the people would have a greater sense of participation in their own government.

One member of the Commission, Mr. Derek Senior, produced a memorandum of dissent in which he proposed a two-level system comprising (a) thirty-five directly elected regional authorities responsible for the planning-transportation-development complex of functions, for capital investment programming, and for police, fire and education; and (b) 148 directly elected district authorities responsible for the health service, the personal social services, housing management, consumer protection and all other functions involving personal contact with the citizen. In four areas regional and district responsibilities would be exercised by the same authority.

Size and Rateable Resources of the Provinces

Province	Area (sq. mls.)	Population (Thousands)		Rateable Value 1968	
		1968	1981	Total (£000)	Per head £
NORTH EAST (5 unitary authorities)	3,639	2,749	2,926	100,045	36·4
YORKSHIRE (10 unitary authorities)	5,631	4,849	5,271	170,664	35·2
NORTH WEST (6 unitary authorities and 2 two-tier metropolitan areas)	5,402	6,990	7,640	267,830	38·5
WEST MIDLANDS (4 unitary authorities and 1 two-tier metropolitan area)	5,169	5,164	5,803	213,403	41·3
EAST MIDLANDS (4 unitary authorities)	4,574	3,017	3,372	118,229	39·2
SOUTH WEST (8 unitary authorities)	9,408	4,061	4,515	165,853	40·8
EAST ANGLIA (4 unitary authorities)	5,889	1,990	2,391	71,625	36·0
SOUTH EAST (17 unitary authorities and Greater London)	10,619	17,053	18,552	1,112,125	65·2

These two levels would be complemented, for other purposes, by (i) directly elected common councils at grass roots level, representing existing parishes and towns or parts of towns small enough to have a real feeling of community and to act as a sounding board for opinion; and (ii) five appointed provincial councils with members predominantly nominated by the regional authorities within their areas and responsible for long term strategic planning but having no executive powers.

Mr. Senior also proposed the removal of advanced higher education and parks from local government control, but the acquisition by local government of all branches of the health service, all roads other than national motorways, the management through executives of all ports and airports outside the London Metropolitan Region, and the discharge of all the functions of river authorities.

On 11 June, 1969 the Prime Minister said that the Government accepted in principle the main recommendations of the Royal Commission and aimed to reach decisions on the main structural reforms as soon as possible. In doing so the separate proposals for the reorganisation of local government in Wales and in Scotland would have to be taken into account. The 1967 White Paper on Wales had proposed county amalgamations and, more significantly, had retained the county boroughs. The Report of the Royal Commission on Scotland (Cmnd. 4150), published in September 1969, proposed a two-tier system of seven regional and thirty-seven district authorities and non-statutory community councils if required, but rejected the all-purpose unitary authority and a single all-Scotland authority. Meantime, in July 1969, the Northern Ireland Government had produced its proposals for reshaping Ulster's local government system and had favoured a unitary structure of seventeen area councils based on the interdependence of town and country.

There had thus crystallised four distinctively different local government structures for the four parts of the kingdom. Whereas Scotland and Northern Ireland are likely to retain their separate systems, the Secretary of State for Wales was required "to make a further urgent review of the structure in Glamorgan and Monmouthshire" (which contained all the Welsh county boroughs) to work out a pattern which would "avoid the continual division between county boroughs and administrative counties". In October 1969 the Prime Minister announced the appointment of a Secretary of State for Local Government and Regional Planning, with responsibilities for housing, local government, regional planning, land use, transport and the environment generally; this "overlord" would take "personal charge of the consultations with the principal local authority organisations about the future of local government" and a White Paper would be produced "giving the Government's conclusions about the main principles in Maud and the main structural change that will form the basis of legislation".[15] The White Paper was published in February 1970 and its proposals are summarised in Chapter 10.

---

[15] *Parliamentary Debates*, Vol. 790, No. 1., 28 October, 1969.

CHAPTER 3

Local Government in Greater London

1. The City and its Environs to the Nineteenth Century

Throughout its long history the City of London has displayed a singular ability to withstand external threats to its independence and an unwavering tenacity in preserving its unique governmental system. As early as A.D. 61 it was already "a town of the highest repute and a busy emporium for trade and traders" and it developed to become the centre of provincial government under the Romans.

Its fortunes declined after the Roman departure in A.D. 410 and little is known of its fate during the subsequent centuries when the teutonic invaders established their communities throughout the present home counties. As the emergent kingdoms of the Saxons crystallised into being, London was gradually resurrected and its commercial life and community organisation developed together. Its growing prosperity attracted the plundering Danes in A.D. 839 and again after 1010, but the City survived and continued to maintain its autonomy and privileges. Deriving its power from trade and finance, its leaders excluded even the monarch, and it is significant that the restored Saxon dynasty in the person of Edward the Confessor established his governmental seat not in the City but beyond its walls at Westminster.

From William the Conqueror the City received a charter ratifying the rights and privileges of its citizens, and in 1132 a further charter recognised its full county status and granted unrestricted freedom in the choice of a Sheriff.

By this time the City's ward structure was almost fully formed, with twenty wards in existence in 1130. By the beginning of the thirteenth century there were twenty-four wards; in 1394 Farringdon was divided into two wards and in 1550 Bridge Without was created, bringing the complement to twenty-six. The last named ward no longer exists, but an alderman still represents it. Each ward had its wardmote comprising one hereditary alderman, who generally gave the ward his name, and common councilmen whose numbers varied according to the size of the ward. They performed such public services as existed and had wide powers in preserving the peace and for imposing sanctions.

In 1141 the citizenry confederated into a single community and London's first mayor was appointed in 1192 to supersede the Sheriff of London and Middlesex who had formerly governed the City.

Territorially, the City has barely changed since the Norman Conquest, with its boundaries enclosing an area of 677 acres. Its governmental machinery originated during the years chronicled above and its present constitution reflects the outward semblance of a far distant age.

The City of London possesses no charter of incorporation but is a corporation by prescriptive right, and functions through three institutions which themselves originated in the ancient assemblies of the Folkmoot, the Husting and the Wardmote:

A. *The Court of Common Hall*

This was developed from the Congregation of all freemen who elected the main municipal officers. By the thirteenth century the assembly had become too large for Guildhall, and attendance came to depend upon a personal summons issued by the Mayor and Aldermen.

In the fourteenth century prominent citizens in the wards were also summoned, but by the mid-fifteenth century only Common Councilmen and "other powerful and discreet citizens" were called upon to attend.

In 1467 the masters and wardens of the guilds were invited, and eight years later the liverymen of the companies replaced the Ward notabilities. This privilege was confirmed by statute in 1725 requiring electors to be freemen and liverymen of at least one year's standing.

A Common Hall is summoned by precept from the Lord Mayor to the masters and wardens of the Livery Companies, and on 29 September the assembly nominates two Aldermen who have served as Sheriffs to be presented to the Court of Aldermen who elect one Lord Mayor, two Sheriffs, a Chamberlain, Bridgemasters, Aleconners, and Auditors of the Chamberlain's and Bridgemasters' Accounts are elected on 24 June by the Court of Common Hall.

B. *The Court of Aldermen*

This is generally believed to have developed from the weekly meetings of the pre-Conquest Court of Hustings where each Alderman, representing his Ward, discussed matters of common concern and determined municipal policy for the federal City.

The Court provided centralised and unified civic administration, and became responsible for the organisation and control of essential public services until the seventeenth century. They possessed great powers and exercised judicial and administrative functions.

Nowadays the Aldermen are elected by the Ward voters, unlike those in any other local authority, and hold office for life. The Court meets about fifteen times a year and is presided over by the Lord Mayor. Their functions are still extensive and include *inter alia*, the final choice between the two candidates presented by the Liverymen for the office of Lord Mayor; the adjudication of disputed elections of Common Councilmen and on alleged election irregularities; the approval of the terms of the livery companies' charters of incorporation; the granting of consent to the wearing of livery; and the administration of justice in their capacity as J.Ps.

C. *The Court of Common Council*

It was customary for important decisions at the Folkmoot or the Court of Hustings to be put before the citizens, or commonalty, for assent, and it is from such direct democracy that the Court of Common Council originated. Ward representatives later came to be consulted by the Mayor and Aldermen and in the thirteenth century the concept of representation was extended by summoning representatives to discuss matters affecting the City.

Further developments between 1319 and 1384 led to the establishment of a permanent Common Council, chosen by the citizens of the wards "to treat the arduous affairs affecting the Commonalty". The court persisted and grew in power over the following centuries as an elected, though strictly limited, representative council when regressive oligarchic control characterised the management of local affairs throughout the remainder of the kingdom.

During the seventeenth century it superseded the Court of Aldermen as the main governing body, and absorbed its major executive and administrative functions.

To-day it consists of the Lord Mayor, twenty-five other aldermen and 159 Common Councilmen. Working through more than thirty Committees, the court undertakes (i) all the ordinary functions of a London Borough (q.v.) financed by rates, and (ii) a number of special activities financed by revenue from the City's Cash and Bridge House Estates—such activities include the running of the Corporation's four City Schools, Open Spaces outside the City like Epping Forest, and four City Bridges, etc.

These municipal institutions and the men who served them guided the fortunes of the mediaeval city to an unparalleled eminence in power and prosperity. In their dual role as leaders of great merchant companies and as mayors or aldermen, they governed London with the same shrewdness which had built their trading empires.

Outside the city the Saxon communities provided the nuclei of many of Greater London's towns and villages. These were firmly established by the eighth century, as were the shire outlines of Essex, Middlesex, Kent and Surrey.

London was excluded from the Domesday Survey of 1086 but the parishes on the periphery were well documented. The drift of population from country to town had already begun, but the city's jurisdiction extended no further north than the bars which had been set up on the roadways outside the city walls by the thirteenth century or earlier. South of the Thames, Southwark had developed as a strategic bridgehead settlement in Roman and Anglo-Saxon days, becoming a busy concentration of prosperous workshops during the early mediaeval period as Chaucer's pilgrims gathering at *The Tabard* would have seen.

Communities of such substance were few, however, and the growth of the city's suburbs into the afforested hinterland was gradual. The local services which existed were based upon the same customary communal activities which typified the rest of the country.

By the late sixteenth century the population of London and its environs had grown to approximately 300,000; and the expansion of commercial activity stimulated the growth of many towns such as Uxbridge, and London expanded rapidly westwards and down-river to Stepney, Deptford and Woolwich. To the *Liberties* adjoining the city walls were attracted the poor migrants from the shires and Europe, and overcrowded slums developed.

The opportunity occasioned by the Great Fire of 1666 for the systematic rebuilding of the City was not taken, and the suburbs spread outwards as land speculation and building increased. The population had grown to 674,350 by 1700, and although many of the outlying communities were still rural in character and continuing to supply London with their produce, by the end of the seventeenth century the signs of a coming industrialism could be seen in embryo in the dockyard towns of Deptford and Woolwich.

The coaching era stimulated further extension into the outskirts during the eighteenth century, and in some directions an almost continuous development stretched from the city to a distance of five or six miles. Many of the outlying towns such as Twickenham, Richmond and "Royal" Kensington were themselves growing to meet the spreading London perimeter. The movement was mainly westwards towards the City of Westminster whose jurisdiction began at the Strand. Unlike the City of London, whose 12,000 ratepaying householders democratically elected their aldermen and common councillors, the City of Westminster was not self-governing but was controlled by twelve burgesses appointed for life by the High Steward. Their control was tenuous, however, and their powers were gradually being absorbed by the J.Ps. and the parish vestries in the area. The titled, the wealthy middle class, the civil servants and the professional men came to reside in the fashionable "Squares" around Covent Garden, Piccadilly, St. James's, and the rich merchants, closely followed by the upper middle class, established their country houses anywhere within a twenty mile radius of the City of London.

2. The Nineteenth Century

The land to the south of the river was opened to the speculative builders after the construction of Westminster Bridge in 1750, Vauxhall Bridge in 1816, Waterloo Bridge in 1817, Southwark Bridge in 1819, Hammersmith Bridge in 1827 and the new London Bridge in 1831. To the east in Bethnal Green an estate was built for the locally employed weavers, and in the eastern and northern suburbs rows of working-class cottages became more common. By 1835 the built-up area of the metropolis, Cobbett's "Great Wen", had extended to approximately twenty-two square miles, with a population of over one million people. They were ill-served by about 172 vestries and a confusion of *ad hoc* bodies, the latter comprising seven boards of commissioners of sewers, nearly one hundred paving, lighting and cleansing boards, a number of boards of guardians set up by the 1832 Poor Law Reform Act, several commissioners of highways and bridges, and numerous turnpike trusts, commissioners of police and of woods and forests, grand juries, inquest juries, leet and annoyance juries, the Middlesex bench of magistrates and the salaried police magistrates.[1]

The suggestion that the City of London should follow the practice of the newly created boroughs (under the 1835 Municipal Corporations Reform Act) and assimilate the surrounding suburbs, was rejected by the City Corporation who saw no reason to relinquish its exclusive status for the dubious privilege of becoming responsible for the problems of such a vast and heterogeneous conurbation. To have done so would have entailed a radical alteration in the character of City government and this suggestion was steadfastly and successfully rejected, as were so many future attempts to change the City.

In 1854 a Royal Commission reported on the problems of control posed by the multiplicity of distinct communities which made up the

---

[1] W. A. Robson, *The Government and Misgovernment of London*, Allen & Unwin 1948, p. 21.

vast urban sprawl of Geater London and by the unco-ordinated activity of 300 or so different *ad hoc* bodies which "carried out what parody of local government there was".[2] Such problems, the Commission felt, would not be solved by bringing the entire area of 75,000 acres with a population which by now had grown to 2,800,000 people living in 260,000 houses under the aegis of an extended City Corporation. They recommended the establishment of a body with responsibility for certain services over the entire area, and to this end the Metropolitan Board of Works was created by the Metropolis Local Management Act of 1855.

The Metropolitan Board of Works comprised forty-five members and a paid chairman, the members being indirectly elected for three years by the vestries of the larger parishes and by the district boards which represented combinations of the smaller parishes. The Board was given responsibility for drainage, paving, cleansing, lighting and improvement in the area of the former Metropolitan Commissioners of Sewers (1848). This area comprised approximately 117 square miles with its central areas in Holborn, Westminster, Kensington, the Thames-side parishes and parts of the East End and south-east districts being fully built over, but over a half of the entire area was undeveloped land. The Board had no control over the City of London.

The Board's main task was to build a sewer system to stop sewage entering the Thames, and within a decade a main drainage system had been constructed to outfalls outside the town. The Board also took over control of the river embankment, many of its bridges and the prevention of Thames floods; it undertook metropolitan street construction and improvements[3]; and it ran the fire engine establishment of the London fire insurance companies from 1866, and in 1867 the Society for the Protection of Life from Fire; by Acts of 1874 and 1875 it was given power to regulate offensive trades and explosives in the metropolis; it was the authority under the 1875 Artisans and Labourers Dwelling Act, and under other legislation controlled the height and frontage line of buildings; and for building control purposes the Board divided London into sixty-seven districts.

Despite the extensive improvements accomplished, the Metropolitan Board of Works had a number of defects. It was indirectly elected; there was no central government control; and, in particular, it lacked executive authority over the vestries and district boards who were frequently neglectful in executing their responsibilities for street paving, cleansing, watering and lighting. Additionally, there

---

[2] K. B. Smellie, *A History of Local Government*, Allen & Unwin, 1949, p. 180.
[3] Roads from Blackfriars Bridge to Westminster Bridge, from Lambeth to Vauxhall, Southwark Street (1864) and Holborn Viaduct (1869).

co-existed other major *ad hoc* bodies in the Metropolitan Asylums Board (1867), the London School Board (1870) and the Port of London Sanitary Authority (1872). The result was a lack of standardisation and coordination of services with irresponsibility and neglect characterising much of the work of the minor authorities.

Meanwhile, major population changes had been further stimulated by railway developments after 1836. Terminals were built at London Bridge, for the Greenwich line, in 1836; at Euston in 1838 and at Cannon Street in 1866. The Victoria and Hungerford Bridges, completed in 1862 and 1864 respectively, brought passengers from the South to Victoria and Charing Cross; the Liverpool Street and Holborn Viaduct of 1874, and the Blackwall Tunnel of 1897, linking Poplar with Greenwich also helped to promote Victorian London's growth. It was now easy for the town-worker, whatever his economic status, to flee the overcrowded centre and set up his family in one of the many contrasting architectural assortments of Victorian suburbia which suited his pocket. The commuters who swarmed into London added to the centre's traffic congestion for they needed conveyance from the railway terminals to their work. After years of violent opposition Charles Pearson's "sewer railway", the underground system, was eventually begun in 1860 by the North Metropolitan Railway Company, and the line from Paddington to Farringdon Street was opened in 1863. Railways extended to the suburbs and with direct access to the commercial centre business premises were established in the environs, and communities quickly grew around the source of employment. Row upon row of terraced houses, supplemented by the conversion of many of the elegant residences of former years into tenements, accommodated working-class families, and within a few decades rural serenity gave way to densely populated towns.

Many of the work-hungry immigrants to Greater London brought poverty with them and, if unemployed for any length of time, they would gravitate to nauseous tenements and insanitary overcrowded slums, creating social problems which the parish vestries were incapable of remedying. Population growth rates were unprecedented; West Ham grew from 2,500 in 1801 to 267,000 in 1901, a century when 130 factories were established there; even the comparatively sedate Hammersmith grew from 25,000 to over 150,000 in the second half of the century alone; Willesden, on the Metropolitan line, grew from 750 in 1851 to 16,000 in 1871 and 115,000 in 1901; and Walthamstow, after the laying of the Chingford line in 1870–73 increased from 11,000 in 1871 to 97,000 in 1901.

Population increases on this scale coupled with the obvious inadequacies of local government to cope with the manifold problems necessitated radical remedial action. The Local Government Act, of 1888 attempted to resolve the situation with the creation of a new authority to replace the Metropolitan Board of Works.[4] The area of the Metropolitan Board of Works became the Administrative County of London and the Board's powers were slightly increased and vested in the new London County Council made up of 124 councillors[5] and twenty aldermen. The main new powers were the right to oppose bills in Parliament, to appoint medical officers and to contribute to the maintenance or enlargement of highways. A number of *ad hoc* bodies such as the Metropolitan Asylums Board, the London School Board, the Boards of Guardians, Burial Boards, the Thames and Lee Conservancy Boards, and the Metropolitan and City Police Forces remained, as did the vestries and district boards. The City was included in the London County Council for administrative purposes, but for "non-administrative" purposes (i.e., functions performed by quarters sessions, J.Ps. coroners, sheriffs, etc.) it remained a separate body.

The reluctance of the legislators to extend the powers of the London County Council beyond those noted, or to limit the number or powers of the multiplicity of authorities which had contributed to the abuses and disunity of the previous administration was largely motivated by the fear that such a large council in the capital was becoming dominated by radical interests. This same fear is alleged to have influenced Balfour's London Government Act of 1899 which divided the county of London into twenty-eight metropolitan boroughs on the basis of the old vestry outlines. This act gave the metropolitan boroughs the same powers as county boroughs in promoting and opposing bills, and, according to Professor Smellie:

> "everything was done to make them a political and administrative counterweight to the possible prestige of a reforming London County Council".[6]

The two-tier pattern of government completed by the 1899 Act remained in existence for over sixty years. The principal powers of the London County Council were: housing, which service was operated in conjunction with the metropolitan boroughs, town and country

---

[4] The Board had become progressively corrupt and a series of scandals involving improper transactions culminated in an investigation by a Royal Commission in 1888.

[5] Two councillors for each of London's sixty Parliamentary divisions plus four members elected by City electors.

[6] K. B. Smellie, *op. cit.*, p. 183. See also W.A. Robson, *op. cit.*, pp. 84–99 for account of hostility against London County Council.

planning, education, welfare services, parks and open spaces, entertainment, finance[7], care of children, health services, fire service, civil defence, main drainage, municipal trading, bridges, youth service and bye-laws. The metropolitan boroughs, each with its mayor, aldermen[8], and councillors, were responsible for housing, public health, libraries, rating, bye-laws, entertainments, finance, roads and highways, parks and open spaces, baths and washhouses, and recreational facilities.

Several *ad hoc* bodies administered services both within and outside the London County Council area, and foremost amongst these were the Metropolitan Police Force, whose jurisdiction covered most of London with the exclusion of the City, the Metropolitan Water Board, the London Transport Executive operating over a radius of twenty five miles from the City, and the Port of London Authority.

Suburban London, however, soon grew beyond the 1888 boundary, spilling into the adjoining local authorities, and an impression of this outward growth is given by the following table of census returns.

POPULATION OF INNER AND OUTER LONDON FOR SELECTED
YEARS, 1851–1961

Census Year	Inner London		Outer London	
	Popl. '000's	Per cent popl. change	Popl. '000's	Per cent popl. change
1851	2,363	—	322	—
1881	3,830	+62	940	+192
1901	4,536	+18	2,050	+118
1951	3,348	−26	5,000	+144
1961	3,195	−5	4,977	−0·46

For convenience, Inner London is equated with the London County Council area, and Outer London with the Registrar General's conurbation (720 square miles), but excluding Inner London. The table shows clearly how the former has decreased from its peak in 1901 and the latter continually increased. Similarly at the centre, the

---

[7] L.C.C. derived its income from precepts upon the metropolitan boroughs and the City Corporation, grants-in-aid, rents, charges and payments and trading undertakings.

[8] Aldermen numbered one-sixth of the councillors on the metropolitan boroughs and on the L.C.C.

City of London, which had experienced steady depopulation from the seventeenth century, declined from 120,000 in 1801 to 26,000 in 1901, and by 1966 had a night population of 4,580.

This overflow of population outwards from the centre has been accelerated during the present century by a number of factors: slum clearance and rehousing policies; redevelopment and the replacement of living areas by office accommodation, particularly in the commercially prestigious central area; the advent of the low-priced family car and the ubiquity of omnibus and underground railway services have increased individual mobility; the rash of speculative building between 1918 and 1939 which doubled the built-up area of London;[9] ribbon development along new arterial and by-pass roadways; air raids during the Second World War and consequent population dispersal; shortage of attractive building sites; natural population increase; the employment growth; the continual attraction of London for immigrants from the provinces and beyond. All these factors and others have combined to increase and redistribute the population, from the City and the metropolitan boroughs of inner London to the ever-expanding communities in the outer zone, and in the process engulfing all Middlesex and parts of Essex, Kent, Surrey and Hertfordshire.

3. The Reorganisation of London Government

During the inter-war years a number of inquiries and a Royal Commission (the Ullswater Commission) into local government in Greater London proved abortive. Meanwhile the problems of this vast amorphous area, of approximately 720 square miles and a population of over eight million, multiplied. Within this urban agglomeration over ninety local authorities carried out their separate functions, with varying resources and degrees of efficiency, and no single overall authority existed to co-ordinate services and be responsible for the problems of the area as a whole, particularly in the sectors of housing, roads and town and country planning.

Concern for these problems led, in the post-war years, to the 1945 Reading Committee's examination of the number, size and bound-aries of the metropolitan boroughs and the distribution of functions between them and the London County Council. The Committee was finally dissolved because it could not separate the problems of the London County Council from those of Greater London as a whole. In 1946 the Clement Davies Committee came to the conclusion that a

---

[9] J. T. Coppock and H. C. Price, *Greater London*, Faber & Faber, 1962, p. 29.

review of the London region should be undertaken by a local government commission, but no action followed. Finally, in opening the debate on the three White Papers of 1957, referred to on page 38, *ante*, the Minister of Housing and Local Government indicated his intention to set up a Royal Commission to examine the problems of Greater London.

In November, 1957 the Royal Commission on Greater London was established with six members under the chairmanship of Sir Edwin Herbert (now Lord Tangley). Their unanimous report was issued in October, 1960 and in its 400 pages the inadequacies of the existing structure were analysed and recommendations for their resolution detailed.

The Royal Commission noted that:

> "The machinery is untidy and full of anomalies. There is over-lapping, duplication, and in some cases, gaps. . . . The fact that local government in London does manage to hang together and avoid a breakdown says much for the British knack of making the most cumbrous machinery somehow work. . . . We are convinced that the choice before local government in Greater London is . . . to abdicate in favour of central government, or to reform so as to be equipped to deal with present-day problems. A surrender to central government . . . would be the death-knell of local government in the review area. Local government means local self-government."

The reforms which the Royal Commission advocated entailed a major structural reorganisation and included:

1. The abolition of London and Middlesex county councils.
2. The creation of a Council for Greater London which would include the London County Council area, nearly all Middlesex county council, the county boroughs of Croydon, East Ham and West Ham, and the metropolitan areas of Essex, Kent, Surrey and Hertfordshire.
3. The amalgamation of the ninety-five local authorities in the area to fifty-two, to be termed Greater London Boroughs.
4. The retention by the City of London of its powers and functions, the Court of Common Council to possess the same powers as a Greater London Borough.

In addition, detailed suggestions were made relating to the constitution of the new authorities and to the allocation and administration of functions.

The Report was studied by the Conservative Government for more than a year and the opinions of over a hundred interested local authorities were heard before a White Paper was issued in November, 1961. It stated that the Government generally accepted the Commission's main recommendations but added that the boroughs should be larger and therefore fewer, and that the educational arrangements were not satisfactory. The White Paper concluded with a declaration of the Government's intention to examine the details further with local authorities before legislative proposals could be presented to Parliament, and added that "the change-over should be made at the earliest practicable date". Some days later the Minister of Housing and Local Government sent a circular to all interested local authorities detailing the Government's proposals for a Greater London of thirty-four boroughs each with a population of 180,000 to 360,000.

Opposition to the Government's plans came mainly from the following sources:

A. *The London County Council*

With a Labour majority for nearly thirty years, the London County Council had "resolutely refused to discuss" with the Herbert Commission, "any of the wider issues of the government of London as a whole," and stuck firmly to the proposition that " 'London' and the Administrative County of London are synonymous terms and that the London County Council is the government of London".

The opposition had not abated by March, 1962 when at the end of an eighteen-hour debate at County Hall, the second longest in the council's history, the London County Council adopted a resolution by its General Purposes Committee which said that the Government's proposals would offer few, if any, practical advantages to offset the disorganisation and disruption of existing services which would be entailed, and requested the Prime Minister (Harold Macmillan) to receive a deputation as a matter of urgency.

The Prime Minister received the deputation in April but despite the appeal made to reconsider the proposals, he felt that no fundamental changes to the plan were necessary. This was followed in July by a further resolution by the London County Council to refuse to co-operate with the Government in implementing the reorganisation.

B. *Certain Affected Authorities*

Middlesex county council was also unwilling to agree to its own demise, stating in February, 1962 that "there was no justification for destroying the fabric of local government in Middlesex and indeed in Greater London", and requesting the Government to "think again so as to . . . avoid the enormous disruption which could well have a paralysing effect on the public for many years to come". Similarly, Surrey County Council urged the Government not to proceed with its proposals, "the drastic nature of which cannot be justified."

C. *The Parliamentary Labour Party*

The Party announced its opposition to the plan shortly before a two-day debate in February, 1962 on a Government motion "taking note" of the White Paper proposals. One of the plan's bitterest antagonists was Lord Morrison of Lambeth, who as Herbert Morrison had been for many years leader of the council's Labour group and Chairman of the London County Council. During the debate on the White Paper he said:

> "Hitler tried to destroy London and failed. Now the Conservative Party, for Party political reasons, is trying to destroy the municipality of the Capital City. It is my belief and hope that they will no more succeed than did Hitler".[10]

Another former chairman of the London County Council, Lord Latham, later said of the Bill that it was

> "the most insidious ever introduced in the history of local government . . . conceived in malice, born in iniquity, and will function in confusion . . . may the wrath of the people descend upon those who have done this wicked thing . . ."

The Government's final pattern for Greater London was drawn up by an independent panel composed of the Town Clerks of Plymouth, Cheltenham, Oxford and South Shields. They investigated objections and suggestions by the local authorities involved and their recommendations were accepted by the Government without modification.

The London Government Bill was published on 22 November, 1962, and during its passage through Parliament some 1,000 amendments were suggested in the House of Commons, it occupied four days in a Committee of the Whole House and twenty-one sittings in Standing Committee. Additionally, the House of Lords considered 785 proposed amendments. The Bill was strongly opposed at all stages by the Opposition in both Houses, and was before Parliament for eight months before the "guillotine" was applied, and it received the Royal Assent on 31 July, 1963.

The main provisions of the London Government Act 1963 are:

1. The creation of thirty-two new administrative areas to be known

---

[10] Lords, Vol. 238, col. 189, 14 March, 1962.

as London Boroughs which were to be the primary units of local government.

2. The area comprising the London Boroughs, the City and the Temples was to constitute an administrative unit to be known as Greater London.

3. The administrative counties of London and Middlesex, the eighty-five metropolitan boroughs, county and municipal boroughs, and urban districts within the Greater London area would cease to exist on the creation of the Greater London Council.

4. The independent position and status of the City of London would remain unchanged, the Common Council having the powers of a London Borough Council.

5. The first elections for Greater London councillors were to be held in April, 1964 and for the London Boroughs in May, 1964. The new councils were to continue side by side with the old authorities and would take over their full functions on 1 April, 1965.

6. The establishment of the Inner London Education Authority, a special, i.e., virtually autonomous, committee of the Greater London Council, to provide the full range of educational services, including the youth employment service, for Inner London. In each of the twenty outer London Boroughs education and youth employment would be borough services. There was to have been a review of the I.L.E.A. system before 1970, but this provision has been repealed (s. 2 of Local Government (Termination of Reviews) Act 1967) and the I.L.E.A. will continue in being.

7. As the administrative counties of Essex, Hertfordshire, Kent and Surrey were to be reduced in size and would consequently lose population and rateable value to Greater London, these counties would be able to obtain transitional financial assistance from the G.L.C. if the effects of the reorganisation caused the county rate to rise by 6*d*. in 1965–66.

8. A Staff Commission would be established to safeguard the interests of local government employees affected by the reorganisation.

(a) *The Greater London Council*. This consists of the "Dais", 100 councillors and sixteen aldermen. The first election was held on 9 April, 1964, with each of the thirty-two London Boroughs being an electoral area and returning two, three or four councillors, according to the size of the electorate. For this election the Cities of London and Westminster were joined to form one electoral area.

At the election 44·2% of the Greater London electorate of 5,466,756 voted, and the resulting political composition of the Greater London Council was: sixty-four Labour councillors and eleven Labour aldermen, and thirty-six Conservative councillors and five Conservative aldermen. Councillors hold office for three years and retire together; aldermen number one-sixth of the council and are elected

6

by the councillors from among their number or from persons qualified to be councillors, and eight retire every third year.

At its first meeting on 27 April, 1965, the Council elected its first Chairman, Sir Harold Shearman, J.P., a Vice-Chairman and a Deputy Chairman, the three being collectively known as the "Dais". (b) *The London Borough Councils.* By the end of January, 1964, final approval had been given to the names of the thirty-two London Boroughs which were to form Greater London (see map). Details of the amalgamations which produced the new boroughs, their population and rateable values are as follows:

Inner London Boroughs

1. WESTMINSTER (Paddington, St. Marylebone, Westminster)	270,140	£108 million
2. CAMDEN (Hampstead, Holborn, St. Pancras)	246,000	£35,250,000
3. ISLINGTON (Finsbury, Islington)	259,600	£19,450,000
4. HACKNEY (Hackney, Shoreditch, Stoke Newington)	254,300	£14,409,000
5. TOWER HAMLETS (Bethnal Green, Poplar, Stepney)	204,000	£14,582,000
6. GREENWICH (Greenwich, Woolwich—south of Thames)	230,100	£12,440,000
7. LEWISHAM (Deptford, Lewisham)	291,670	£11,620,000
8. SOUTHWARK (Bermondsey, Camberwell, Southwark)	310,600	£17,866,000
9. LAMBETH (Lambeth, Wandsworth—eastern part)	340,800	£19 million
10. WANDSWORTH (Battersea, Wandsworth—western part)	335,000	£15,384,000
11. HAMMERSMITH (Fulham, Hammersmith)	217,400	£13,993,000
12. KENSINGTON AND CHELSEA (Kensington and Chelsea)	220,600	£24,990,000

Outer London Boroughs

13. WALTHAM FOREST (Chingford, Leyton, Walthamstow)	248,500	£11,555,000
14. REDBRIDGE (Ilford, Wanstead, Woodford, Chigwell—southern part, Dagenham—northern part)	248,600	£12,365,000
15. HAVERING (Hornchurch, Romford)	249,300	£11,492,000

16. BARKING (Barking—eastern part, Dagenham—southern part)	178,900	£9,858,500
17. NEWHAM (Barking—western part, East Ham, West Ham, Woolwich—north of the Thames)	264,000	£14,500,000
18. BEXLEY (Bexley, Crayford, Erith, Chislehurst and Sidcup—northern part)	212,900	£10,083,000
19. BROMLEY (Beckenham, Bromley, Chislehurst and Sidcup—southern part, Orpington, Penge)	294,300	£15,187,000
20. CROYDON (Coulsdon and Purley, Croydon)	328,300	£17,909,000
21. SUTTON (Beddington and Wallington, Carshalton, Sutton and Cheam)	167,400	£9,185,000
22. MERTON (Merton and Morden, Mitcham, Wimbledon)	189,000	£10,834,000
23. KINGSTON UPON THAMES (Kingston upon Thames, Malden and Coombe, Surbiton)	186,300	£9,459,000
24. RICHMOND UPON THAMES (Barnes, Richmond, Twickenham)	182,000	£10 million
25. HOUNSLOW (Brentford and Chiswick, Feltham, Heston and Isleworth)	209,100	£15,013,000
26. HILLINGDON (Hayes and Harlington, Ruislip-Northwood, Uxbridge and Yiewsley, West Drayton)	232,000	£15,428,000
27. EALING (Acton, Ealing, Southall)	303,800	£17,125,000
28. BRENT (Wembley, Willesden)	296,600	£19,678,000
29. HARROW (Harrow)	209,500	£10,974,000
30. BARNET (Barnet, East Barnet, Finchley, Friern Barnet, Hendon)	316,400	£21,600,000
31. HARINGEY (Hornsey, Tottenham, Wood Green)	258,400	£13,222,000
32. ENFIELD (Edmonton, Enfield, Southgate)	271,600	£17,240,000

Twenty-three of these Boroughs have a council membership of seventy, while the remainder vary from sixty-five (Barnet, Bexley and Harrow) to fifty-six (Waltham Forest). Each London Borough Council consists of a Mayor, Deputy Mayor, Aldermen and Council-

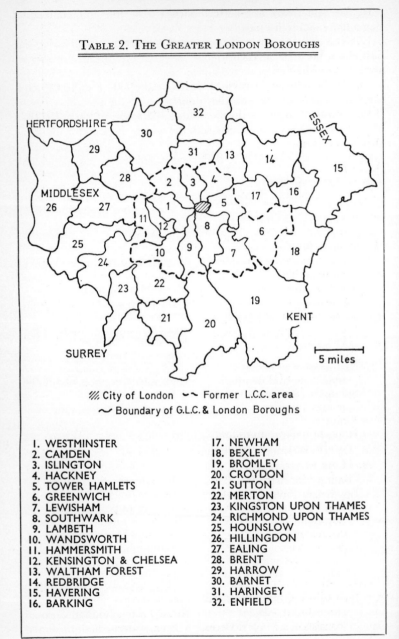

TABLE 2. THE GREATER LONDON BOROUGHS

HERTFORDSHIRE

ESSEX

MIDDLESEX

KENT

SURREY

5 miles

///// City of London ⌒⌒ Former L.C.C. area
⌒ Boundary of G.L.C. & London Boroughs

1. WESTMINSTER	17. NEWHAM
2. CAMDEN	18. BEXLEY
3. ISLINGTON	19. BROMLEY
4. HACKNEY	20. CROYDON
5. TOWER HAMLETS	21. SUTTON
6. GREENWICH	22. MERTON
7. LEWISHAM	23. KINGSTON UPON THAMES
8. SOUTHWARK	24. RICHMOND UPON THAMES
9. LAMBETH	25. HOUNSLOW
10. WANDSWORTH	26. HILLINGDON
11. HAMMERSMITH	27. EALING
12. KENSINGTON & CHELSEA	28. BRENT
13. WALTHAM FOREST	29. HARROW
14. REDBRIDGE	30. BARNET
15. HAVERING	31. HARINGEY
16. BARKING	32. ENFIELD

lors, the Aldermen numbering one-sixth of the councillors. All councillors will retire together every three years.

(c) *Powers and Duties.* As these boroughs were intended to be the primary units of local government their responsibilities are greater than those of the former metropolitan boroughs. The Greater London Council, for its part, was to be made responsible for the "greater strategic tasks" which required planning over the area as a whole. The Common Council of the City of London received the powers of a London Borough Council. Services for which the London Borough Councils and the Greater London Council were separately responsible were:

London Borough Councils

Personal Health Services.
Maternity and Child Welfare, Mental Health, etc.
Welfare Services—care of aged, handicapped, blind and homeless
The Children's Service
Libraries
Cemeteries and crematoria
Registration of local land charges
Allotments
Registration of births, marriages and deaths
Swimming baths and wash-houses
Refuse collection
Inspection of premises for health and overcrowding
Control of vermin, pests and infectious diseases
Disease of animals
Sanitation
Noise and smoke abatement
Weights and measures
Food and drugs
Street Markets and slaughterhouses
Street cleansing
Administration of Shop Acts
Licensing of various establishments, e.g. employment agencies
Information services about the Borough
Elections and registration of electors

Greater London Council

London Fire Brigade
London Ambulance Service
Refuse disposal (London Borough Councils may do this until 1967)
Land drainage—in the London excluded area
Thames flood prevention
Smallholdings
Licensing—Motor vehicle and driving licences, Petroleum storage licences,
Places for public entertainment, Tracks for betting
Supplies Services—purchase and supply of goods and equipment for the G.L.C., the I.L.E.A., the London Borough Councils, if required, and other public bodies
Royal Festival Hall, etc. on South Bank

Greater London Council—continued

Iveagh Bequest, Kenwood
Geffrye Museum, Hackney
Horniman Museum,
  Lewisham
Marble Hill House,
  Twickenham
Crystal Palace

Scientific Services for the
  I.L.E.A., the London
  Borough Councils, if requir-
  ed, and other public bodies
Research and intelligence
  organisation for Greater
  London

Services for which responsibility was to be shared comprised:

Planning: The Greater London Council was the overall planning authority and was required to produce the strategic Greater London Development Plan. It would deal with or give directions on planning applications which were of major importance in the planning of Greater London. The London Borough Councils were the local planning authorities and were required to produce Borough Development Plans within the framework of the strategic Greater London Development Plan. They would receive all planning applications and deal with all those which were not reserved for Greater London Council decision.[11]

Roads: The Greater London Council was responsible for the construction, improvement, maintenance and lighting of main roads (other than trunk roads) in Greater London and for all Thames bridges, other than the four City bridges. It would delegate some of its road functions to the Borough Councils who would be responsible for the construction, improvement, maintenance and lighting of roads other than main and trunk roads.

Traffic: The Greater London Council was the overall traffic authority for roads in Greater London and would authorise traffic management schemes, traffic control, speed limits, pedestrian crossings on main roads, traffic signs, and street parking schemes. It could also provide off-street car parks. The London Borough Councils could provide on- and off-street car parking. They would provide and maintain traffic signs and signals, road markings, pedestrian crossings, subways and metered parking places. The Transport (London) Bill, 1968, provided for the complete reorganisation of public transport in Greater London, the G.L.C. becoming the overall planning authority for London's internal transport

---

[11] The Greater London Development Plan, published in March 1969, gave priority to the improvement of housing, roads and communications, and aimed at pegging the population of Greater London at 7·3 million in order to maintain an adequate labour force.

facilities—buses, underground, highways, traffic and parking arrangements.

Housing: For the time being the Greater London Council had all the housing powers of the London County Council and its stock of houses (about 220,000). The Greater London Council was required to survey the housing needs of Greater London, help to provide houses and employment for Londoners both in London and in the new and expanding towns, maintain a housing exchange bureau, and could make loans for house purchase. The London Borough Councils had full housing powers within their Boroughs, including the provision of new houses, improvement schemes, slum clearance and loans for housing purchase. They took over some 338,000 houses from their predecessors.

Parks: The Greater London Council took over all the parks and varied activities provided by the London County Council; but some of them might later be transferred to the Borough Councils. The Greater London Council had power to provide new parks and open spaces that were of more than local significance. It also took over Green Belt land formerly vested in the London County Council and the Middlesex County Council. The London Borough Councils have power to provide parks and open spaces within their Boroughs and they took over all parks and open spaces provided by their predecessors.

Sewerage and Sewage Disposal: The Greater London Council took over all main sewers and sewage disposal works in the Greater London Council sewerage area including the control of discharges of trade effluents to sewers. In general the London Borough Councils were responsible for sewers other than main sewers, and had control over drains.

Civil Defence: The Greater London Council was responsible for the auxiliary Fire Service and the ambulance and first-aid sections of the Civil Defence Corps and would co-ordinate transport for the dispersal in an emergency of children and their mothers, and young persons. The London Borough Councils each provide a Civil Defence division including headquarters, rescue, welfare (dispersal and care of the homeless and emergency feeding) and wardens' sections.

Building Preservation Orders: The Greater London Council and London Borough Councils had power to make and enforce Building Preservation Orders for buildings of architectural and historic interest.

Control of Building Construction: The Greater London Council was responsible under the London Building Acts for the control of the construction of buildings in inner London. It delegated some of its functions to the inner London Borough Councils. The twenty outer London Borough Councils control the construction of buildings in their Boroughs.

Entertainments: The Greater London Council and the London Borough Councils had power to provide entertainment of any kind including the provision of theatres, concert halls and dance halls.

Education: See provision 6 on p. 69.

The standard attained by the councils in the provision of these services depends largely upon the degree of co-operation which exists between the thirty-two borough councils and the Greater London Council. The London Boroughs Committee was therefore formed as a voluntary association of all the London Borough Councils: (a) to provide a forum for the discussion of common problems and for the provision of common advice; (b) to enable the London Boroughs to speak with one voice when necessary to Government Departments; and (c) to provide a means whereby the Greater London Council can discuss problems affecting the Boroughs without having to go to each of them individually.

The remodelling of local government in Greater London by the 1963 Act constituted the first major reform in the structure of English local government since the late nineteenth century. The legislation was radical and its implementation fraught with major difficulties, particularly during the 1964–65 interregnum when many complex problems had to be resolved. The reorganisation was aided by Labour's council election successes which mollified the former political controversy and supposedly replaced it with "the gentle dew of constructive co-operation". (*The Times*, 1 April, 1965).

The Act was not without its critics, however, who questioned, for example, the reduction in the size of the Greater London Council area originally envisaged by the Herbert Commission; the decision to perpetuate the aldermanic system; the large constituencies and the limited responsibilities of the Greater London Council councillors; the reduction in the number of council seats within Greater London and its significance for democratic representation; the motivation behind some of the amalgamations; the division of responsibilities between the Greater London Council and the Boroughs; the role and future of the I.L.E.A.; or even whether the entire operation was too radical or not radical enough.

If, however, one accepts the Herbert Commission's assessment:

> "that the choice before local government in Greater London is, in truth, to abdicate in favour of central government, or to reform so as to be equipped to deal with present-day problems",[12]

then the structure which emerged, despite any imperfections, was an endorsement of representative local government over centralised control. This was particularly significant at a time when local government faced a progressive diminution of its control over local services and their transfer to government departments or regional bodies. The reorganised London government system was therefore seen as "an act of faith"[13] which the Greater London Council and the London Boroughs would have to justify.

One appraisal of subsequent developments was made by the London School of Economics Greater London Group,[14] and it concluded that the two-tier system in Greater London had "some clear advantages over this system it replaced". The G.L.C. area was viable, its size and resources enabling it "to undertake certain overall functions essential in a great city", while the size and resources of the Boroughs were adequate for the exercise of their functions. The allocation of more important functions to the Boroughs had had an "invigorating effect" upon them and there had been "a general levelling up of standards". Where the respective responsibilities of the two tiers were clearly defined, the system appeared to be working satisfactorily. Differences had occurred, however, where functions had overlapped, more especially in housing, planning and highways, and the London Boroughs Association had played "a notable part" in securing inter-tier co-operation and resolving difficulties. Despite the "obvious merits" which had resulted from the change, however, the "reforms appear to have made little impact on the voting behaviour of the electorate, save in the outer boroughs for the G.L.C. elections". Nevertheless, the

> "general consensus of opinion among those most closely concerned with their implementation is that the London Government reforms are proving a success, though it must still be some time before their full potentialities are realised".

---

[12] The Herbert Commission, para. 707.
[13] *The Times*, 1 April, 1965.
[14] The Greater London Group, "The Lessons of the London Government Reforms", Research Study No. 2, H.M.S.O., 1968.

CHAPTER 4

Local Self-Government

The efficiency of our local government system rests not so much upon a trained bureaucracy as upon the voluntary efforts of community representatives. To them is entrusted a large measure of autonomy and responsibility for the translation of group needs into municipal action. Local government is, in effect, local self-government, and the voluntary principle is one of its pivotal characteristics. As will be seen later, not all representatives are directly elected by the public, but those who comprise the majority, the councillors, are so elected; and it is the way in which the franchise is exercised which largely determines the quality of the representation and the nature of the control which is exercised over the administration of local services.

1. The Local Government Franchise

Much of the law relating to local government elections is consolidated in the Representation of the People Acts of 1949 and 1969. British subjects and citizens of the Irish Republic who are 18 years of age, are entitled to vote at local elections, providing they are not legally disqualified and their names are on the Register of Electors for the authority. The Register is compiled annually by the Electoral Registration Officer (often the Clerk to the local authority), who lists the names of those of voting age on the qualifying date, 10 October, and those who attain voting age during the subsequent twelve months (the date of attaining voting age being indicated). A preliminary register is issued and those who have been omitted may then apply for inclusion; in addition, objections will be heard against the inclusion of individuals. The registration officer decides upon these questions, but there is a right of appeal first to the County Court and then to the Court of Appeal. The final register is then published, coming into effect on the following 16 February and is tenable for the following twelve months.

Prior to the Representation of the People Act, 1969, people who lived outside the local authority but who occupied rateable land or premises of a yearly value not less than £10 within the authority, and were not disqualified in any way, also qualified to be registered and to vote within that authority. The 1969 Act abolished, with effect from the 1970 register, the non-resident franchise and property qualification for candidates at local government elections. This does not apply, however, in the City of London. A person may not vote more than once in the same electoral area at any local government election; and at an ordinary election for any local government authority which is not a single electoral area. (Note, however, that a parish voter may vote in three elections, viz. for the parish council, the rural district council and the county council.) Service voters and Crown employees outside the kingdom and their wives may be registered as voters and may appoint proxies to vote on their behalf. Other absentee voters may apply to the registration officer for permission to vote by post, and since the 1969 Act this has been extended to rural district elections, previously excluded, and to voters who are unable to vote personally by reason of religious observance. The 1969 Act also changed the registration rules to entitle a person to be registered as an elector immediately on reaching the age of 18 and to vote in any subsequent election.

Persons not entitled to be registered or to vote include: persons under 18 years of age, aliens, persons convicted of treason or felony, persons of unsound mind, and, for a five-year period, persons convicted of corrupt and illegal practices at elections. Mental hospital patients and prisoners are not qualified as residents for voting purposes. Peers are not disqualified from local government elections.

2. Frequency of Elections

Local authority elections are held annually or triennially, depending on whether one-third of the councillors retire each year, as in county and non-county boroughs, or whether they retire en bloc every third year, as in administrative counties and parishes. Urban and rural district councils may have one-third of their councillors retiring annually or they may, if the council has passed a special resolution by a two-thirds majority and this has been accepted by the county council, retire en bloc.

Administrative county council elections are held in the week which begins with the Sunday before 9 April. County and non-county borough council elections are held throughout England and Wales on a day fixed by the Home Secretary in the week which begins with the Sunday before 9 May. The date of urban and rural district council elections is decided by the district council and its county council, and will, like borough elections, be held in the week which begins with the Sunday before 9 May. Parish council elections are held on a day arranged by the County Council in the week which begins with the Sunday before 9 May.

3. Candidates for Election

Unlike members of Parliament who may have no particular connection with the constituencies they represent, the law relating to local government elections requires a more positive identity of interest between the candidate and the area he wishes to represent. Not only must he be a British subject of full age (i.e. 21 years), but also be qualified in one of the following ways:

1. By registration as a local government elector for the area of the local authority for which he is a candidate; or

2. By residence within the area of the local authority during the whole of the twelve months preceding the election; for parish councils only, this qualification may be modified to include residence in the parish or within three miles of its boundaries since 25 March in the year preceding election year.

In addition, there are disqualifications which render persons unfit for candidature, and from the many disqualifications which formerly existed, the following still apply:

1. Persons holding any paid office or other place of profit in the gift or disposal of the local authority in question or any of its committees. This will exclude mayors, chairmen or sheriffs who are paid allowances.

2. Bankrupts or debtors who have made a composition with their creditors.

3. Persons surcharged within five years before election or since election by a district auditor to an amount exceeding £500.

4. Persons who within five years before election or since election, have been convicted in the United Kingdom of any offence and sentenced to imprisonment for not less than three months without the option of a fine.

5. Persons disqualified by legislation relating to:

    (a) Corrupt practices e.g. personation, bribery, treating or undue influences, making a false declaration regarding election expenses, or

    (b) Illegal practices, e.g. payment for the conveyance of electors to the poll; the employment of paid canvassers, incurring expenses in excess of the allowed limits, failure of a candidate or his election agent to make certain declarations and returns.

6. In a borough council, being an elective auditor of the borough.

4. Council Elections

The election of councillors may be held:

(a) Annually or triennially, as indicated above, or

(b) To fill casual vacancies which may be occasioned by a councillor's death, his disqualification, his resignation, his election to the office of alderman, his failure to discharge his duties by six consecutive months, or his unauthorised absence from the authority's meetings. The bye-election so caused, is conducted in exactly the same manner as the ordinary elections unless: (i) the vacancy occurs within six months of the termination of the office of the out-going councillors, in which case the seat remains vacant until the ordinary election; or (ii) the vacancy occurs on a parish council, whereupon the council will co-opt a qualified person to fill the vacancy until the ordinary elections are held.

The election campaign formally commences when the Notice of Election is released by the returning officer who organises the local election. He sees that all statutory requirements are complied with and arranges polling stations and the requisite equipment, their manning, the swearing-in of staff and the announcement of the result. For county council elections the returning officer is appointed by the council; in boroughs, one alderman acts per ward but where there is no ward division, the mayor holds the position for the entire borough; and in district councils the clerk undertakes this duty.

Candidates for election may have a variety of motives for offering their services to the local authority, and often they may be supported by a local political organisation. Nomination papers signed by a proposer, a seconder and eight other electors for that area must be handed to the returning officer by noon on the fourteenth day before the election; in rural districts and parishes the nomination papers need only be signed by a proposer and seconder, both electors for that area, and are submitted on the sixteenth day before the election. By the Representation of the People Act 1969 the nomination paper, and ballot papers, may contain a description of the candidate, subject to a maximum of six words, and the restriction prohibiting reference to a candidate's political activities is removed. Nominations must be accompanied by the candidate's written consent to his nomination, by a witness's signature and by a statement of the candidate's qualifications for election. The papers are examined by the returning officer who determines the validity of the nominations.

Each candidate is required to appoint an election agent to handle his campaign, although he may act as his own agent providing he informs the returning officer of his intention at least twelve days before the election.

At this stage, it may be apparent that there is no need for an election campaign because the number of nominations corresponds exactly with the number of vacancies to be filled, in which case the returning officer declares the nominated candidates elected. Alternatively, there may be fewer nominations than vacancies, in which case he declares the candidates elected and fills the remaining vacancies with the retiring councillors who, at the previous election, received the highest number of votes.

Where the nominations exceed the vacancies, a poll must be held by ballot, and the campaign is mounted in the days prior to election day. The agent and his voluntary workers organise support for their candidate by posters, speaking at election meetings and acting as polling or counting agents on election day. Prohibited practices include, amongst others, the indiscriminate sticking of posters, coercion, intimidation or bribery, and payment for cars to convey electors to and from the polls. The candidate, and particularly his agent, must record all election expenditure and ensure that the statutory limitation of £30 together with an additional 1s. 0d. for every six entries in the register of electors, is not exceeded. The limitation at a G.L.C. election is £200 plus 1s. 0d. for every four entries in the electoral register.

Despite the activity displayed by the voluntary workers and the high polls recorded at parliamentary elections, the local authority elector tends to display a remarkable reluctance to participate in the democratic process. The Registrar General's statistical returns for 1958 and 1967, years when triennial elections were held, show that on average in no type of authority did half the electorate exercise a vote (See Table 3). Even more perturbing, however, is the high number of uncontested seats. The result is that the proportion of the total electorate being able to record a vote is much lower than the number qualified to vote, and if we refer to the 1967 poll, the comparative figures for voters as a percentage of *all* local government electors in those local authorities are: county councils 28 per cent, county boroughs 39 per cent; municipal boroughs and urban districts 23 per cent and rural districts 15 per cent. Such figures and the resultant minority councils cast doubt on such statements as "local government is the backbone of democracy".[1] Indeed the Maud Report commented (para. 39): ". . . our local government does not appear to be especially democratic".

The poll returns for individual authorities show a wide variation, for example, from 9·69 per cent in a new London Borough in 1964 to 84·3 per cent in a Welsh urban district in 1962[2]; and the general

---

[1] Quoted in *The Municipal Journal*, 30 July, 1965, p. 2588.
[2] *Ibid.*, 6 August, 1965, p. 2670.

TABLE 3. PERCENTAGE OF ELECTORATE VOTING IN CONTESTED ELECTIONS, AND CONTESTED AND UNCONTESTED SEATS, 1958 AND 1967

Local Authority	1958			1967		
	Unopposed Councillors Returned	*Contested Seats*	*% of electorate voting in contested areas*	*Unopposed Councillors Returned*	*Contested Seats*	*% of electorate voting in contested areas*
Administrative Counties	2,444	1,568	33·3	1,956	1,822	38·7
County Boroughs	250	1,092	40·3	55	1,470	40·3
Municipal Boroughs and Urban Districts	2,211	4,666	42·9	1,250	4,768	42·8
Rural Districts	8,613	2,848	46·2	7,656	3,762	42·8
TOTAL	13,518	10,174	38·6	10,917	11,822	40·4

Source: *The Registrar General's Statistical Review of England and Wales* for relevant years.

tendency is for the percentage voting to fall as the size of the authority increases, though this is not an invariable rule.

Apathy is the decisive factor and many commentators wonder how democratic local government can be when the poll is so low and uncontested seats so numerous. Yet, at the same time as the Local Government Information Office resolved to combat this "creeping paralysis", a contrary viewpoint was expressed by an Ipswich alderman at the 1965 annual conference of the Association of Municipal Corporations:

"Low polls usually mean the electorate is satisfied; high polls often occur when there is something to grouse about".[3]

There may be a degree of truth in this, but public apathy remains an eroding influence upon local democracy.

A number of remedial suggestions have been put forward to attract voters to the booths, and these include: the holding of all local elections on the same day with wireless, T.V., and newspaper commentary providing the necessary stimuli to increase turnout; the retirement en bloc of all councils and the holding of triennial elections; the dissolution of all councils when Parliament is dissolved and the elections of councillors and M.Ps. on the same day and on the same ballot paper.[4] The Maud Report recommended that in all authorities councillors should retire together and the system of triennial elections should be applied in all types of local authority. In the new system advocated by the Redcliffe–Maud Commission it was proposed that all members of all main authorities should be elected on the same day, and that an inquiry should examine whether three years or four would be a better term of office for the main authorities and whether spring or autumn would be a better time for holding elections.

One further suggestion which has received considerable publicity and excited some controversy is the changing of the electoral system to that form of proportional representation known as the single transferable vote. Despite the alleged drawbacks of the system in parliamentary elections, its advocates suggest that the disadvantages would not operate in local government elections.[5]

5. Councillors

Before the new councillor begins his three year term of office he has to make a declaration of acceptance which says:

---

[3] *The Municipal Journal*, 1 October, 1965, p. 3329.
[4] Professor J. A. G. Griffith, "Local Democracy: A Sorry State" in *New Society*, 14 February, 1963.
[5] For some of the main arguments see "Electoral Reform in Local Government", by E. A. Rowe in the *Municipal Journal*, 16 July, 1965 and J. Harvey and L. Bather, *The British Constitution*, Macmillan, 1963, pp. 71–72.

"I (name) of (address), having been duly elected to this office of councillor for the (local authority) hereby declare that I will take the said office upon myself, and will duly and faithfully fulfil the duties thereof according to the best of my judgement and ability."

Similar declarations have been made by 43,000 councillors who to-day, for no monetary reward, direct the activities of over 2 million council employees from rent collectors to teachers and town clerks to rodent officers, and spend on the public's behalf £2,700 million a year, which is more than Britain's defence budget.[6] Within their local authorities they are accorded the status and deference which one might expect from an office which, according to one opinion, "is one of the highest forms of voluntary service in the community."[7]

Yet of all society's roles that of the councillor would appear to be one of the most frequently maligned by the unsatisfied public. The following excerpt from an examiner's report reveals a sad stereotype which is all too prevalent an impression in the public mind:

"Most saw him as little more than an incompetent ignoramus and were consequently somewhat handicapped in assigning him with anything but a very minor, for some even superfluous, place in local administration."[8]

The opinions of young students may not always be regarded as authoritative signposts to the truth, and one might question their objectivity. More validity may be attached to the following assessment, based upon a personal working knowledge, by the President of the Society of Town Clerks:

"He (the councillor) receives no personal advantage from his office, but the demands on his time are ever increasing. He is under closer scrutiny and more liable to be called to account for his actions. He invariably suffers financially from the time he gives to council work, and he can expect no public gratitude for his service. If the public realised the sacrifice, the honest endeavour, and the shrewd judgement which is put at their disposal, they would be less grudging in their thanks, and show more humility in their criticisms."[9]

The public's attitude towards their councillors reflects an amalgam of their own personal experience and assimilated local folklore, their

---

[6] *Observer*, 21 November, 1965.
[7] *The Councillor's Handbook*, a guide for new councillors prepared by the Municipal Journal Ltd.
[8] Report on the Intermediate Examinations of the Institute of Hospital Administrators, *The Hospital*, vol. 61, no. 9, September, 1965, p. 498.
[9] *Guardian*, 3 June, 1965.

7

perceptions being modified by the extent to which their expectations have been satisfied by the council. The public's attitudes are ambivalent: they accept the office as the keystone of the council's structure; they recognise him as a community leader who gives substance to the anonymity of the council's officers, and they may appreciate that without his voluntary acceptance of the time-consuming and enervating work there could be no semblance of democratic control over the administration of local services. Conversely, the councillor can be the focus of all criticism. He is arraigned for erecting incompetence into a system and indicted as a power-seeking, corrupt functionary by those who are incapable of accepting altruism as a valid motivation for voluntary work.

Councillors are expected to help run the local authority in the best interests of its inhabitants, and this requires them to express community opinions in the council and committee meetings; to bring individual grievances to the appropriate departmental officers and follow up any subsequent action; to disseminate sound advice and communicate council proposals to the public; to promote the economic development of the authority by attracting new employment opportunities; to provide ample social and leisure facilities; to act as watchdog over the expenditure of public money by preventing excessive spending, by scrutinising chief officers' proposals, by evaluating priorities; to act as a local ombudsman; and generally to create a viable and efficiently administered community. A tall order requiring high administrative ability—and all for the price of nominal expenses.

It is no small wonder that so many people are reluctant to stand for office, and in March, 1964, a committee under the chairmanship of Sir John Maud was appointed to look into this and related problems. Its terms of reference were:

> "to consider how in the light of modern conditions local government might best continue to attract and retain people (both elected representatives and chief officers) of the calibre necessary to ensure its maximum effectiveness."

Reasons postulated for the reluctance to serve, and which the committee investigated, included distaste for party allegiance or publicity; the lengthiness of committee proceedings; the inconvenient times of meetings and transport difficulties; the feeling that local authorities have insufficient freedom to do what they should do; the financial loss involved and the absence of any adequate arrangements for payment of members; and the unwillingness of some employers to release employees to serve on councils.

One frequent criticism of councillors is that many are too old and unrepresentative of the different age groups comprising the electorate. The Maud Report[10] confirmed earlier research[11] and showed that "members do not reflect the community in terms of age, sex, occupation or education. Members tend to be drawn from the older sections of the population; their average age is 55 and that of women members is somewhat higher. Over a quarter of the adult male population are in the 21–34 age group but only a twentieth of men members are of this age. Over half the men members, but less than a third of the adult male population, are over the age of 55. Members of rural district and county councils are on the average even older as are the aldermen. Comparatively few women serve on local authorities; over half the adult population are women but only about 12 per cent of members are women.

"A fifth of all members are retired people but the proportion of retired people who are members of rural district and county councils is significantly higher." There are also marked occupational contrasts with the population. "For example, employers and managers, and farmers and professional workers, occupy a larger proportion of seats in the councils than their proportion in the general adult male population. But the converse is true of skilled and unskilled manual workers."

The main obstacle to a balanced age and occupational representation is the reluctance of people to become candidates. The factors which affect recruitment are: the time involved[12] (although this covers a number of attitudes), inability to stand for election where one works because of residence elsewhere, the deterrent effect of party politics, absence of training, financial hardship involved, difficulties of release from employment, and the times of meetings.

It is possible that the current reformist spirit in local government may influence some of the more enlightened local authorities to modify those customary practices which tend to exclude the younger professional and manual workers and to introduce improvements in

---

[10] *Management of Local Government*, Vol. 1, Report of the Committee, H.M.S.O. 1967, Chapter 6, and Vol. 2, *in toto*.

[11] For example, Mary Stewart, *Unpaid Public Service*, Fabian Occasional Paper, No. 3, 1964.

[12] In *Town Councillors* by A. Rees and T. Smith (Acton Society Trust) the authors, on the basis of a sample of thirty Barking councillors, comment on the effect of council work on family life. The councillors had an average of fifty main committee meetings annually as well as council meetings, sub, joint and consultative committees and about sixteen hours "homework" a month. The sort of people with whom they may perhaps be compared, in terms of the amount of time spent away from home, are heavy drinkers or commercial travellers.

evening meetings, better allowances, streamlined agendas, clerical assistance—which could make council service more attractive to these groups.

Already some local authorities are embarking upon improvements which only a few years ago would have encountered opposition. One example is the increased attention which is being paid to training of councillors. The expansion of local government work and the complexity and scope of services rendered obviously requires well-informed councillors if they are to carry out the job they were elected to do. Sweden has led the way in this respect with its centralised school for councillors which was established in 1956 and in ten years had provided 27,000 delegates—45 per cent councillors and the remainder local government officers—with courses on local service legislation, administrative procedure, planning and anything else requested by their local authority associations.[13] There was no comparable body in Britain to provide formal training seminars for members, but since the 1960's there has been a slow but progressive build-up of interest in *ad hoc* courses provided by universities and technical colleges. An additional stimulus has been given by the establishment in 1967 of the Local Government Training Board whose provincial training officers have organised courses for members, officers and manual staffs. These have been well complemented by the training activities of such bodies as the Royal Institute of Public Administration, LAMSAC, the Association of Councillors, the Institute of Local Government Administrators, and the Institute of Local Government Studies (Inlogov) at Birmingham University.

A further attraction to those who presently could not afford to stand for council service is the suggestion that a more adequate scale of remuneration should be paid. Since the 1948 Local Government Act, a councillor receives a nominal allowance for food and travel, and a financial loss allowance which amounts to a maximum daily rate of £3 5s. In December 1969 the Government agreed to raise the amount to £4. This system has been frequently criticised particularly as it does not apply to such councillors as housewives or the self-employed. Besides being unsatisfactory the law governing the allowance is ambiguous as to how far councillors can claim for hypothetical earnings which they would have made had they not been engaged on council duties. Whilst the above amounts may constitute a reasonable recompense for members of small authorities, membership of large authorities often entails many hours of attendance weekly at various meetings and a disproportionate amount of travelling

---

[13] *The Municipal Review*, January, 1965 pp. 28–33.

time[14]; in particular, committee chairmanship can be a full-time occupation and thus deserving of some greater allowance. As *New Society* has commented:

> "Our concept of local representation still seems to be rooted in the 19th century assumption of an inexhaustible supply of leisured gentlemen ready to undertake council work".[15]

A more realistic approach is taken in some other countries—a municipal councillor in Paris receives £540 a year and his opposite number in New York City gets £2,500 a year. In this country, political parties may make up the loss suffered by councillors, and this can amount to a considerable sum; Mary Stewart found that 29 per cent of her sample named sums between £25 and £1,000 as their losses in one year.

The opinions presented to the Maud committee were mixed. Lancashire County Council favoured financial recompense but N.A.L.G.O. did not, and other opponents of payment have made an exception for committee chairmen because of the responsibility they bear. Meanwhile, the Greater London Council sought powers to pay councillors an allowance and a bi-party group of members discussed the idea at ministerial level and was assured of a sympathetic reception when parliamentary powers were sought.[16]

The Maud committee's interim report on allowances for elected members, published in June, 1966, pointed out that 87 per cent of councillors questioned never claimed the existing allowance, probably because they were unable to demonstrate financial loss. The committee proposed in lieu an annual expense allowance for councillors, fixed by the local council, and a simplified quarterly claim for travel expenses on which councillors would *not* be required to give details of their journeys. In thus making the councils responsible for deciding the rates of allowances, the proposal, in words attributed to Sir John Maud,

> "runs counter to the general trend of practice in local government in Britain and does strike a blow for trusting the elected representatives of the country."[17]

---

[14] Mary Stewart's survey indicated monthly average council work of 44 hours for county councillors, 40 hours for county borough councillors, 20 hours for municipal and metropolitan boroughs; travelling time: 19 hours and 9 hours for C.C. and C.B. councillors respectively. See also Chap. 6.

[15] *New Society*, 14 February, 1963.

[16] *Municipal Journal*, 22 October, 1965, p. 3537.

[17] *The Times*, 22 June, 1966.

The committee opposed the payment of salaries to council members but in its final report recommended that members of the Management Board should be paid part-time salaries. Additionally, it was not thought necessary to make recommendations on the payment of committee chairmen.

There is always some danger that payment might attract the job seekers who would be keen to grab the "spoils of office" but the benefits which might accrue from the attraction of a better age and occupational cross-section of the public to council service would more than compensate for the odd corporation carpetbagger who slipped through to committee chairmanship. It is fitting that the last words on this aspect and on the role of the councillor should be those of Paul Smith, the former Town Clerk of Bognor Regis and the Secretary and founder of the Local Government Reform Society. Writing about the reform of local government and the need to protect the system from abuse, he said:

> "In considering the problem as a whole, one must not forget the enormous contribution which most local councillors make towards the proper running of their towns by attending committees at all hours of the day and night and by looking into local problems and complaints on behalf of the public. This contribution is invaluable—it absorbs most of a councillor's spare time—yet it is unpaid and, to a great extent, not recognised by the vast majority of people.
>
> "As great as the need of local government reform is the duty of the public to realise the debt owed to its councillors. The status value of a monetary standard is accepted for almost all other forms of service: is this not the time to seriously consider the giving of appropriate financial recognition to these trustees of the public for all the sacrifices made in the interest of service to the community? This would not be a 'quid pro quo' but rather an earnest of our respect for their trust".[18]

6. Indirect Election

Whereas councillors are elected by the public, the holders of the offices of alderman, mayor and council chairman are elected by the councillors and not by the public.

(i) *Aldermen*

Aldermen are elected by the councillors from existing councillors or persons qualified to be councillors. They number one-third of the

---

[18] *The Times*, 16 August, 1965.

number of councillors[19], or a quarter of the full council, and serve for six years; a half of their number retire every third year immediately after the election of new aldermen. Their duties do not differ from those of councillors, except that those in boroughs which are divided into wards act as returning officers at local authority elections.

The aldermanic principle is exclusive to administrative county, county borough and non-county borough councils, and was introduced by the Municipal Corporations Act 1835, to provide borough government with an element of stability and continuity. Its introduction was violently opposed by the Whigs but the Conservatives feared that the councillors' tenure of three years in office was too short a time to guarantee stable local government and consistency of policy over a longer period. One quarter of the council appointed for six years would provide, it was felt, the necessary consistency and continuity of experience. Whig opposition was blocked by the House of Lords and ever since the office has attracted controversy.

Not that the office is without advantages. The system does fulfil to some extent the original aim for continuity of personnel and policy. It is, moreover, an office of great status deriving added prestige from its antiquity and its association in the public mind with "elder statesmen". It allows people of proved merit in many disciplines, and others with experience in various administrative capacities, but who may not wish to become involved in election campaigning or party politics, to be brought on to the council and to use their experience to the advantage of the public. Moreover, the office can be awarded by the council, on the public's behalf, to those who have distinguished themselves or brought benefit to the locality as industrialists, businessmen, social workers, etc. There is also the advantage, more theoretical than real, that in county councils where the elections are held trienially a completely new council could be elected, lacking in experience and detailed knowledge of their predecessors' policies; a half of the aldermen would continue in office for the following three years and could provide invaluable guidance.

Against these advantages, however, must be set the disadvantages:

1. The office, being filled by the choice of councillors, is plainly undemocratic in character.

2. The election of certain councillors or outsiders may cause jealousy among those not elected, and create grudges and vendettas which can only work to the detriment of council harmony and service to the public.

---

[19] In London the ratio is one alderman to six councillors.

3. In boroughs where one third of the councillors are elected annually, there can be no sudden change of council to disrupt continuity. The prime justification thus breaks down.

4. Appointments are rarely made from the electorate, the office generally being reserved for councillors.

5. Appointments are often allocated on the basis of seniority and not ability, with the result that many aldermen are very old. Mary Stewart's sample showed that 80 per cent of the aldermen on two county councils were over 60, more than a third over 70, and three were over 80 years of age.

6. Aldermen can dominate the council. Often the most powerful are elected aldermen and once elected they remain until they choose to retire. Because of seniority, they eventually sit on more committees than do councillors and monopolise a disproportionate number of committee chairmanships.[20]

7. The system is abused extensively for party advantage, particularly when the party in control dead-heats or is defeated at the polls. Aldermanic votes are then used by that party "to entrench itself in power for a further term to flout the will of the people".[21]

This last aspect has been the main source of controversy. In 1949, the Labour group in the L.C.C. retained control by packing the aldermanic seats although it had only sixty-four councillors against sixty-four Conservatives and one Liberal. In the metropolitan borough of Lewisham in 1959, the elections resulted in the Conservatives gaining twenty-eight seats and Labour twenty-seven seats; there was, however, a majority of Labour aldermen and their votes plus the casting vote of the mayor secured the election of an increased number of Labour aldermen, and Lewisham had a Labour-controlled council. A similar occurrence took place in Wolverhampton, but two High Court judges ruled that the election of seven aldermen, including the mayor, was invalid. Another practice is to bring back to the council councillors who are defeated at the elections; e.g. in the Huddersfield County Borough in 1961, when two former Labour councillors were defeated but returned as aldermen. *The Economist* wrote at the time of the Birmingham dead-heat in May, 1961, which resulted in a compromise between the two party leaders to allow Labour to retain effective power:

> "It is by no means unknown for local parties with an actual minority of elected councillors to hang on to office for three more years because they have enough aldermen to swing the vital vote."[22]

---

[20] A. Rees and T. Smith, *Town Councillors*, Acton Society Trust, 1964.
[21] Henry Brooke, *Guardian*, 10 October, 1961.
[22] *The Economist*, 20 May, 1961, p. 755.

Such incidents as these should not be regarded as isolated cases, and there have been frequent demands for legislative action to prevent the misuse of the system. Some local authorities have joined in with cries for reform or abolition of the office. In 1964, Abingdon borough council passed such a resolution as did Oxford City Council.[23] Abingdon went further and circularised every member of the Association of Municipal Corporations to ascertain the degree of support for a memorandum to the Maud Committee, suggesting that if abolition were unpalatable, a number of reforms might be considered. These included making the title of alderman an honorary one, to be bestowed by the council at their discretion upon a limited proportion of senior members without altering their legal status as members of the council retiring every three years; reducing the proportion of aldermen to councillors, presently one to three outside London, to one to six; electing aldermen at the polls in the same way as senators in the American Congress; and ensuring that anyone defeated at the polls should be ineligible for aldermanic election during the following year.

Of the 247 replies to the Abingdon Memorandum, 121 were against change or offered no observations, forty were in favour of abolition or would welcome other reforms as an alternative, sixty-four were in favour of retaining the office subject to some change, and twenty-two were prepared to leave the matter to the Maud Committee or the Association of Municipal Corporations. In a supplement to the Memorandum, the Town Clerk of Abingdon Municipal Borough summed up the result and referred to a questionable attempt to regulate aldermanic elections:

> "It is interesting to note that a number of towns in opposing camps, for instance Abingdon and Preston, attempt to regulate aldermanic elections by Standing Orders. It is submitted that these are ultra vires in the sense that a person could be validly elected Alderman in contravention of such Standing Orders if the provisions of the appropriate statute have been complied with. The very fact that such towns have deemed it necessary to formulate Standing Orders repugnant to the statute to try to regulate these elections, suggests that the present law is in need of some revision.
>
> "The result may perhaps be fairly summed up in a single sentence by saying that there is an overwhelming majority for retaining the office of Alderman, since only 26 Cities and Boroughs are in favour of outright abolition; but that there is a strong and increasing demand for reform of the law

---

[23] *New Society*, 24 December, 1964, p. 17.

relating to the nature, methods of election and tenure of the office."

It is not the office so much as the abuse of the system which makes it imperative that some such legislative measure be undertaken. The office is undeniably undemocratic, but there are advantages to compensate for this. The temptation which the office affords to the unscrupulous to manipulate aldermanic elections, however, can only tarnish the image of local authorities and contribute to a negation of the democratic principle upon which local government is founded. The view of the Maud Committee was that the system had "no logical justification" and that it should be abolished. The Redcliffe–Maud Commission reiterated the proposal and said that there would be no "place for aldermen on local councils, whose basic function is to be directly representative of local people".

(ii) *The Mayor and Council Chairman*

The formal hierarchy of each council is headed by an indirectly elected mayor or chairman, offices which combine the functional aspects of chairmanship, mediation and guidance and the ceremonial duties associated with being the authority's chief representative.

A mayor, resplendent in the traditional and colourful regalia of office, is exclusive to county and municipal boroughs. He is elected by the council at its annual meeting in May from its own aldermen and councillors or from persons qualified to be aldermen and councillors for that borough. Invariably the mayor-elect will have been selected some time before, by a special mayoral selection sub-committee or a private informal meeting, and the basis for selection may be seniority on the council, or it may be for party advantage; rarely, the office may go to an extra-council elector by virtue of his public eminence. The May election is thus more a conventional ritual than a formal contest.

Once elected, he presides over all council meetings and may call a meeting at any time. He has precedence in all places in the borough, unless in the presence of the Lord Lieutenant of the County; he votes at aldermanic elections even if an alderman himself, despite the prohibition against aldermen voting for aldermen; and he represents the borough to all individuals and bodies from within and without the authority, symbolising to them its corporate life. The range of his duties will require his full-time attention, and will therefore entail him in a considerable personal financial loss; the borough may then pay him a reasonable remuneration to offset his obligations and, in a large borough, he may have a mansion house and a mayoral car at his disposal.

At his own discretion he may appoint a deputy mayor, from the aldermen or councillors, and mayor's chaplain. The deputy mayor's name will be notified in writing to the council and he will carry out the mayor's duties when the mayor is unable to act or the office is vacant, but may not take the chair at council meetings, unless so authorised by the council. His office will continue until the mayor's successor is appointed.

The distinctive title of Lord Mayor has been granted to the mayors of twenty-one cities in the country by royal letters patent as a mark of prestige, but there is no special local government significance.

All other local authorities, the administrative counties, urban districts, rural districts and parishes, are presided over by chairmen who will undertake much the same functional and ceremonial role as the borough mayor, but without looking so sartorially decorative. The chairman of a county council is elected annually by the council from among the county aldermen or councillors, or from persons qualified to be county aldermen or councillors. The chairman of an urban or a rural district council is elected annually by the council from among the councillors or from persons qualified to be councillors. Parish council chairmen are similarly elected annually from among the councillors or from persons qualified to be councillors; parish meeting chairmen are chosen annually at the parish meeting, and they preside over all assemblies of the meeting.

Chairmen and mayors were *ex officio* J.P.s, but the Justices of the Peace Act 1968 took away this entitlement, except in the cases of the Lord Mayor and aldermen of the City of London, and empowered mayors of boroughs and the chairmen of the G.L.C., county councils and district councils to carry out certain acts (e.g. authenticating signatures on documents) which can be carried out by J.P.s on the supplemental list. The retiring age was to be progressively reduced from 75 to 70 and provision was also made for the payment of a financial loss allowance.

Vice-chairmen must be elected by county councils and may be elected by district councils from council members. Each vice-chairman will hold office until immediately after the election of a chairman at the next annual meeting of the council. Subject to any standing orders made by the authority, the vice-chairman may execute any duty normally performed by a chairman.

The office of mayor or chairman is the highest honour which any authority can grant members of its electorate. The vast majority of the office-holders have exercised their duties with competence, and, conscious of their pre-eminent position and the responsibilities which have been vested in them, have been able to dissociate themselves from party ties and have generally fulfilled the public's expectations.

Unfortunately, as with the aldermanic role, the system can be, and sometimes is, abused by local party organisations. To-day the office is infrequently given to members of the general public but tends to be reserved for councillors and aldermen on the basis of seniority or as a political reward. The determination of the succession has in certain local authorities become an occasion for heated political wrangling and manoeuvring, with the dominant party exercising a virtual monopoly over the office. The office may then become a source of grievance to the opposition and its incumbent the focus of transferred antipathy.

This attitude will be heightened when the balance of power between parties on the council is marginal and the mayor or chairman is required, in his capacity as chairman of the meeting, to give his casting vote on important issues of policy which have divided the parties or when aldermen are to be elected and the power balance is likely to be affected. In formal groups, one of the chief characteristics of chairmanship is impartiality, but the influences acting on a political appointee may well be too great for him to remain scrupulously neutral. Recorded instances of such partiality are few, but where power is at stake any opportunity to increase it becomes a strong motivation for the unscrupulous.

It is thus essential that he rises above any suspicion of party involvement, and many office-holders have consequently severed their membership and all contact with local party organisations during their year of office. Moreover, in order to minimise accusations of bias and also to devote their full energies to the duties of the office, they have freed themselves of their responsibilities as councillors and suspended their membership and chairmanship of council committees.

The offices of mayor and chairman can personify all that is good in local government, but it is the individual incumbent himself, by his ability, self-discipline and, above all, his awareness of his responsibility to the public, who will ennoble or discredit the image which the public receives.

7. Party Politics in Local Government

The foregoing account has made a number of references to the influence of party politics on the membership and balance of power in the council chamber, and it would be apposite at this stage to attempt to assess its contribution to local government. One opinion has appraised its influence in the following terms:

"A new trend in local government theory can be drawn. . . . A majority of seats on a council, however small, is now taken to be a mandate for absolute control. It is the Parliamentary outlook. Everything follows logically from this. It is seen at its most consistent in places like Bristol, where Labour takes full control even with a majority of four; but, when in a minority, moves into straight opposition. The idea is—no sharing of responsibility, no co-operation."[24]

There is much evidence in the larger authorities to substantiate such a view; but the vast majority of local authorities are small and less tightly organised politically, and many have no political divisions at all. Moreover, one should not assume that political allegiances necessarily imply a continual atmosphere of party polemic and bitterness, for much council work, particularly in committee, is characterised by a spirit of co-operation and moderation.

Nevertheless party divisions do exist, and have been a significant feature of local government for many years. Local political associations came into being with each successive extension of the franchise in the last century, particularly after the Reform Act of 1867 increased the electorate by millions in the fast-expanding industrial towns.

At first the associations were most strongly organised in the larger provincial cities and industrial centres of the North and Midlands where, by the 1870s, municipal elections were being fought on party tickets. Soon such municipalities were also being run on party lines, as for example was Birmingham under the mayoralty of Joseph Chamberlain in 1873.

Local political associations were slightly later in developing in the south of England, but from its inception in 1889 the London County Council was organised on a party basis with the majority party, the Progressives, made up of Liberals and a few Fabians, and the opposition, the Moderates, being mainly Conservatives. The Conservative Prime Minister, Lord Salisbury, fulminated at the London County Council in 1894, as,

"the place where Collectivist and Socialistic experiments are tried . . . a place where the new revolutionary spirit finds its instruments and collects its arms."[25]

---

[24] Roy Perrott, "Whips in the Council Chamber", *Guardian*, 6 August, 1959. Note also the Maud Committee's comment (para. 367): ". . . in none of the other countries are the parties 'permanently embattled in the same way as in many English industrial authorities'."
[25] W. A. Robson, *The Government and Misgovernment of London*, Allen & Unwin, p. 86.

By the time the Labour Party was formed in 1906, party political grouping was primarily rooted in the councils of most large towns. The non-payment of M.Ps. (until 1911) and the well-established national organisations supporting the Conservative and Liberal parties in Parliament, made the idea of a third and embryonic party achieving parliamentary control an extremely remote possibility. Earlier, local Independent Labour Party groups had turned their attention to local government and, primed with Fabian policies, the Labour Party joined in the local fray with no little success. In the 1919 local government elections Labour won 412 seats, gained control of the large county borough of Bradford and of twelve metropolitan boroughs; in contested elections in 1961 Labour gained 43·3 per cent of the votes in comparison with the 44·7 per cent won by the Conservatives and their supporters.[26]

An impression of the political alignment of local councils in England and Wales in 1968 can be gained from the following table based on figures published in *The Municipal Year Book* 1969:[27]

Party control	Types of councils					
	C.B.s	*London*	*C.C.s*	*N.C.B.s*	*U.D.s*	*R.D.s*
Conservative controlled	66	88	14	37	22	4
Labour controlled	17	9	3	10	22	5
Liberal & other Party controlled	0	0	2	1	2	0
Multi-party	8	3	10	16	17	2
Independent	4	0	35	30	32	69
Not known	5	0	36	6	5	20

This table gives no indication, however, of the vast diversity of political opinion and organisation which exists in each local council. An analysis of political activity in four English towns by J. G. Bulpitt confirmed the assessment of A. H. Birch that "local parties are highly

---

[26] Ivor Gowan, "Role and Power of Political Parties in Local Government", *Local Government Today—and Tomorrow* (ed. D. Lofts), *Municipal Journal*, 1962, p. 86.
[27] *Municipal Year Book* 1969, Municipal Journal Ltd. Table derived from B. C. Smith and J. Stanyer, "Administrative Developments in 1968: A Survey", *Public Administration*, Autumn 1969, Vol. 47, p. 364.

individual, conditioned more by their environment than by directives from central office and largely independent in managing their own business".[28] In the four towns, only housing was consistently influenced by party politics, and in "other policy sectors no general pattern of party disagreement emerged". In the main, the "style of local party politics . . . seemed to be determined to a large extent by individual Councillors, the differences between them, and the past political histories of the local authorities". There was no evidence of bitter division between local parties on national party lines, but rather a desire to practise political restraint and avoid divisive issues. "With the exception of the Salford Labour Party all parties appeared embarrassed by their activities in local government. The predominance of patronage disputes suggests a preoccupation with the possession of power, not the use of it for policy purposes."

Bulpitt concluded his informative study with a tentative classification of party systems in local government into positive and negative systems. In the former, party representatives are in the majority and the parties accept a degree of political responsibility for Council work; the positive system can be further sub-divided according to the importance of (a) size and stability of the majority party, (b) the pattern of patronage distribution, and (c) the way in which Standing Orders are interpreted by the Labour Group. Negative systems are where two or more minority parties exist among a majority of Independents, there is little political responsibility for running the council, and "party is merely an electoral device".

Where party control is strongly organised, particularly on the councils of the larger municipalities and cities, "a kind of Parliamentary government in miniature" develops. Within that microcosm "a tougher, parliamentary outlook" prevails where,

> ". . . the party whips crack audibly off-stage; in which policy is decided out of sight and sound of press and public. . . in which there is often an informal 'Cabinet' of leading party men whose influence is unquestionable (or at least unquestioned); in which there is a clear division between the governors and the opposition, both tending to speak with one unified prefabricated voice from the depths of the party machine".[29]

The "voice" is "prefabricated" in that policy decisions are taken at party caucus meetings before the council meets. Here council members of the majority party, together with non-council members of the local party organisation, who may or may not have voting powers,

---

[28] J. G. Bulpitt, *Party Politics in English local Government*, Longmans, 1967.
[29] Roy Perrott, "Whips in the Council Chamber", *Guardian*, 6 August, 1959.

hammer out policy. Individuals may express their differing view-points in private, but once a line of action has been decided, individual members are expected to abide by the majority decision and to vote accordingly when the council meets. Failure to do so may result in expulsion.

The Labour group which controlled Leeds City Council had a highly organised party caucus which met at the "epitome" meeting before the council meetings and mid-monthly. This meeting "controls council proceedings", wrote Professor Wiseman who continued:

> "It shows also a group which devotes much time to study of the Council agenda and to minutes of committees other than those on which the inquiring member himself serves and which is determined to keep leader and chairman on their toes. The epitome meeting is essential if the majority party is to control the affairs of the Corporation."[30]

Thus the majority party caucus may be seen not only as the real decision-making body but also as an agency for the control of its own members. The council meeting, as a result, tends no longer to be "an instrument for decision but, like the House of Commons, an instrument for propaganda".[31]

Other results of majority party control will be seen in the emergence of the party leader as leader of the council, dominating its meetings, and the party's virtual monopoly of the chairmanships and vice-chairmanships of committees, aldermanic seats, mayoralties and council chairmanships. Sharing these offices on the basis of party strength, with the mayoralty/chairmanship alternating between Labour and Conservative nominees now tends in the larger towns and cities to have become more a residual tradition of the past than a convention to be perpetuated.

Opinions vary considerably as to the necessity and value of party politics in local government, and the following arguments for and against summarise some of these opinions. The case against political groups might include the following arguments:

1. Party politics are unnecessary and irrelevant in local government. Local authorities are primarily administrative, not legislative, bodies which are required to implement policies already decided in Parliament. The areas where local discretion is permitted are not so controversial as to require the confrontation of local party machines and should be decided on the basis of benefit to the community and

---

[30] H. V. Wiseman, "The Party Caucus in Local Government", in *New Society*, 31 October, 1963.
[31] Sir Ivor Jennings, *Principles of Local Government Law*, U.L.P. 1963, p. 129.

not political expediency. In this respect W. A. Robson has written: ". . . party alignments and loyalties tend to become a public nuisance when they are linked up with matters which have no bearing on the work of the Council".[32]

2. Acceptance of the party whip necessarily limits a councillor's freedom of decision and independence of action. Unlike the M.P., he does not have such extensive and tangible election support from the party to repay; his major obligation is thus to the electorate and their immediate, personal and local problems, not to the party machine.

3. The majority party caucus is an undemocratic institution insofar as its deliberations are influenced by the participation of party association representatives; the press and the public are excluded and the local authority's officers are never present to be consulted. Yet its decisions can exercise an important influence over the conduct of major community services.

4. Since the majority party caucus determines what the council does, the council meeting itself is an irrelevancy, and democratic control a hollow sham:

> "Local government is one of the sacred cows of the political mythology about the working of democracy in the United Kingdom. The idea that local government is essentially more democratic than central government lives on despite the singularly undemocratic working of local representation and of local elections."[33]

5. The majority party's decisions at the caucus meetings may be based upon a small majority vote of perhaps one. The image which is presented to the full council and to the public is, however, one of complete unanimity. The electorate will be unaware of the discussion preceding the vote, the alternative proposals expressed, and which council members took an independent line. These latter will be required to approve the narrow majority view, regardless of conscience or principles, at the council meeting, and may even have the additional embarrassment of having to defend as chief spokesman the party's final decision.

6. The majority party's monopoly of offices in the council and the committees may be interpreted by the public as a form of Tammany Hall corruption. Within the council the distribution of the spoils of office may cause jealousy, and the exclusion of worthy opposition members will add to their resentment.

7. Party politics contribute to the community's electoral apathy, help to dissuade able non-party men and women from standing for candidature or for co-option to council committees, and alienate the public from the council's members and officers.

---

[32] *Ibid*, p. 87.
[33] *Public Law*, 1962, Editorial, p. 5.

8

8. In areas dominated by one party, its candidate is certain to be elected, whether opposed or not. The real selection will therefore be the "primary", where a candidate is chosen to stand for the party by the party leaders. They will almost invariably prefer conformists, and the electorate loses all direct influence over the type of candidate who is presented for election. The candidate will thus represent his party and not necessarily his ward.

9. The emergence of a party leader who "guides and controls his party's contribution to the business and debates of the council and ... makes major pronouncements on council policy" may well become a form of autocratic dominance. Professor Gowan continues: "There is some danger that, surrounded by weak colleagues, and with an ineffective opposition, the leader can become the 'boss', and that the party system is then prone to degenerate into 'one-man' government. Such cases are fortunately rare . . ."[34]—but not unknown.

Those who defend the existence of party politics in local government have advanced the following advantages:

i. The party system, with a majority kept on its toes by an effective opposition, the local press and its own internal discipline, provides a local authority with strong and efficient administration. The alternative, a council composed of individualists, would result in compromise decisions which would satisfy no one, least of all the public.

ii. Party organisations give greater definition, vitality and coherence to the conduct of local matters, and "a proposal supported or opposed on party lines, gets a better and more zealous exposition and advocacy, and a more comprehensive discussion than otherwise might be the case".[35]

iii. To expect "the cut and thrust of debate" in the council chamber followed by a free vote to determine the outcome of disputed policies is to display a naïve interpretation of the purpose of a council meeting. The majority group's decision can be questioned in council, and after discussion matters can be referred back to committees for reconsideration, but debate will generally not change the majority group's earlier decision. This does not entail anything novel in our governmental process, and as Professor Wiseman has observed:

> "Debates are to educate public opinion and to enable parties to express their views and stake a claim for future support from the electorate. This argument may be even more valid in local government because the vast majority of decisions are on detailed administrative matters which a large meeting is incompetent to decide. At most it is competent to refer the matter back to the appropriate committee for further consideration."[36]

---

[34] *Ibid*, p. 74.
[35] H. Emerson Smith, "Party Politics in English Local Government," in *Secretaries' Chronicle*, March, 1955.
[36] *Ibid*, p. 10.

iv. Party politics educate the public and make local government understandable to the electorate. Without the spice of party strife in the council chamber, interest in the work of the local authority would be far less than it is; the exclusion of politics would increase the electorate's apathy and the number of uncontested seats. A study of local democracy by R. P. Lowry in "Micro City" in California showed that where personalities and not parties fight local elections, antipathy directed against a depersonalised party might be replaced by open hostility against candidates. An American study may not be strictly relevant to British experience, but a case may be made for the retention of political alignments in British local government. An editorial in *New Society*[37] commented:

". . . the problems of recruiting the right people to local government and arousing public interest are not solved by getting rid of organised politics. The party structure, to some extent, provides politicians with backing to offset personal abuse and enables issues to be seen in less personal terms. And if party politics are removed the electorate appears to feel even less involved in decisions than they do in Britain now. The achievement of effective grass roots democracy demands that local government should be made more, not less, a part of national political life."

v. The caucus meeting, far from rendering individual councillors politically impotent, provides them with an opportunity to speak their mind, without fear of misquotation in the press or mis-interpretation by the public or the council's officers, and to persuade their colleagues of the validity of their proposals. Similarly, they may ventilate constituents' grievances and those of local minority groups and make their leaders aware of ward or area difficulties. Such an opportunity is not available in the council meeting where a rigid timetable has to be maintained and "backbench" councillors have little opportunity to speak. Moreover, the caucus meeting's detailed analysis of the council agenda, which comprises the minutes of all committees, is not only personally valuable in providing councillors with a survey of the entire gamut of council affairs, but, more significantly, allows them to question committee chairmen on the content of their minutes so ensuring that proposals are dissected. If the replies of a chairman are unsatisfactory, the minutes may be referred back to the committee for reconsideration. Finally, where a party has a substantial majority on the council, leaders may become complacent or may assume oligarchic control; the caucus meeting permits members to exercise control over their leaders without committing the party to unseemly debate in the council before the opposition and the public.

In conclusion it may be said that debate on the necessity for party politics in local government will continue as long as politics remain an

---

[37] 14 January, 1965.

integral feature of local administration, and there is no indication that its incidence is diminishing. Party allegiance need not be detrimental to the efficient working of local authorities, and may indeed make significant contributions to local government.[38] Political power, however, can be abused, and the surest safeguard against its abuse rests with a discerning and responsible electorate.

---

[38] *Management of Local Government* (Maud Report), Vol. 1, paras. 32–33: "The presence or absence of local parties does not determine the quality of local government . . . England manages relatively well, though there is evidence that in a minority of authorities parties tend to have too much of a stranglehold in day-to-day operations. . . ."

CHAPTER 5

The Local Government Service

1. General Introduction

Local authorities employed over two million people in 1969. These constituted one-twelfth of the nation's working population and included solicitors, architects, midwives, teachers, work-study officers, accountants, labourers, dustmen, engineers, park attendants and many others who are essential to the efficient working of local authority services.

Within this diverse employment range a distinction is made between those in "the local government service" and the remaining employees. The "service" as such is made up of officers, that is

> "those who participate in the administration and management of Local Authority services, and whose duties are of an administrative, professional, technical or clerical nature".

Excluded from the "service" classification are the manual workers, or "servants", and also teachers and the police, who, in J. H. Warren's words "are usually thought of as belonging to separate and well-defined services of their own".[1]

It is important to note this distinction between the "service" and the remainder, and to realise that while the efficiency of local authority services depends upon the many specialist abilities of its officers there is a far larger body of personnel who perform essential duties, and more often under the critical gaze of the public. All are included in Table 4 which represents the total number on the pay-rolls in each of the main departments and services of local authorities in June, 1969.

Councils are empowered to appoint such officers as they "think necessary for the efficient discharge of the functions of the Council". In addition to these discretionary appointments there are certain statutory appointments. Under Part IV of the Local Government

---

[1] J. H. Warren, *The Local Government Service*, Allen & Unwin, 1952, v.

TABLE 4. NUMBERS EMPLOYED BY LOCAL AUTHORITIES AND IN POLICE FORCES IN ENGLAND AND WALES—JUNE 1969

Department or Service	MALES		FEMALES		Total males and females
	Full-time	Part-time	Full-time	Part-time	
Education department:					
(a) Lecturers and teachers	183,072	57,127	206,359	86,342	532,900
(b) Other staffs (clerical, school cleaners, school canteen staff, etc.)	66,750	19,289	114,432	328,914	529,385
Water supply	10,763	36	621	288	11,708
Construction	110,239	234	1,354	280	112,107
Transport services	53,655	126	6,196	549	60,526
Health services, day nurseries, children's, aged persons' and other homes	40,054	3,923	97,471	94,027	235,475
Restaurants and canteens (excluding school canteens); orchestras; entertainments; amusement parks; race courses; golf courses, etc.	6,208	1,884	4,466	4,461	17,019
All other local authority departments	382,065	19,099	91,174	40,940	533,278
Police forces (inc. Metropolitan Police)	87,758	—	3,515	—	91,273
Grand Total	940,564	101,718	525,588	555,801	2,123,671

Source: *Employment and Productivity Gazette*, October, 1969.

Act 1933, county, borough and district councils must appoint a clerk, treasurer, medical officer of health, surveyor (but not in a rural district), and, with the exclusion of county councils, at least one public health inspector. Parish councils may appoint a clerk and a treasurer, but only the clerk, if he is not a member of the council, may be paid. Rural borough councils may appoint a town clerk, a treasurer and any other officers considered necessary. Other acts require the appointment of a chief education officer and a children's officer in counties and county boroughs, and a coroner, a public analyst, inspectors of shops and of weights and measures, and registration and returning officers for elections in all local authorities performing these services.

Fitness to fulfil the specifications of an appointment is generally a matter for the individual local authority to determine, on the basis of its own selection criteria and the availability of candidates, but for some appointments qualifications are prescribed by statute or by ministerial regulations. Medical officers of health, public health inspectors, health visitors, midwives, and inspectors of weights and measures have to be qualified. On the other hand, no specific qualifications are required for clerks to the authority, or surveyors, and all that is required is that each should be a "fit person".

A number of appointments are subject to central government approval. The Secretary of State for Education requires a list of candidates with their qualifications for appointment as chief education officer, and he may prohibit the appointment of anyone he considers to be unfit for the post. Similar powers are granted to the Home Secretary over the appointment of a children's officer. The appointment of a chief constable or a chief fire officer is also subject to the approval of the Home Secretary, while the approval of the Minister of Agriculture, Fisheries and Food is required before the appointment of a public analyst.

In certain cases the dismissal of officers is similarly subject to Ministerial control. The medical officers of health, and the public health inspectors of boroughs and county districts cannot be dismissed without the approval of the Minister of Health; the surveyor's dismissal must similarly be first approved by the Minister of Transport, but only where he contributes to his salary; and the clerk of a county council and the county medical officer of health, although appointed "during the pleasure of the council", cannot be dismissed without the approval of the Minister of Housing and Local Government and the Minister of Health respectively. There is, consequently, considerable security of tenure in such offices, but otherwise the staff is generally engaged "during the pleasure of the council", and the

Local Government Act, 1933, specifically refers in this respect to the county treasurer and county surveyor, the town clerk, borough treasurer, surveyor, and the general staff of a borough, and the clerk, treasurer, surveyor and general staff of a district council. Nevertheless, a local authority and an officer may enter into an agreement, in the terms of the appointment, that neither party may terminate the appointment without reasonable notice.

In addition to the statutory appointments so far considered, there is the larger body of officers recruited according to need. In the *Scheme of Conditions of Service*, known variously as "The Charter" or "The Purple Book", details are given of a new salary structure which came into effect on 1 February, 1967. The new categories of staff are:

A. *Clerical Division*

The General Division and Clerical Grade I are replaced by a new Clerical Grade I which has within it a routine work bar. Progression beyond this depends upon work performed rather than qualifications held. Clerical Grades II and III are retained and a fourth grade has been created to cover posts undertaking the more senior clerical work.

B. *Administrative and Professional Division*

1. Trainee Grade. Introduced to secure a better share of the talented youngsters who will be needed to fill senior posts in the future. It will accommodate officers while studying for their qualifications, and after qualifying they will be expected to be appointed to professional or administrative posts.

2. A.P. Grades. The former Grades A.P.T. I to A (renamed V) have been retained for officers performing professional and/or administrative work and have therefore been renamed A and P Division. Certain technical officers will be transferred to a new division (see D below) Grades A.P. III, IV, and V will be used to from the first stage professional grade for special classes of officer—qualified solicitors, finance staffs, architects, engineers, surveyors, planning staff, valuers, land agents and administrative staff.

3. Senior Officers Grade. Introduced to replace Grades B and C.

C. *Principal Officers*

Introduces two salary ranges to replace Grades D to I. In determining the salary grade for each of the Principal Officer posts the local authority is to choose five consecutive points from either Range I or

II. The salary of the gradings of posts above the level of Range II will be at the discretion of the employing authority.

D. *Technicians and Technical Staffs Division*

A new salaries division of six grades, introduced for officers undertaking work of a technical nature which requires a special kind of training or expertise but does not need to be done by officers with a professional qualification, e.g. draughtsmen, clerks of works, building inspectors, laboratory/workshop technicians. It excludes posts of a professional nature filled by unqualified officers.

E. *Typists and Machine Operators*

F. *Miscellaneous Classes*

Eight salary grades replace the former scales for a range of occupations including education welfare officers, school meals supervisors, etc.

The salaries of the Clerk to the authority, the medical officer of health, the chief education officer, the treasurer, the chief architect and the engineer and surveyor when above Range II (q.v. C above) are at the discretion of the employing authority, but within minima which are related to the population size of the local authority. It should be noted too that the remuneration of Clerks to county councils must by statute be approved by the Minister of Housing and Local Government, and of certain medical officers of health and inspectors by the Minister of Health. In the health and education services the appropriate minister will make orders or regulations to which local authorities have to adhere, but where there are no legal provisions the only requirement in law is that the local authority "may pay ... such remuneration as they may determine". In practice, however, the terms and conditions of employment of local authority staff are negotiated at a national level by employer and officer representatives to the National Joint Council for Local Authorities' Administrative, Professional, Technical and Clerical services, and these are implemented by most local authorities.

2. The National Joint Council (formed in 1944 and sometimes referred to as the National Whitley Council) comprises sixty-three members, of whom thirty-two represent the employers and thirty-one the officers, appointed as follows:

A. *Employers' Side:*

One representative of the employers' side of each of the Provincial Councils (excluding the Greater London District).

Four representatives of the employers' side of the Greater London District Whitley Council.

Seven representatives from the Association of Municipal Corporations.

Five representatives from the County Councils Association.

Two representatives from the Urban District Councils Association.

Two representatives from the Rural District Councils Association.

B. *Officers' Side:*

One representative from the employees' side of each of the Provincial Councils (excluding the Greater London District).

Four representatives from the employees' side of the Greater London District Whitley Council.

Eight representatives of the National and Local Government Officers' Association.

Three representatives of the National Union of General and Municipal Workers.

Two representatives of the National Union of Public Employees.

One representative of the Transport and General Workers' Union.

One representative of the Confederation of Health Service Employees.

An independent Chairman is appointed for three years by the Minister of Housing and Local Government and has no voting rights.

C. *Functions of National Joint Council:*

"To secure the largest possible measure of joint action for the consideration of salaries, wages and service conditions of officers within the scope of the Council and to consider such proposals in reference to these matters as are submitted to them from time to time by the Provincial Councils".

There are thirteen Provincial Councils whose membership varies from district to district, but N.A.L.G.O. representatives are in the majority on the staff side of each Council. Moreover, the Provincial Council representatives on the employees' side of the national council are all members of N.A.L.G.O. In addition, there are local joint committees within these local authorities where the employing authorities afford "facilities for regular consultation with representatives of their staffs on all questions affecting their conditions of service". The Model Constitution, determined by the National Joint Council, outlines the functions of such a committee: to establish regular methods of negotiation for the prevention of differences and their settlement should they arise, but excluding cases of individual discipline, promotion or efficiency; to consider any relevant matters referred by local authority committees or staff organisations; to make recommendations to the appropriate committee relating to the applicability of terms and conditions of service, training and education of officers; and to refer questions to the appropriate Provincial Council, provided the local authority approves, and inform it of any matter which is of more than local interest.

Alongside the tiered negotiation structure for officers there is the National Joint Council for Local Authorities' Services (Manual Workers) which since 1919 has negotiated wages and conditions of service for local authority manual workers and is organised on Whitley principles. It excludes craftsmen whose national rates and conditions are negotiated by their unions and local authorities pay the agreed rates and any additional local differentials which appertain. Other groups of employees have their own negotiating machinery in: Joint Negotiating Committee for Chief Officers of the Local Authorities—representing finance officers, engineers and surveyors, chief education officers, chief architects and the deputy clerks of boroughs and county districts; Joint Negotiating Committee for Town Clerks and District Council Clerks (excludes Clerks to County Councils); Burnham Committee—for teachers; National Joint Council for County Council roadmen; National Joint Council for Local Authorities' Fire Brigades; Whitley Functional Councils for the Health Services; Joint Committee for Water Engineers' Salaries; the Police Council and so on. On these bodies the officers are represented by their own trade unions or professional bodies.

The Charter states that, "Negotiations between individual local authorities and unorganised workers are impracticable" and consequently recommends local authorities to recognise the organisations which are represented on the National Joint Council, adding that "the interests of local authorities and their staffs are best served by individual officers joining their appropriate organisations, it being understood that the organisation he joins is a matter for the unfettered judgment of the individual officers."

The predominant union in local government is, of course, N.A.L.G.O. which was founded with 8,000 members in 1905 from the federation of the Municipal Officers' Association, a number of Municipal Officers' Guilds and the Association of Municipal and County Engineers, and was certified as a trade union in 1920. The Association's name was changed in 1952 from the National Association of Local Government Officers to the National and Local Government Officers' Association, "to take into account its newly extended membership to staffs in nationalised health, electricity, gas and other services". In 1964, affiliation to the T.U.C. was agreed by ballot after having been rejected by members on a number of occasions since 1921. It is the fourth largest trade union in Britain and the largest white-collar union in the world with a membership which has doubled since 1948 to 373,000 in 1969, of whom about 210,000 work in local government. It is organised in 1,406 branches in twelve districts. Its assets are valued at more than £1½ million and its income, mainly from members' subscriptions, amounts to over £¾ million a year.

3. The Departmental Structure

Local authorities are organised on a departmental basis, with each function, service or group of related services being the responsibility of a particular department. The departmental hierarchy is headed by a chief officer who delegates sectors of work to his section heads, and is himself responsible to a committee of councillors and aldermen for the detailed day-to-day work of the department. Some departments such as that of the Clerk or the Treasurer provide a common service to all other departments. Departments such as education or public health provide a specific service. Certain departments may combine common and specific functions—the engineer's department will be solely responsible for roads and serve other departments.

There would be little point in describing a typical departmental lay-out or the structure of any one department, because each local authority is to a large extent unique and its organisational forms are determined by statutory requirements, and the stimulus of purely local needs. Moreover, the pattern of organisation within a department will reflect the chief officer's ideas of the best form of organisation, the availability of manpower, its efficiency and the persistence of customs, practices and procedures from the past. Briefly, however, the range of responsibilities of the following chief officers might include:

A. Clerk of the local authority: co-ordination of the activities of all departments; servicing of committees; legal advice and work regarding purchase or sale of property, promotion of bills, representation of the council at inquiries, etc.; public relations; manning and establishment work, secretarial services; licensing; safeguarding council records.

B. Treasurer: Council finance and accounts; advice on financial policy; costing; internal audit; calculation and make-up of wages; collection of rents on council property; preparation of annual estimates of income and expenditure; ensures all payments are legal.

C. Engineer and Surveyor: Construction and maintenance of council properties including roads, bridges and sewage disposal works; refuse disposal; building maintenance works; street lighting; construction of parks, baths, stores; and sometimes responsibility for town and country planning and control over architectural and housing provision activities.

D. Chief Education Officer: Administration of all schools and colleges maintained and assisted by local education authority; education services; youth employment; school meals and supplies; youth clubs; engagement of teachers; appointment of school caretakers; museum, art gallery and library provision.

E. Medical Officers of Health: Statutorily responsible for the oversight of Public Health Services generally, which include the personal health services, school medical service, clinics and prevention, notification and treatment of disease, also welfare services for the old, blind and mentally handicapped; and is usually, through the Public Health Inspectorate, concerned with bad housing, clean air and general environmental health.

F. Public Health Inspector: Responsible by statute for environmental public health conditions, including prevention of nuisances, inspection of meat and other food supplies, supervision of lodging houses, inspection of unfit dwellings, sampling of water supplies, clean air duties and, if directed by the Local Authority, supervision of refuse collection and disposal.

4. The Clerk

At the centre of the administrative network is the principal officer, the Clerk to the local authority. His conditions of service state that he "shall be the chief executive and administrative officer of the council and shall be responsible for conducting the whole of the work of the council". The office originated in towns in the thirteenth century but there are few references to the post in borough charters before 1600. His duties were varied but he was commonly required to translate and convey all communications from Westminster to the townsfolk; he had to know the law and represent his borough in disputes with Westminster and other boroughs; he had to be able to write and spell in order to keep the town's rolls, and copy deeds, wills and charters; and he was sometimes required to manage the town's accounts. As his duties increased so did his influence, and the opportunities for various corrupt and irregular practices within a closed and self-perpetuating corporation were always present. The report of the

Royal Commission of 1833 considered these irregularities and when the Municipal Corporations Reform Bill was drafted the town clerks' position and their tenure, generally for life, were acrimoniously debated. The 1835 Act embodied a compromise between the radical Whigs and the protective Tories and laid down that the town clerk would in future "hold his Office during (the Council's) pleasure", that he would be a "fit Person", and that he could not be a council member nor a treasurer, elected auditor or assessor. His duties were specified, the main being the counter-signature of orders for payment, responsibility for the compilation of the Freeman's Roll and the publication and distribution of Burgess Lists, and he was required to send a summons to each council member to attend council meetings.

Almost invariably, town clerks still continued to conduct their own private legal practices, but the addition of public health, sanitation and various other services in the nineteenth century made it increasingly difficult for them to maintain a dual role. Their statutory town duties were increased only slightly by the Municipal Corporations Act 1882, which made them responsible for keeping the charters, deeds, records and documents of the borough, and for supervising the nomination procedure for local elections and giving notice of election; they were also required to prepare and submit an annual return of receipts and expenditure to the Local Government Board. By the Local Government Act 1929, the Clerk became responsible for the supervision of the registration of births, deaths and marriages, while the Representation of the People Acts between 1918 and 1949, made him the key figure in the conduct of parliamentary and local elections; the Land Charges Act 1925, added to his responsibilities that of registering local land charges, and the Housing Act and Public Health Act, both in 1936, specified for the Clerk certain duties of a clerical nature.

Administrator or Lawyer?

The Clerk's duties are, consequently, manifold and important, and single him out as the central figure in the chief officer echelon. However, overshadowing his three basic functions of lawyer, secretary and spokesman, is a fourth major function—that of co-ordinating the work of the different departments within the authority. Co-ordination is essentially an administrative technique, and the assumption that this talent is best exercised by legally trained clerks is felt by many to be quite unwarranted. As the scope of local government became wider and more complex it became increasingly necessary that one official should be entrusted with the task of co-ordinating administration. The Royal Commission on Local Government (the

Onslow Commission) concluded in 1929 that the most suitable
co-ordinating officer was the Clerk and while

> "the balance of convenience points to the selection of a clerk with
> legal qualifications", the Commissioners also felt that it would
> be "regrettable if such a requirement were maintained to the
> exclusion of candidates who might bring into the services of an
> authority abilities of a high order".

In 1934, the Hadow Committee report on the qualifications,
recruitment, training and promotion of Local Government officers,
which "exerted a considerable influence in official circles"[2] as far
as the local government service was concerned, took the same view
as the Onslow Commission, stating:

> "The essential qualifications of the clerk is administrative ability.
> He should be a person of broad and constructive outlook,
> interested in the wider issues of local government, skilled in
> negotiation, and he should ordinarily have had experience of
> administrative work".

The report added that

> "too much importance should not be attached to the legal
> qualifications. We recognise its practical convenience, but we
> do not consider it essential where the Clerk's administrative
> duties are sufficiently heavy to occupy practically his whole
> attention, and a legal staff is employed".

To insist on legal qualifications would exclude

> "persons of high administrative ability whose experience has
> been gained in other work".

The reports of the Treasury O. and M. Division on Coventry city
council in 1953 referred to the need for a town clerk, acting in the
capacity of a Chief Administrative Officer and to

> "changing the nature of the principal post", adding that it
> "would no longer be appropriate for the holder of the post also
> to be the Council's Legal Adviser because that would serve to
> obscure the purely administrative nature of the post and weaken
> it by the association of unrelated activities".

It was felt that the effect of making the post wholly administrative
would, incidentally, improve staff morale and corporate spirit by

> "throwing the post open for future generations on the basis of
> their administrative abilities and not primarily of their pro-
> fessional or technical qualifications".

---

[2] J. H. Warren, *op. cit.*, p. 73.

The town clerk of Coventry disagreed with these views stating that

"there is practical advantage and economy in the association of the administrative side of the office with the purely legal work..."

Subsequently, however, the designation was changed to town clerk/ chief administrative officer with power to intervene in administration where he considered it necessary in an endeavour to carry out the duties which the Council required him to assume.

The controversy over whether the town clerk should be trained as a lawyer or whether an administrator should be appointed, or whether two distinct offices should be created with the legal adviser subordinate to the chief executive will undoubtedly continue. In the meantime, tradition had been flouted with the appointment in July, 1965, of the Ford Motor Company product planning manager, who had no legal training, to become the 'Principal City Officer with Town Clerk' of Newcastle upon Tyne, at a salary of £9,500. He would head the city's administration and co-ordinate a £175 million development programme. Nottingham followed with the appointment of a town clerk with the additional title of 'Chief Executive Officer', and a salary in excess of £7,000; while at Basildon the late Alma Hatt, after twenty-one years as clerk to the council, was to become its first Chief Executive Officer paying "exclusive attention to the direction, promotion and co-ordination of the council's programme", and was succeeded by David Taylor, an ex-N.C.B. industrial relations officer. Oxford appointed an accountant as chief officer, and Stafford, Luton and Sheffield have changed the town clerk's title to include 'Chief Executive Officer'.

5. The City Manager

Some of these designations were popularly referred to in the press as "city managers" and there was much speculation about the apparent similarity of the new appointments with that office and the applicability of that office to English local government. There are approximately 2,000 city managers in America, increasing at the rate of seventy new adoptions each year,[3] and managers are appointed also in Ireland and West Germany. The U.S. City Manager occupies the same position as the president of a business corporation, which may be likened to the Board of Directors. He is the Chief executive and theoretically

"the council is responsible for policy, the Manager for execution and advice on policy".[4]

---

[3] *Local Government Chronicle*, 12 November, 1966.
[4] T. E. Headrick, *The Town Clerk in English Local Government*, Allen and Unwin, 1962, p. 213.

The councillors are usually fewer than fifteen, however, and there are no committees, so that the Manager has wide discretion in matters of detail and is

"in complete control of the executive arm of local administration".

He appoints and may dismiss all technical officers, and can create, merge, dissolve, or rearrange departments to increase efficiency. The departments report to him and he

"takes a particular interest in the financial matters of the administration. He supervises the budget preparation and the consideration of supplementary estimates".

Financial management, as distinct from financial policy, is left to the accountant who is, however, responsible to the Manager and not to the Council.

The system was created to counteract corruption and inefficiency, but its unmodified application in Britain would require:

(a) the abolition of the committee system which is fundamental and based on statute;

(b) the subordination of the chief officers to the chief executive and the diminution of their duties as laid down by statute, and the removal of their security of tenure;

(c) a severe restriction in the size of the council—this and the abolition of the committee system could make it even more difficult to attract good councillors;

(d) the reduction of democratic control to a minimum, the weakening of local lay leadership and the destruction of political organisation in local government;

(e) the vesting of complete authority for policy implementation, formulated by the council, in one man who would be wholly responsible for allocating council work to a department, in place of the present routing of work from the council to the committee and a department.

C. H. Chipperfield, a principal in the Ministry of Housing and Local Government, studied the city manager system in operation in America and concluded that it had more vices than virtues and that only the vices would thrive here.[5] In Britain, he claimed, there were virtues in the local government system which were not possessed to such an extent in America, and which might be destroyed if the city manager system were introduced. These virtues are: political responsibility; political parties which reflect real differences of opinion within the electorate; an active involvement of a reasonable proportion of socially conscious people in local government; and

[5] *Public Administration*, Summer, 1964, p. 128–131.

9

"a stable balance between the political and executive powers and a more just appreciation . . . of the benefits of co-operation both with other local authorities and with the central government".

It is unlikely that the city manager system will be introduced without modification into Britain. If it were, it would need to be preceded by legislation to abolish committees and to define the relationship between the manager and the statutory officers. The appointments in Britain of a chief executive, with uniquely wide powers of managerial control and direction over administration, have borne little resemblance to the dominant American city manager and have involved no radical disruption of the committee system nor a derogation of the chief officers' powers. The chief executive's role has invariably been enlarged as one integral aspect of a number of changes in a council's internal administrative machinery which were felt to be needful. The widening of the area of recruitment to those who have no legal qualifications is a separate issue, and as the role becomes more administrative, and many clerks have within their own departments legal sections staffed with solicitors to deal with conveyancing, contracts, land charges and prosecutions, a legal training for the principal officer becomes irrelevant. T. Dan Smith said:

> "It is essential that local government now sees the need to appoint senior officers with authority to organise comprehensively, to settle disputes, iron out difficulties and remove bottlenecks, in other words, a chief of chief officers, a City Manager. Local government can have no hope of dealing adequately with its problems until this is done".[6]

The Reports of the Maud and Mallaby Committees and the Redcliffe–Maud Commission have all recommended a clerk or chief executive who should be the official head of its staff and who should be chosen from all professions including the lay administrators. Whether industrialists or solicitors are appointed in the future is immaterial, provided that proved administrative ability of a high order becomes the main criterion for selection and that the appointee is given sufficient power to achieve executive co-ordination and to provide consistent overall policy advice.

6. Relationship with Public and Council

The "Code of Conduct" laid down in "The Charter" requires local government officers to give their "undivided allegiance" to the employing authority, to display the "highest standard of conduct",

---

[6] The Association of Municipal Corporations, September, 1965.

to be "honest in fact," and "beyond the reach of the suspicion of dishonesty". He must not "subordinate his duty to his private interests", nor must he "make use of his official position to further those interests", and he should be "courteous to all". It concludes by stating: "The public expects from the local government officer a standard of integrity and conduct not only inflexible but fastidious".

As a public servant an officer has to conform to a scrupulous standard of propriety in his relationship with the public and the authority which employs him. He is statutorily required to account for all moneys and property in his charge; he must declare any direct or indirect pecuniary interest in any contract into which his employing authority is preparing to enter or has entered; and he must not exact or accept any fee or reward in his official capacity other than his due remuneration.[7]

The case of *Attorney-General* v. *De. Winton*[8] held that a borough treasurer is not a mere servant of the council but owes a duty to the public and stands in a fiduciary relation to the burgesses as a body. He must therefore disobey an order from the council which calls for illegal payment, and responsibility for such a payment rests on him personally.

In the case of *Re Hurle-Hobbs ex parte Riley and Another* in 1944 Lord CALDECOT, C.J. remarked that the Town Clerk

> "may be said to stand between the Borough Council and the ratepayers. He is there to assist by his advice and action the conduct of affairs in the Borough".

If he sees the Council's actions may lead to an improper or unlawful act he must intercede with his advice.

Advice may sometimes be unpalatable, and an officer may lose the support of the elected representatives by his opposition to their wishes. He is nevertheless a servant of the council and is answerable to them for his actions. In the Bognor Regis inquiry of 1965, Mr. J. Ramsay Willis, Q.C., stated that the clerk to the council should express his opinion in a manner that would not embarrass his council, and once his view was known to them he should leave them to come to their own decision. It was the duty of councillors to formulate policy and they were directly responsible to the ratepayers at the polls.

Allegations of corruption and maladministration are not uncommon, however, particularly in connection with town and country planning and local authority contracts, but there is little evidence as

---

[7] Local Government Act 1933, sections 76 (pecuniary interest) and 124.
[8] [1906] 2 Ch. 106.

to their incidence. In respect of councillors, the Maud Committee Report referred (para. 107 of Vol. 5) to "the general picture . . . of a high standard of honesty . . . even where members are subject to strong local pressures", although an attitude survey carried out for the Committee showed that 25 per cent of the electors felt that people became councillors "because they wanted to make money for themselves" (Vol. 3, Table 132). Yet there was no mention of officers although it has been said that "the scope for malpractice by officers is as great, if not greater, than that by members". The law relating to corrupt practices is the Public Bodies Corrupt Practices Act 1889, and of the nine persons prosecuted under this Act between 1964 and 1967 (inc.) seven were found guilty; and all of the eight prosecuted under s.76 of the Local Government Act 1933 were found guilty. The data relating to surcharges and irregularities reported by the District Auditors show that between 1957 and 1966 there were 145 surcharges involving £67,707, of which only six were wholly or partly reversed on appeal to the minister, and 390 irregularities which led to 290 officers consequently ceasing to hold office. This latter number is small in comparison with the total numbers employed, but "it is not entirely negligible".[9]

In July 1969 the Prime Minister announced the Government's intention to extend the ombudsman system to investigate complaints of maladministration in local government and to make reports. He said:

"... the activities of local authorities impinge upon the daily life of the citizens directly and over a wide range and the introduction of a system analogous to that of the Parliamentary Commissioner into the local government sphere would be a major extension to the citizen's right to redress."

It was suggested that similar officials were being considered to investigate complaints in the health service and against the police, and that it would be unnecessary to await the implementation of the Redcliffe–Maud Report before the local ombudsmen were appointed. The Prime Minister added that a start might be made in London and possibly other large cities before local authority boundary changes were implemented. The Greater London Boroughs of Haringey and Havering had already appointed ombudsmen in 1968. Further support for the idea was provided in November, 1969, when in a pamphlet *The Citizen and the Council*, "Justice", the British

---

[9] D. E. Regan and A. J. A. Morris, "Local Government Corruption and Public Confidence", *Public Law*, Summer, 1969.

Section of the International Commission of Jurists, recommended a team of at least six commissioners or ombudsmen working from a central office.

In addition, much could be done to eradicate the secrecy which surrounds some of the actions and decisions of councils by opening their committee proceedings to the public and the press (as advocated by the Local Government Reform Society), with certain scrupulously controlled exceptions. Local authorities could also give greater attention to establishing full-time public relations departments (there were only 64 public relations departments or officers in April 1968) and developing their scope, and to utilising the professional services of the Local Government Information Office. In this respect too, local radio will stimulate communication between public and council, and the eight already functioning have given much attention to municipal affairs. Lastly, councils could make more use of information exhibitions, news sheets, handbooks, lectures by councillors and officers, brains trusts, demonstrations, citizenship awards, etc. to stimulate interest in local government.

7. Committees on the Management and Staffing of Local Government

In response to a request from the Local Authority Associations the Minister of Housing and Local Government set up in 1964, two committees of inquiry. One, under the chairmanship of Sir John Maud, considered

> "in the light of modern conditions how local government might best continue to attract and retain people (both elected representatives and principal officers) of the calibre necessary to ensure its maximum effectiveness."

The terms of reference of the second committee, headed by Sir George Mallaby, were:

> "To consider the existing methods of recruiting local government officers and of using them; and what changes might help local authorities to get the best possible service and help their officers to give it".

A circular issued by the Ministry of Housing and Local Government added that the Mallaby Committee was expected to examine

> "any special difficulties in getting and keeping staff for particular services; ideas for the greater employment of graduates; the career prospects; movement between authorities and the

opportunities for promotion; any reasons for unwillingness of people to enter or remain in local government service. They will not be concerned with the pay of staff. Training schemes and the question in particular of administrative training for professional staff will certainly concern them; and also the desirability of a Staff College for local government."

The Mallaby Committee published its report *Staffing of Local Government* in March, 1967, having received information from a variety of sources during its three years' work. These included 145 submissions of written evidence (nine from local authorities), oral evidence from private individuals and various bodies, replies to postal questionnaires to a sample of local authorities and a sample of N.A.L.G.O. members, and visits to local authorities and other institutions at home and abroad.

After setting out the conditions of service and existing staffing situation, the bulk of the report analysed possible developments which would affect staffing in the context of the national shortage of manpower and particularly of skilled and trained personnel. The Committee detailed recommendations in the realisation that they would not all be applicable to all local authorities but "that action can generally be initiated on them without any new legislation and without awaiting the results of other enquiries which are now being conducted". The Committee thus recommended that local authorities should accept certain "propositions and responsibilities".

Regarding *recruitment* local authorities should recognise the growing need to recruit graduates as trainees for professional and administrative posts and the danger of not doing this. They should consequently place more emphasis on recruitment from universities and colleges. School-leavers should be attracted by good training schemes and opportunities to obtain administrative and professional qualifications. The necessity to offer comparable rewards and attractions to those offered by competing employers should be accepted. Consideration should be given to offering an extension of talks and lectures on local problems and developments to the schools, and to giving senior pupils the opportunity of seeing local authority work at first hand by means of holiday attachments. Close contacts should be maintained with schools' careers masters, youth employment officers, and registrars of technical colleges, supplemented by publicity for local government careers organised on a national scale. Attention should be paid to the timing of approaches to school leavers, undergraduates and the secretaries of appointments boards, and to the quality of their advertisements and publicity material. Local authorities need to note changes which affect the recruitment and use of medical practitioners in other branches of the National Health Service. Individual local authorities should consider making joint arrangements between themselves for the recruitment, appointment and training of staff.

With reference to *career prospects*, local authorities should ensure that the prospects of the school leaver trainee, are, when he has qualified, the same as those of his graduate counterpart, and that the technician is given a proper place beside the professional officer. Subject to the size of the local authority and the scope of its responsibilities, the lay administrative officer should be provided with a career which would take him to the second or third tier position in the department and he should be equal in salary and status with his professional colleagues at those levels. All senior posts in education departments, excepting that of Chief Education Officer and those concerned with advisory work with schools, should also be available to him. The Clerkship of an authority, being mainly an administrative post, should be open to all professions including the lay administrative officer.

On the matter of *selection procedure*, the Mallaby Committee stated that local authorities should consider seeking advice from outside assessors when appointing principal officers and their deputies. Interviewing panels of elected members for the selection and appointment of principal officers and their deputies should be small, while principal officers should be responsible for selecting and appointing their staff up to and including third tier level, making full use of the specialist advice available in the Clerk's Department.

Recommendations relating to *training* were extensive. Local authorities should accept responsibility for arranging training facilities and enabling their officers to make full use of them. It is the Clerk's responsibility to see that adequate training schemes exist. Adequate facilities for continued general education as well as professional training should be provided for direct entrants from schools, and selected well-qualified candidates should be sponsored for full-time university degree courses. When fixing departmental establishments allowance should be made for training needs. Principal Officers should be responsible for ensuring that adequate arrangements are made for the training of their staff, and training officers should be of senior status. Local authorities should arrange for a Local Government Training Board to be established on lines suggested by the L.G.E.B. Working Party on the Cost of Training, with training levies and grants spreading the cost of training more equitably as with the Industrial Training Boards.

Induction training should be provided for new entrants, and local authorities which have the facilities should offer recognised courses of professional training by means of full-time, sandwich, block-release or day courses.[10] Professional officers should have opportunities to gain the widest possible experience in their own and related departments, and in selected cases receive periods of secondment to other local authorities, industry, commerce and public employment generally. The D.M.A. should be recognised as an "in-service degree" with a bias towards public administration, and its conduct should remain with the L.G.E.B. Training for the lay administrative officer should take into account both the work to be performed and the diversity of backgrounds of trainees, and should include practical experience, general studies and specialist studies in administrative subjects.

Facilities should be provided for clerical and machine operating staff to improve their educational standards and their technical proficiency, and able clerical staff should be encouraged to attain the standard necessary for entry to the trainee grade. Senior officers should receive formal training in management to suit their particular needs, and local authorities should consider the extent to which they can train their own staff for computer operation and for other specialist work in management services. Refresher training should be provided to keep officers abreast of developments, to retrain displaced officers and for married women or others returning to employment.

On the *use of staff* fourteen recommendations were made, some specifically directed to particular services or officers. More generally, the Committee recommended local authorities to examine their establishments to see whether and to what extent work could be done without loss of efficiency by staff without full professional qualifications; to draw on private resources for specialist services when the flow of the particular specialised work is irregular; to recruit married women; and to facilitate the use of cars and to see that necessary ancillary assistance and equipment are provided. Greater use should be made of management services not only to assist decision-making but also to enable scarce resources to be used to the full, and smaller local authorities should enter into joint arrangements for the provision of management services.

With regard to *internal organisation* the Clerk is recognised as head of the council's paid service and has authority over all other depart-

---

[10] Note the comments in Reports Nos. 29 and 45 of the Prices and Incomes Board which emphasised the lack of an awareness in local government of the need for formal training in management, although there was evidence of low labour utilization, inefficiency, management which was remote, and lacking in quality, managerial expertise and cost consciousness.

mental heads so far as this is necessary for the efficient management and execution of the council's functions. Clerkships should be open to all professions and occupations. Consideration should be given to reducing the number of separate departments by placing under one officer a group of departments with related functions; appointments of officers to such positions should have particular regard to their managerial abilities. Local authorities should devolve much wider administrative responsibility on principal officers, and make adequate arrangements for central establishment control. A central establishment organisation in a local authority should provide a number of executive services for individual departments and for the authority as a whole. The Maud Report, which appeared two months later, similarly emphasised the need for the reform of internal organisation, and the main proposals affecting the officers are considered in the next chapter.

Staff mobility should be encouraged between local authorities and other branches of the public service, with periods of secondment or attachment to government departments and statutory corporations. Qualified and experienced officers from the private sector should be recruited.

The Ministry of Housing and Local Government was recommended to examine the possibility of amending the law to permit the delegation of statutory functions to principal officers. Lastly, it was hoped that Local Authority Associations would give particular consideration to: setting up a Central Staffing Organisation to keep staff training needs under review and to perform a number of functions in relation to recruitment and training; determining how adequate facilities for training officers in establishment work could best be provided; establishing a central body to co-ordinate the resources of the various agencies concerned with the provision of, or advice on, the management services; establishing high level courses on the lines of those provided by the Imperial Defence College and making approaches to the Treasury and others likely to be concerned; and pressing for the implementation of the proposals of the Ministry of Labour Committee on the Preservation of Pension Rights to assist in the recruitment of professional staff.

Few of the Mallaby Report's recommendations required changes in the law or in the structure of local government, and could therefore be implemented immediately. "There is no obstacle", said Sir George Mallaby, "except apathy. . . ."[11] Of all the recommendations, a major impetus was given to training by the creation from the

---

[11] *Local Government Chronicle*, 20 May, 1967.

L.G.E.B. of a Local Government Training Board which had its inaugural meeting in September, 1967. It has since established a grant and levy system on the pattern laid down by the industrial training boards formed since the passing of the Industrial Training Act 1964. The L.G.T.B. remains a voluntary board,[12] however, and its success will depend upon the extent to which individual local authorities provide the necessary financial support and participate in the efforts of its provincial officers.

Local government is not unique in having neglected formal training in the past, and much investment in training is required if its staff is to be adequately prepared for the manifold tasks which have to be performed. The National Board for Prices and Incomes criticised managerial inadequacy and low labour utilisation in local government and emphasised the need for training at all levels,[13] and there is now distinct evidence of an increase in training activity.

Of the remaining Mallaby proposals, those relating to internal organisation were reiterated by the Maud Report and have provided local authorities with new guidelines for experiment and for giving the officers an effective responsibility for the day-to-day administration of services and a larger measure of decision and control. A greater awareness is also evident of the need, expressed by the Maud Report, for "a systematic approach to the processes of management", and in this respect the work of such bodies as LAMSAC in the areas of work and method study, job evaluation, computer usage, etc., and INLOGOV in providing high-level managerial courses, can have a major influence upon the quality of local government personnel and consequently upon the service provided to the public.

---

[12] Note the widening of the L.G.T.B.'s scope as a result of the decision of the House of Lords in "the R.A.C. case" in May, 1969 (q.v. *L.G.T.B. Bulletin* No. 7, August, 1969). Note also the T.U.C.'s backing in September, 1969 of the demand by NALGO, NUPE and NUGMW for a statutory board, one NALGO delegate stating that 400 local authorities had refused to pay the levy.

[13] Reports No. 29 and No. 45, 1967.

CHAPTER 6

Administration by Committees

The Third Schedule to the Local Government Act 1933, requires all councils to hold one annual meeting and at least three other meetings during a year "for the transaction of general business". The increasing complexity of a local authority's work, however, demands more frequent meetings than the statutory requirement and many councils meet once a month. Generally, the larger authorities hold their meetings during the day, the urban and rural districts often in the evenings; while parish meetings may not be held before six o'clock in the evening.

In the time available during these meetings, it is obvious that council members would be unable to administer council services in detail nor devote the requisite attention to the current problems of each service; and, indeed, the full council does not attempt to do so. The function of the full council meeting is to decide questions of policy and principle and to use its general power to appoint such committees as it thinks necessary to undertake any general or special work.

Local administration is based upon the committee system which is a partnership of council members and permanent officers working in close collaboration. To its committees the council may delegate any of its functions except the power of levying, or issuing a precept for, a rate, or of borrowing money. The council will also determine the numerical strength of each committee, its term of office and the scope of its work. Providing it is not a finance committee, the council may also invite persons who are not members of the local authority to become co-opted members of a committee, but at least two-thirds of a committee's membership must be council members. In addition, a local authority may be compelled by Act of Parliament to establish certain standing committees to administer statutory services.

It may be found that the work of some committees which deal with large areas of responsibility may be more effectively managed if there is a further delegation to sub-committees of sectors of the total service administered. This may be done only if the council has conferred on the committee the right to delegate to a sub-committee,

TABLE 5. FORMER COMMITTEE AND SUB-COMMITTEE STRUCTURE OF CHESHIRE COUNTY COUNCIL

KEY: M—Membership total.
     CO—Number of co-opted members.
     *—Minutes not reproduced in main minutes submitted to council.

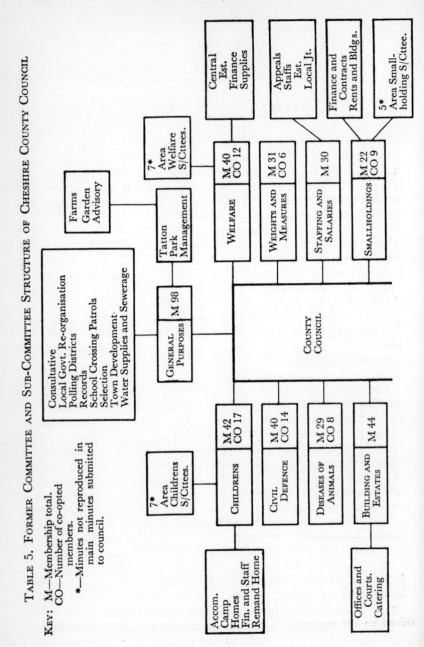

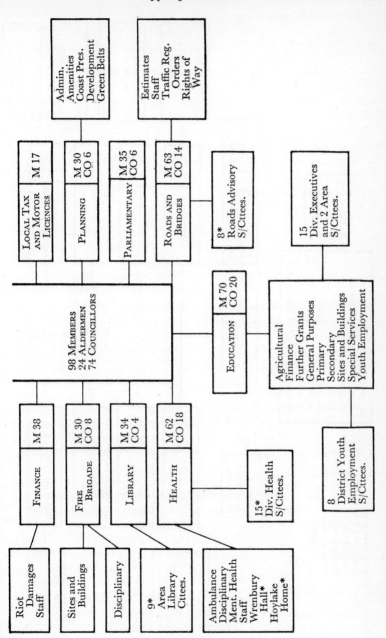

Admin.
Amenities
Coast Pres.
Development
Green Belts

Estimates
Staff
Traffic Reg.
Orders
Rights of Way

LOCAL TAX AND MOTOR LICENCES | M 17

PLANNING | M 30 CO 6

PARLIAMENTARY | M 35 CO 6

ROADS AND BRIDGES | M 63 CO 14

8* Roads Advisory S/Cttees.

15 Div. Executives and 2 Area S/Cttees.

98 MEMBERS
24 ALDERMEN
74 COUNCILLORS

EDUCATION | M 70 CO 20

Agricultural
Finance
Further Grants
General Purposes
Primary
Secondary
Sites and Buildings
Special Services
Youth Employment

FINANCE | M 38

FIRE BRIGADE | M 30 CO 8

LIBRARY | M 34 CO 4

HEALTH | M 62 CO 18

15* Div. Health S/Cttees.

8 District Youth Employment S/Cttees.

Riot
Damages
Staff

Sites and Buildings

Disciplinary

9* Area Library Cttees.

Ambulance
Disciplinary
Ment. Health
Staff
Wrenbury
Hall*
Hoylake
Home*

generally specified in the council's standing orders, or if the sub-committee has statutory authority, for example, the education committee may have sub-committees for primary schools, secondary schools, further education, and so on.

Thus each council, with perhaps the rare exceptions of a small district council or parish which are able to cope with all their work in full session of the council, will have a number of committees and sub-committees differentiated according to specified "vertical" services, for example, education, public health, housing, highways, and on the basis of common-to-all "horizontal" services such as finance, establishments, supplies, or works and buildings.

1. Types of Committee

A. *Statutory Committees*

Their appointment is required or authorised by the statute which establishes a particular service. For example, the Local Government Act 1933, requires the appointment of a finance committee in every county council; the Education Act 1944, requires every local education authority to have an education committee; every county and county borough council must have a health committee under the National Health Service Act 1946, and a welfare services committee under the National Assistance Act 1948; while under the Municipal Corporations Act of 1882 every borough council had to appoint a watch committee.

B. *Standing Committees*

These are permanent committees appointed annually to deal with a particular and continuing function, e.g. finance, health, parks, housing or libraries. There will generally be one such committee for each department or group of departments with related functions.

C. *Special Committees*

These are appointed to deal with a particular task or problem of a temporary nature and are discontinued when their work is completed, for example, an unemployment relief committee during a local trade recession, a Coronation committee, or, in Wales, a National Eisteddfod committee in the host town for liaison with its organisers.

D. *General Purposes Committee*

Strictly, the general purposes committee should not be categorised separately as it is a standing committee, but since its membership is often restricted to the chairmen of the mandatory and permissive committees listed above, it requires special mention. This committee, sometimes called the parliamentary committee or the steering committee, deals with general policy matters and has important co-ordinating functions where party organisation is strong or where there are matters arising which are of common concern to more than one committee. Its membership guarantees its high prestige and power, and it is frequently likened to the "cabinet" of local government, with its chairman having almost prime ministerial status.

E. *Joint Committees*

Joint Committees are formed by two or more local authorities for any purpose in which they are jointly interested, providing it is not the responsibility of a statutory committee, and which can best be administered over a wider area than that of the separate authorities. They have no independent financial powers nor are they corporate bodies. Examples include joint burial committees and joint sewerage committees.

2. Committee Membership

The composition of statutory committees is governed by the terms of the statute which establishes the service and there are wide variations in membership. The watch committee of a borough must comprise council members, their number must not exceed one third of the council and the mayor must always be a member[1]; education committees and sub-committees may contain specified numbers of co-opted members; the National Assistance Act 1948, requires women members on any committee set up under its provisions. Non-statutory committees may consist wholly of council members or they may have up to one third of their membership co-opted from members of the public who must be qualified to serve as councillors for that authority. Finance committees must wholly consist of members of the appointing local authorities.

The council's standing orders will generally specify the method to be adopted for the appointment of committee members, and the procedure will vary from one authority to another. Members may be appointed by a selection committee which recommends names to the council; or there may be one representative from each ward, parish or area appointed to each committee; a system of proportionate representation based upon the respective strengths of the parties or some form of balloting may be adopted; or individuals may be left to

---

[1] Municipal Corporations Act 1882.

persuade a consensus of the committee membership to accept them. Standing orders will usually specify also the minimum or maximum number of committees upon which a council member may serve, and it might vary from two to ten. Membership of the more "important" or "interesting" committees, such as Education, Finance, Planning, Health, is coveted, and disappointment with not being appointed to these may cause friction and jealousy in the council chamber.

The key figure in the committee is the chairman. He controls its meetings, speaks on its behalf at council meetings and elsewhere and maintains a constant liaison with the chief officer of the department which executes the committee's decisions. He may be elected by the committee at its first meeting or by the full council, and his appointment is generally by seniority, on the dubious premise that long service engenders executive ability, or by merit based upon his familiarity with committee procedure and a long acquaintance and interest in the work of a particular committee, or as a reward for service to the dominant political group. There is no limit to his tenure of office, unless a term is stipulated in the standing orders, but an indefinite period should be avoided. It may be beneficial insofar as his experience should develop with each passing year, but he is also likely to become so "efficient" as to act independently of his committee, while meantime depriving enterprising committee members of the opportunity for advancement and chairmanship experience. For the same reasons, the tendency for the leading council figures to collect chairmanships should be avoided.

The chairman's relationship with his committee's chief officer and the senior departmental officers is critical, and should not be thought of in terms of a dominant-submissive partnership. The officers will execute the committee's instructions, but committee chairmen and members would be rash to ignore the advice of their officers or to attempt to impose excessive limits on their areas of discretion in making decisions on the committee's behalf. K. C. Wheare has stated that:

> "In practice the administrative function will be shared between the committee and the higher officials. It may be that in law the committee could make every decision and give every instruction; in practice it cannot be done. And it cannot be done, not only because no committee could give the time to cope with such detail, but because no good official could be expected to tolerate a situation in which he had no discretion, initiative or responsibility."[2]

---

[2] K. C. Wheare, *Government by Committee*, Clarendon Press, 1955, p. 176.

The Treasury O. and M. Division's second report on Coventry[3] emphasised the need for the devolution of responsibility to chief officers:

> "To do so would . . . speed up and simplify administration without in any way weakening control."

The relationship between committee chairman and chief officer is, moreover, a subtle one,

> "more subtle than the cliches about the distinction between policy and its execution".[4]

Ultimate responsibility will remain, however, with the committee and its chairman who will have to substantiate its recommendations and defend its actions, if it has delegated powers, to the full council.

Finally, a good committee chairman must be: experienced in local government, have served a lengthy apprenticeship, know procedure and be aware of precedent; have the welfare of the locality foremost in his mind; appreciate the mixed abilities of his committee members and the degrees of efficiency of his officers, get the best out of each and mould them into an efficient team; maintain good working relationships with his officers between meetings; and realise that his ability as a leader can directly affect the efficiency of his committee.

Disqualifications and disabilities

A person who is disqualified from being elected or being a member of a local authority is disqualified from being a member of a committee or sub-committee of that authority, but a teacher or anyone holding an office in a school or college maintained by that authority may become a member of the council's education committee or public libraries committee.[5]

If a member of a local authority has a pecuniary interest, direct or indirect, in any contract or proposed contract or other matter, and is present at any meeting of the local authority at which the contract or matter is being considered he must disclose the fact and must not take part in its consideration or discussion, nor may he vote on any question relating to it.[6]

---

[3] *Public Administration*, vol. XXXII, Spring 1954, p. 67.
[4] Sir William Hart, *Some Administrative Problems of Local Government*, I.M.T.A., 1965, p. 8.
[5] Local Government Act 1933, section 94.
[6] *Ibid.*, section 76. Note, however, the intention of the Minister to give general permission to councillor-tenants to speak and vote on housing matters (738 H.C. Deb. 258–259).

3. The Council's relationship with its Committees

Whenever a council creates a non-statutory committee, the need to specify the extent of that committee's control over the service for which it is responsible poses an immediate problem. If the council delegates full executive responsibility for administering a service, the council faces the risk of relinquishing its overall control and becoming a mere rubber-stamp to the decisions of a committee which may come to regard itself as a separate *ad hoc* authority independent of the appointing council. The problem and its inherent dangers have been expressed thus:

> "It is most important that a right balance should be struck between the powers of a council and the powers of its committees. If too much power is given to committees, they will begin to act as independent bodies; they will be reluctant to co-operate with other committees of the council; there will be a lack of co-ordination in council work; and there will be attempts at empire building or committee imperialism at the expense of each other. This is, indeed, the great danger in administration by committees. . . . There are many reasons for it, but it is certain that a good foundation upon which such difficulties and tendencies flourish is the grant of delegated powers of administration to committees of councils. It encourages them to believe that they are little councils in themselves."[7]

Appreciating the likelihood of such consequences, a council may hedge its delegation of executive powers with restrictions, requiring the committee to submit its reports to the council for formal approval, or not granting a committee the right to delegate its executive powers to a sub-committee. A council need not delegate any of its executive powers and may merely require from the committee recommendations upon which the council may base its decisions. This, however, would then necessitate the council itself having to re-examine all the facets of a matter under decision and apart from the time-wastage involved, the advantage of prior analysis at the committee level would be largely minimised.

Standing orders have thus tended to confer a limited executive power which permits a committee to make decisions on routine matters which are then formally approved by the council, whilst only matters of principle or those involving exceptional expenditure require council attention exclusively. Control is still retained over routine matters by the circulation to council members of committee minutes, reports and recommendations (these are also available to

---

[7] K. C. Wheare, *op. cit.*, p. 175–176.

the press and the public), before the full council meeting; at this meeting also the committee chairman will rise to move that his committee's minutes, reports and recommendations be approved, and any member present, not being a member of that committee, may indicate his dissent and a discussion upon which a vote will be taken could follow.

In the case of statutory committees, these may have executive powers granted to them which only they can exercise and not the appointing council; nor may the latter express its disapproval of the committee's acts. A police committee for a county police force can compel a county council to raise the money it requires and obtain particular premises. In boroughs maintaining their own police force, the watch committee, two-thirds of which will comprise council members, is the police authority for the borough, and its acts do not require council confirmation, although the council will retain financial control. In such cases, no council approval is required by the committees but they are required to report their proceedings.

4. Co-ordination between Committees

A large local authority is likely to have over a dozen main committees and a large number of sub-committees, and in order to ensure that (a) the work of one is not duplicated by another, or (b) that a committee's actions are not contrary to council policy, or (c) that a committee adheres to its terms of reference, or (d) that it does not deliberately work in isolation, jealously resentful of the encroachment of other committees upon its sphere of action, the council may exercise its overall control, achieve committee coordination, and integrate committee and departmental effort in a number of ways:

1. by clear definition of the functions and responsibilities of each committee and sub-committee;
2. by the establishment of a senior committee made up of the chairmen of all other main committees;
3. by the secretarial role of the Clerk to the Council's department and the work of the committee clerks, which lead to a standardisation of procedures. The integration of administration is facilitated by regular chief officers' meetings convened by the Clerk to the Council;
4. by such "horizontal" committees as the finance committee, co-ordinating all spending, and the establishments committee and planning committee which will provide common services to all departments and advice to all committees;
5. by the requirement that all committee reports and recommendations are submitted to the full council for formal approval;

6. by party political allegiances which may help to unite members and bind committees in support of party policy, while regular party group meetings should ensure co-ordination of effort.

5. Admission of the Public and the Press

Before the Public Bodies (Admission to Meetings) Act 1960, which came into force on 1 June, 1961, the general public had no statutory right to attend local authority meetings. They now have a right to be present unless excluded by special resolution of the authority concerned.

Under the Local Government Act 1933, the only local authority meetings the public had a right to attend were those of parish councils and parish meetings and even parish councils could resolve to exclude the public at any time without reason. Some authorities did nevertheless admit the public as a matter of grace.

The Press on the other hand had a right to be present except at meetings of committees and sub-committees. The exception did not apply in the case of education committees nor in the case of joint committees or boards acting under delegated powers [Local Authorities (Admission of Press to Meetings) Act 1908]. The 1908 Act gave the local authority the right to exclude, temporarily, the press from any meeting if a resolution to that effect was passed by a majority of the members present, when, in their opinion, in view of the nature of the business to be transacted, it was in the public interest to exclude them. The Public Bodies (Admission to Meetings) Act 1960, stipulated that when press representatives attend meetings which are open to the public they must be given reasonable facilities for reporting the proceedings and a copy of the agenda.

6. The Advantages and Disadvantages of the Committee System

The committee system is fundamental to local administration in England and Wales, but it is not without its defects. It is necessary, therefore, to evaluate the merits and demerits of the system in order to appreciate the experimental changes which are currently being made by some local authorities to their committee structure.

The main advantages of the committee system are said to be:

1. The division of a complex range of work amongst committees and sub-committees ensures a more detailed and effective coverage of council services and responsibilities, and permits the full council, during the limited time of its meeting, to concern itself with policy matters without being overwhelmed by too much detail.

2. Division of the work amongst members, often according to their own interests, leads to specialisation in a narrow range of services (according to the number of committees a member serves). The consequent development of skill brings greater personal satisfaction and allows the member to make a more effective contribution to the work of the committee and to the community as a whole. The council officers serving the committee will thus be advising not uninformed amateurs but members who have some awareness of the technical aspects of the service and its problems, and also a knowledge of the relevant legislation.

3. As in the House of Commons, lack of time generally prevents the "backbench" councillor in the larger authorities from speaking at full council meetings, but he is given ample opportunity to participate in discussion at committee meetings. It is here that he will first prove his abilities and make his greatest contribution to the locality; for it is in the committee room that the spadework is done which will affect community services, not in the more formal and rarified atmosphere of council meetings where the public gallery witnesses only a rather sedate fraction of local government at work. Wheare says:

> "If there is to be any reality in the idea of democratic government, it is essential that as many people as possible should have an opportunity of taking part in governmental processes. Committees provide that opportunity".[8]

4. Co-option is required on some committees, and, with the exception of the finance and watch committees, permitted on all others. This allows individuals who have a specialist knowledge of the committee's work to participate in its deliberations without having to stand for election or take on the full responsibilities of council membership. Moreover, where party organisation is strong, co-opted members have no need to toe the party line and may thus express their views with critical detachment. Authoritative opinion may more effectively lead the majority group to reconsider a matter than would the suspected opinions of the minority group's spokesman. Unfortunately, there is little use made of the power to co-opt, and a similar reluctance by members of the public to serve as co-opted members.

5. Committee members will represent different areas of the local authority, different shades of political opinion, different interests and classes. Such a cross-section of opinion should ensure that varying community interest will be taken into account before recommendations are framed or action taken.

6. The committee system brings into partnership the chief officers experienced in their own sphere of activities, and the representatives whose uppermost concern should be their community's interests.

---

[8] K. C. Wheare, *op. cit.*, pp. 171–172.

"Bureaucratic sense must justify itself before the questioning of common sense",

says Wheare[9], and the combination of specialist knowledge and community responsibility should produce administration which is at once efficient and personal, and sensitive to the needs and problems of groups and individuals in the area.

7. The informality of procedure and discussion at committee meetings, in contrast with the formal rules of debate observed at council meetings, the absence of the press and the public, and thus the absence of any necessity to "speak to the gallery", enable members to discuss matters in a far more relaxed and extrovert manner.

Against such merits should be balanced the alleged disadvantages of the system:

i. Delegation of executive authority to committees can give rise to such abuses as "committee imperialism", lack of co-operation between committees and co-ordination between services, and independence of council control which may ultimately affect the quality of the service and result in a tarnished image of the council in the public's eyes.

ii. The permissive power of co-option is rarely used because of the reluctance of council members to have a meritocracy critical of their perhaps unsophisticated efforts or their unquestioning acceptance of party group decisions. Co-option also offers opportunities for abuse by allowing fellow-travellers, defeated councillors, or even acquaintances to take a part in committee work when they may know little and care less about the service administered by the committee. Where co-option is obligatory, for example on the education committee, academics could provide what would amount to a gratuitous consultancy service, but they may still be regarded with suspicion by the elected members. Finally, co-opted members may be disruptive of genuine group harmony, may be intolerant of the financial restrictions which frequently bedevil a committee's work, and carry no responsibility as far as the public is concerned if their specialist schemes misfire.

iii. Council membership is a part-time activity which makes extensive demands upon time. Lack of time coupled with membership of several committees means that committee meetings must be arranged at intervals of perhaps four to six weeks or more. In the meantime, decisions are awaited by the council's officers and action is being delayed, departmental work is being disrupted and the public becomes increasingly more resentful of apparently unjustifiable delays in routine matters. As an administrative technique, the committee system in local government creates bottlenecks, frustration

---

[9] *Op. cit.*, p. 172

and inefficiency, which will increase when sub-committees are involved in the chain of delegation.

iv. The extension of the council's functions stimulates the creation of extra committees and sub-committees, which in turn make greater demands upon the council members' time. The alleged advantage that committee membership increases a member's opportunity to specialise in segments of the council's work may in fact be more of a textbook dream than reality, for the division of a member's energies over a range of services and his attempts to keep abreast of legislative and technical developments may place too great a burden upon him. He is, when all is said and done, generally a part-timer with a living to earn elsewhere, and his committee work may constrain to an excessive involvement in detail and a deterioration in the quality of his work, particularly where policy decisions are required. Additionally, committee work may leave him little time to meet his constituents with any regularity and prevent him from following up their complaints and keeping a watching brief over his constituency.

v. The creation of separate committees for separate services tends to isolate the operation of departments. Basildon Urban District Council, for example, felt "it important that as the size of their administration grows they continue to maintain a common service with a common aim, namely the benefit of the community". As committees increase in number, problems of co-ordination increase unless a council attempts to rationalise its committee structure by grouping services which have a broadly similar purpose. Such rationalisation, however, will entail the reduction in the number of committees and the consequent surrender of chairmanships, together with their status, prestige and power, and these are not lightly forsaken.

vi. Committees produce a vast amount of paperwork which members should assimilate. Basildon Urban District Council found that their committee members received 350 pages of reports in six weeks, plus internal progress reports, government publications and policy documents from outside bodies. All this reading, if conscientiously done, makes further inroads on time.

vii. Committee meetings in many authorities are held during the evening and require the presence of officers who have already completed a full day's work. Even when meetings are held during the day, senior officers often have to make time to attend and to have reports prepared, which then have to be produced by typists, clerks and machine operators. The cost involved in such operations is not inconsiderable, and in terms of energy expenditure and frustration the cost may be incalculable!

viii. The monopoly of committee chairmanships and the holding of a majority of seats on the more important committees by the dominating party introduces a further element of discord between the majority and the aggrieved minority. Commital to a party line and the leadership of a strong chairman could also stultify discussion within a committee and undermine its purpose.

ix. The lack of information emanating from committee meetings because of the exclusion of the press and the public has caused much dispute and can prompt public suspicions of committee corruption. Of the complaints received by the Local Government Reform Society during 1965, 13 per cent of them related to secrecy over council committees and documents,[10] and after the Bognor Regis inquiry in November, 1965, there were newspaper recommendations that committee meetings at which councillors voted on tenders and planning decisions should be open to the press and the public, and receive publicity.[11] Many councils feel, however, that reporters are only seeking items for sensational criticism, or that meetings are often treated as routine calls for junior reporters. For their part, the press are irked by the absence of information and feel they have a public duty to gain entry to committee meetings or at least to receive early statements after committee meetings, instead of after council meetings which have ratified committee decisions. There is a need here for councils to study the 1961 circular on the Public Bodies (Admission to Meetings) Act, and for a sensible arrangement to be worked out between senior editorial staff and council members and officers in each locality.

Such features of the committee system are clearly detrimental to effective administration. The Committee on Management was similarly critical, commenting that: "The virtues of committees are, at present, outweighed by the failures and inadequacies of the committee system" (para. 128). Its report refers to the absence of a co-ordinating and unifying central body comprising a selected few members to provide an authority with overall direction and control. Instead there is a proliferation of committees constituting a system which is "a contrivance for decentralising the various functions of the council and for creating a number of microcosms of it to meet problems as they arise". Such dispersal of direction and control among committees, with each committee in turn having its own supporting departmental hierarchy, results in a general lack of unity in the authority's work—"There may be unity in the parts, but there is disunity in the whole" (para. 97).

The report adds that the committee system also contributes to the misuse of the authority's officers. The requirement that statutory functions cannot be further delegated to officers is extended in some authorities where "a vast range of administrative decisions are taken by members in committees". The effect is to inhibit the devo-

---

[10] *The Times*, 13 December, 1965.
[11] *Ibid.*, 24 November, 1965.

lution of administrative discretion on officers, which "in practice means that any member or officer has convincing arguments for insisting that matters, however minor, shall be considered at committee level". There is a reluctance therefore to attempt to distinguish between major issues and day-to-day matters, between "policy", which is the province of the members, and "administration", the province of the officers. "We believe that the lack of clear recognition of what can and should be done by officers, and of what should be reserved for decision by members, lies at the root of the difficulties in the internal organisation of local authorities" (para. 101). Such a lack of distinction between the respective roles and responsibilities of members and officers leads to overlapping, waste of time and energy, and constitutes a gross misuse of skills, manpower and money, and further acts as a disincentive to qualified people entering the local government service.

The difficulty, and perhaps impossibility in some cases, of distinguishing between policy and administration in the social and political context of the locality is stressed. Where members and officers are doubtful, they will "play safe", particularly where there may be possibilities of appeal against decisions, and the matter will be added to a committee's agenda. Further reasons for increasing the agenda would include the sensitivity of members to neighbours' reactions, a desire to appear to have a full knowledge of what the authority is doing, a sentimental or personal interest in particular matters, or to fill in the detail of caucus decisions; officers may also put up issues for discussion " 'just to create an interest', for 'tactical reasons' or because of an unwillingness to accept responsibility" (para. 111).

The Parkinsonian tendency of committees to concentrate on the trivial is also noted, "because they come easily within the reach of their understanding and to avoid discussion of major questions because of the difficulties which they involve". This, however, highlights the problem of determining at what level of decision-taking a committee can relinquish direct responsibility because of the principle that members are ultimately responsible for the conduct of affairs in the authority. "The committee system . . . does not lend itself to the careful selection of the key-points at which control should be exercised by those who are ultimately responsible; it leads to the indiscriminate submission to committees of material for information, mingled with material for deliberation or for decision—a hugger-mugger of the important and the trivial."

Reference is also made to the demands and the cost of the committee system. The number of committees in authorities varies, averaging nineteen in county councils and twenty-one in county boroughs; the average number of sub-committees is high, with forty-seven in county councils and forty in county boroughs, one authority having 160 sub-committees! Wide variations are found in the nature of sub-committee work and the number of members on each. Demands upon members' time are great, with an average of over six council and committee meetings a month in counties and over nine per month in county boroughs; the duration of each meeting could be an hour or as much as five and a half hours. Total time spent on council business for the member could vary from over thirty-four hours per month in a rural district to seventy-six hours in a county borough, but with only a quarter of this time actually in attendance. This was seen to be another disincentive towards offering oneself for local authority service. Lastly, the volume of paperwork was noted, with one county borough sending out 700 sheets a month to each member (1,000 if he were on the education committee), at an estimated total cost of £2,000 a month.

7. Modifications to the Traditional System

Dissatisfaction with such characteristics of the committee system had already stimulated a few councils to pioneer radical modifications in their internal organisation. Newcastle upon Tyne appointed a "city manager" or "Principal City Officer with Town Clerk" (Mr. Frank Harris) in 1965. He envisaged a change in the traditional relationship between members and their chief officers, the latter being delegated "complete responsibility for running his own show . . . (and) . . . responsibilities shall be widened so that far less committee time is devoted to detail and more time is available for well-considered policy decisions".[12] He planned to reduce the number of committees from thirty-six to eight, and of these two would be key committees or "planning bases" at which controversial party issues would be determined by political party groups before being presented for debate. The two committees would be (a) the *Municipal Relations Committee*—with responsibility for internal organisation, parliamentary work and by-laws, public relations, registration, administration of justice and the sole control of staff; and (b) the *Resources Planning Committee*—responsible for the general control of long-term planning, budgeting, town and development planning, financial control and administration. The remaining six committees would be responsible for public safety, health and social services, education and leisure, housing, public works and transport, and civic enterprises.

---

[12] *Local Government Chronicle*, 24 July, 1965.

THE PROPOSED ORGANISATION

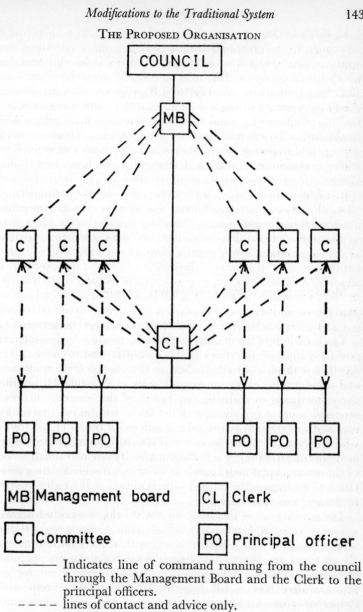

| MB | Management board | CL | Clerk |
| C | Committee | PO | Principal officer |

——— Indicates line of command running from the council through the Management Board and the Clerk to the principal officers.

– – – – lines of contact and advice only.

This diagram does NOT imply that one committee has only one principal officer associated with it or that each principal officer has necessarily a single committee to refer to.

Basildon U.D.C. also appointed a Town Manager, abolished all sub-committees (excepting three education sub-committees) and approved the creation of an *Executive Committee* of nine members which would occupy a structural position between the council and all normal committees. Tamworth M.B. proposed a *Resources Planning Committee*, working through a management group of ten members, and a reduction of committees from nine to four. Bedford M.B. established a *Management Committee* to guide the authority's overall strategy and to permit better control and direction of all committees within that strategy. Similarly, Camden borough set up an *Advisory Committee* to exercise overall co-ordination.

In addition to reducing the number of committees the need for allocating co-ordinating and directive powers to a central committee is given explicit recognition in the above proposals. The Committee on Management said that committees and sub-committees should be kept to a minimum, with no more than six committees in the larger authorities, that they should be deliberative and not executive or administrative bodies, except for exceptional purposes, and that they should each deal with a group of subjects. Additionally, all but the smallest authorities should appoint a *Management Board* of between five and nine members which would have wide powers delegated to it.

The functions of the management board would be: (a) To formulate the principal objectives of the authority and to present them together with plans to attain them to the council for consideration and decision; (b) to review progress and assess results on behalf of the council; (c) to maintain, on behalf of the council, an overall supervision of the organisation of the authority and of its co-ordination and integration; (d) to take decisions on behalf of the council which exceed the authority of the principal officers, and to recommend decisions to the council where authority has not been delegated to the management board; and (e) to be responsible for the presentation of business to the council subject always to the rights of members under standing orders.

The significance of this body for the existing committee organisation would be: (a) Committees should not be directing or controlling bodies nor should they be concerned with routine administration; (b) no committee should have more than fifteen members (including co-opted members); (c) committees should be deliberative and representative bodies; (d) committees should take executive decisions only in exceptional circumstances when the management board requires them to do this—these fields of decision-taking should be strictly defined by the management board and it should be made clear that the committees issue instructions to the officers only on these matters; and (e) the number of committees should be drastically reduced and similar or related services should be grouped and allocated to one committee. Para. 168 states: ". . . we believe that in an all-purpose authority it should be possible to reduce their number to about six", and suggests—Planning and development, Housing, Works—including highways and traffic, Education and culture, Health and welfare, and Public protection.

Board members would individually assume responsibility for the running of a particular service, as well as for speaking for a particular service and department on the Board and in the council; they could become "municipal ministers". The advantages were suggested to be: the establishment of a close working arrangement between the management board and principal officer; and difficult issues could be brought rapidly to his notice and decisions swiftly taken. On the other hand, some serious disadvantages were visualized: the board member could become so involved in affairs that he might become full-time and require an office and supporting staff to do his work; he could become the real, but untrained, head of department, with the principal officer his subordinate, so reducing the discretion and responsibility of the principal officer; the present dispersal of responsibility among committees would be replaced by the fragmentation of "ministerial responsibility"; and perhaps most serious was the impossibility of reconciling "the supervisory and co-ordinative role of the Clerk with the primary allegiance of principal officers to individual management board members".

Certain safeguards were therefore necessary: the board's chairman must ensure that his colleagues, by acting independently, did not break the unity of the board; and secondly, the relationship between the Clerk and the principal officers which creates organisational unity must not be thwarted by the development of independent arrangements between a principal officer and a board member.

Reactions to the proposed organisation were varied. The presidential address to the Institute of Baths Management attacked the management boards which "were likely to provide a Tammany Hall type of control".[13] On the other hand, Sir Andrew Wheatley, a member of the Committee on Management, agreed with the concept of a management board but felt that the proposal went further than was necessary. It would invest "far too much power in the small number of members" and "will deprive the greater majority . . . of the opportunity of participating effectively in the formulation of policy and the development of services . . . without the committee

---

[13] *Local Government Chronicle*, 21 September, 1968.

system local government could not work". He wished to retain standing committees and invest them with executive powers, "but on any major issue of policy or new scheme involving capital expenditure they should first report to the management board".

Both A.M.C. and C.C.A. opposed the idea of a management board, the former finding that the proposal left no room for a participating role for elected members if committees were to lose their executive function, and the latter thought it unlikely that candidates for election would contemplate serving for years on non-executive committees. The R.D.C.A. felt the idea was suitable for rural district councils and certain of them (e.g. Wrexham, Grimsby and Newport Pagnell) had gone some way to the establishment of a management board, but had retained committees with more than merely deliberative powers. Many cities and boroughs favoured the creation of a policy advisory or co-ordinating committee, some strengthened or adapted the functions of an existing committee (generally the finance committee), whilst almost all had accompanied the change with a reduction and simplification in the committee structure.[14] The Secretary of the A.M.C. commented: ". . . the board would effectively import cabinet government into local government. . . . By and large, local government has sided with Wheatley . . . very few authorities indeed have been prepared to try the 'full Maud' management board".[15]

Supportive weight was given to this evaluation by a later analysis of organisational changes which had occurred.[16] This showed that although many local authorities had accepted Maud's analysis of the problem, they had not accepted the proposed solution and had favoured instead Sir Andrew Wheatley's proposal. Of the eighty-three county boroughs asked for information, forty-two of the seventy-seven respondents rejected the management board proposal "either implicitly by adopting some other approach to the problem of policy co-ordination, or explicitly by giving reasons for rejection", and the reasons were fairly consistent: "(1) Conflict with collective responsibility of councillors; concentration of power; undemocratic. (2) Divisions of councillors into two classes (those on the management board and the remainder). (3) Discontent and frustration of councillors not on management board. (4) Effect on recruitment of

---

[14] B. C. Smith and J. Stanyer, "Administrative Developments in 1967: A Survey", *Public Administration*, Autumn 1968, Vol. 46.

[15] J. C. Swaffield, "Local Government Changing", *New Society*, 19 September, 1968.

[16] R. Greenwood, A. L. Norton and J. D. Stewart, "Recent Changes in the Internal Organisation of County Boroughs: Part 1 Committees", *Public Administration*, Summer, 1969, Vol. 47.

councillors of high calibre. (5) Inappropriate to local government because based on commercial or central government practice."

Regarding the reduction in the number of committees recommended by Maud, of the thirty-four county boroughs which had completed a revision only Bradford had achieved reduction to six committees, whilst the remainder largely operated with ten to fifteen committees. The size of committees had barely changed from pre-Maud days, but most were in line with the Maud recommendation of a maximum of fifteen members. As far as the allocation of functions to committees was concerned some authorities had barely altered the basic structure, while others had made "incisive analyses of their organisation" and amalgamated related functions, but the "common pattern still differs little from that revealed by the Maud Committee research". There was, however, indication that where committee structures had been reformed "there has been a great saving in members' time and, in so far as officers also attend meetings, of their time too".

Generally it would appear that local authorities accept the Maud Committee on Management's diagnosis of the organisational problems which result from their committee structure, and also accept that greater internal co-ordination is required and could be achieved by allocating wide functions to a policy committee; but it is not accepted that reorganisation should entail a radical change in the powers or functions of existing committees. Although not bound by the recommendations of the Committee on Management, the Report of the Royal Commission commented[17] that its members were "firmly of the opinion that the new main authorities must have a central committee, board or body of some kind, by whatever name it may be called". Additionally, "the case is surely cast-iron for a central body to advise the council on its strategy and priorities, co-ordinate the policies and work of the service committees, and ensure that the best managerial methods are adopted in each department and in the work of the council as a whole". Each of the new authorities should therefore work out the form of central committee most suited to its requirements, and also the division of duties between the central committee and the service committees "which would continue to be at the heart of affairs".

"It is, however, a radical change from traditional practice that we seek. The central committee must be at the core of the administration; and the proliferation of committees must be ended".

---

[17] *Royal Commission on Local Government in England* 1966–69, Vol. 1, paras. 486, 489, 493–5.

CHAPTER 7

Functions of Local Authorities

I. INTRODUCTORY

Local authorities provide a comprehensive range of environmental, protective and personal services which are essential to community life. A local inhabitant may not realise their full extent, yet directly or indirectly they affect almost every aspect of his existence, from the time he is born to the moment he dies.

Although the main functions of each type of local authority will be laid down in public general acts, the powers of local authorities of the same category need not be uniform. Local authorities have no choice but to exercise their obligatory powers to provide such services as education or public health, but other powers are permissive, allowing a local authority to decide whether or not to provide, for example, local entertainments or libraries. Additionally, special powers may be conferred by private local acts, others may be contained in charters which grant towns borough status, while certain local authorities may decide to exercise powers conferred by "adoptive" acts.

Differences in the provisions of county districts of the same status may also be caused by the differing extent to which county councils make use of their powers to delegate functions. Under s. 274 of the Local Government Act 1933, any function may be delegated except (a) one for which the county must itself appoint a committee, or (b) the power to borrow money or issue a precept for the levy of a rate. In certain cases, counties may be required to delegate and in others county districts may claim delegation. Under the Education Act 1944, for example, county councils are required to constitute divisional executives of county districts, while under the Local Government Act 1958, county districts may claim the status of excepted districts for the exercise of education functions if they have a population of 60,000 or more or if there are special reasons. Similarly, county districts may claim the delegation of certain health and welfare functions.

Moreover, the Minister of Housing and Local Government has power to confer the functions of parish councils on parish meetings, borough or urban district councils, and urban district functions on rural districts.

The extent of provision will also vary according to public need and be influenced by the local authority's financial resources and competence, and some functions may be relinquished to a joint authority.

It must be noted, however, that although variations will exist for the above reasons, between authorities of the same status, all the powers are conferred by Parliament and no local authority may provide a service or exercise any powers without statutory authority. Should it exceed the statutory limitations, it will be deemed to have acted *ultra vires* and various sanctions may be applied.

1. Services provided by Local Authorities

Any list of services differentiated according to type of local authority must, by reason of the above qualifications, be little more than an approximate guide. A more realistic impression of the range of services provided by the councils in a typical administrative county, in this case Nottinghamshire, and the distribution of responsibility for their provision, may be obtained from Table 6 (pp. 150–1) All the listed services would be provided by a county borough.

2. Joint Provision

Two or more local authorities may combine voluntarily or be combined by statute or ministerial order to provide and maintain a service for the following reasons:

1. A specialist service may be far too costly for one local council to bear alone, particularly if that service will be used by only a small proportion of its population, for example, a special school for the blind or the deaf. It would be uneconomic for every local authority to provide such schools, but in combination the cost would be shared and all would benefit.

2. Natural physical features may necessitate joint action. For example, the availability of water is determined by topographical features and not local government boundaries, and its collection and distribution necessitate large scale planning, co-ordinated management and combined resources. Similarly, problems of river pollution must be tackled by all the riparian authorities, for the neglect of one could jeopardise the work of the others. Sewerage schemes also need to be determined by the physical characteristics of areas so that

11

TABLE 6. LOCAL GOVERNMENT SERVICES IN NOTTINGHAMSHIRE

Ref. (1)	Services (2)	Local Authorities Responsible for Provision					
		Borough Councils (3)	Urban District Councils (4)	Rural District Councils (5)	Parishes in Rural Districts (6)	County Council (7)	County Council except named District Council in its own area (8)
1	Allotments	●	●		●	●	
2	Approved Schools					●	
3	Baths and Wash-houses	●	●	●	●		
4	Bus Shelters	●	●	●	●		
5	Car Parks	●	●	●	●	●	
6	Cemeteries and Burial Grounds	●	●	●	●	●	
7	Children and Young Persons					●	
8	Civil Defence						Newark Borough
9	Coroners						Newark Borough
10	Disease—Notification					●	
11	Diseases of Animals					●	
12	Disinfection	●	●	●			
13	Education						Mansfield Borough, Beeston and Sutton Urban Districts
14	Fire					●	
15	Food and Drugs					●	
	Local Health Services—						
16	Care of Mothers and Young Children					●	
17	Midwifery					●	
18	Health Visiting					●	
19	Vaccination and Immunisation					●	
20	Home Nursing					●	
21	Ambulance					●	
22	Prevention of Illness					●	
23	Domestic Help					●	
24	Mental Health					●	
25	Housing	●	●	●	●		
26	Libraries	●	●	●		●	Mansfield, Newark and Worksop Boroughs; Arnold, Carlton Hucknall and
27	Lighting of Streets				●		●

No.	Service							Notes
28	Magistrates' Courts						●	Mansfield and Newark Boroughs
29	Museums			●	●			
30	Parks and Pleasure Grounds	●	●	●	●	●		
31	Parking Places for Bicycles and Motor Cycles						●	
32	Planning—Town and Country						●	
33	Police						●	
34	Probation of Offenders	●	●	●	●	●	●	
35	Public Clocks	●	●	●	●			
36	Public Conveniences	●	●	●	●	●		
37	Public Health—Personal and Other Services		●			●	●	Newark Borough
38	Public Seats and Shelters in Roads	●	●	●	●	●		
39	Quarter Sessions						●	
40	Rate Collection						●	
41	Refuse Collection	●	●	●	●			
42	Registration of Births, Deaths and Marriages						●	
43	Registration of Electors						●	
44	Remand Homes						●	
45	Roads, Classified	●	●	●	●			
46	Roads, Unclassified	●	●	●				
47	Road Fund Licences—Collection						●	
48	Road Safety	●	●	●				
49	Sewerage and Sewage Disposal	●	●	●	●			
50	Shops Acts						●	All Boroughs; Arnold, Beeston, Carlton, Hucknall, Kirkby, Sutton and West Bridgford Urban Districts
51	Smallholdings							
52	Weights and Measures						●	Newark Borough
53	Welfare of Aged and Handicapped Persons							

N.B.—In addition to the services detailed above, West Bridgford U.D.C. provide public transport and all the Boroughs and Hucknall U.D.C. operate markets.

sewage disposal works might be sited at common outfalls rather than at more costly and separate outfalls in each area.

3. It is administratively inefficient and financially wasteful for two or more contiguous authorities to duplicate services, e.g. technical colleges in counties and county boroughs might better serve students and ratepayers if inter-college competition for courses were restricted and spheres of responsibility within a specified catchment area agreed.

There are broadly two forms of federal body resulting from the combination of local authorities:

A. *Joint Committees*

Under ss. 91 to 93 of the Local Government Act 1933, local authorities may set up joint committees "for any purpose in which they are jointly interested" and may delegate any of their functions, except the power to levy or issue a precept for a rate, or to borrow money. The number of members, their term of office and the area of their authority will be decided by the constituent councils, who will also defray the joint committee's expenses in agreed proportions. Joint committees are frequently established for temporary provisions.

B. *Joint Boards*

These are generally bodies corporate, with perpetual existence and a common seal; they may sue and be sued, have the power to hold land and to raise loans either independently or through their constituent authorities upon whom they may issue precepts. They are invariably formed for the running of more permanent services.

Joint committees are thus completely dependent upon their constituent authorities, while the joint board is independent of control by its constituent authorities. The distinction is simple but important, and the dependency test will help to identify those joint boards which are loosely referred to as joint committees e.g. the Mersey Tunnel Joint Committee.

There were examples of joint action as long ago as 1696 when Bristol replaced the separate Poor Law administrations of nineteen city parishes with a "Corporation of the Poor" which combined all parishes and their churchwardens. This precedent was followed by several other towns and urban parishes, and legislation in 1722 permitted parishes to combine for poor law purposes. The principle of combination found a number of advocates and many towns, parishes and rural counties established joint authorities. The Poor Law Amendment Act 1834, adopted the principle by creating unions of parishes under the aegis of elected Boards of Guardians and a further major example in the nineteenth century was the forty-five-member Metropolitan Board of Works (1855) providing an array of drainage and highway services for London's vestries, district boards and the City.

After the Public Health Act 1875, which empowered districts to form themselves into a united district for public health purposes, a number of acts included clauses providing for the combination of authorities for housing, education, mental care, electricity supply, town planning, sea fisheries, libraries, cemeteries, fire brigades, etc. The power to establish joint committees and boards was generally neglected, however, and between 1875 and 1939 there were only sixty-five set up by local acts and 190 by provisional orders, 111 of the latter being for isolation hospitals.[1] The *Municipal Year Book* 1966 lists thirty burial boards or committees, twenty joint sewerage boards, one conservancy catchment board, eighty-nine water boards and sixty port health authorities, and in 1967 included a section on educational building consortia and housing groups.

One might have assumed that the convenience and economy effected by joint action would have appealed to cost-conscious councils, but local authorities have not appeared anxious to participate in joint undertakings. They are frequently reluctant to forsake any part of the services which they administer and jealously preserve their autonomous control. Many of the smaller authorities have been unwilling to enter into agreements where their minority representation might be subordinated to the larger authorities, while mistrust of "big brother" and his future intentions have also served to limit effective co-operation. The equitable sharing of costs may also become a contentious issue. The result has been that many local authorities have preferred to administer their own services rather than amalgamate for economy and efficiency.

Governmental attitude to amalgamation has varied, depending on whether it has been contemplating a radical reconstruction of local government or not. In the latter case, in 1945 for example, the government believed it "to be inexpedient to contemplate drastic innovations" preferring "to rely on the existing structure . . . with appropriate machinery, where necessary, for combined action";[2] but the Maud Report (1967) compared the situation unfavourably with foreign practice where there existed "a more relaxed and pliant state of affairs." In Britain, joint action was "not popular", and one effect

---

[1] Elizabeth Howard "Joint Authorities" in *Essays on Local Government*, ed. C. H. Wilson, p. 212.

[2] *Local Government in England and Wales during the Period of Reconstruction* (Cmd. 6579).

of the difficulty "of inducing local authorities to act together, or to combine with outside agencies" was to reinforce "the central government's liking for provisions which allow little latitude". The implication is clear: unless local authorities are prepared to join forces to provide services, and in the process surrender a measure of individual sovereignty, central authorities are more temped "to lay down the ways in which duties are to be discharged".

II. LOCAL AUTHORITY SERVICES

The growth in the revenue and capital expenditure of local authorities in England and Wales is shown in the following table:

Service	Revenue account £m			Capital account £m		
	1956–57	1962–63	1968–69	1956–57	1962–63	1968–69
Education	527	930	1,450	90	129	184
Housing	222	356	640	325	387	795
Trading	185	245	359	45	64	106
Highways	117	183	274	21	60	121
Police and fire	114	183	294	10	14	32
Public health	109	169	274	33	67	115
Individual health	54	87	138	2	8	17
Other services	169	294	496	29	65	90
Totals	1,497	2,447	3,925	555	794	1,460

It is unfortunately impracticable in the available space of this book to discuss each local authority service, and five only of the major services—education, housing, town and country planning, police, and health and welfare services—will be considered within the framework of the appropriate legislation.

1. Education

The education system in England and Wales is administered by the Secretary of State for Education and Science through the Department of Education and Science. The local education authorities are the councils of counties and county boroughs. County councils may delegate certain powers relating to primary and secondary education to divisional executives representing one or more county districts. Under the Education Act 1944 and the Local Government Act 1958 a borough or urban district can claim excepted district status to bring it outside the county scheme of divisional administration and to submit its own scheme. In the Greater London area the outer Boroughs are L.E.As for their boroughs, but the inner Boroughs, the City and the Temples come under the administration of the Inner London Education Authority, a special committee of the G.L.C. Public spending on education almost doubled between 1961 and 1968, reflecting rises in costs as well as expansion in the service, and it is anticipated that expenditure will continue to rise and remain the biggest single item of a local authority's expenditure. Tables 87 and 91 of the *Annual Abstract of Statistics* 1968 showed that in January 1967 there were 7,987,071 pupils on the registers of all schools, of whom 7,328,110 were in maintained primary and secondary schools, and an enrolment of 3,091,000 students in further education establishments maintained or assisted by L.E.A.s or in receipt of a direct grant from the D.E.S.

A. *Development*

Poverty and ignorance among the lower orders of society attracted the attention of voluntary reformers from the S.P.C.K. in 1700 through to John Wesley and the voluntary schools of Lancaster and Bell in the early nineteenth century. The State did nothing to remedy the vast educational deficiencies until Parliamentary Committees were appointed in 1816, and their inquiries revealed the "existence of tractless wastes of educational destitution"[3]. In 1833 parliamentary funds of £20,000 were paid to the National Society and the British and Foreign Schools Society, and very gradually an administrative structure was pieced together until in 1839 the Committee of Council on Education was set up to administer government grants.

The main development in publicly provided primary education dates from the Education Act 1870 which set up directly elected school boards in areas which were short of schools and empowered them to raise a rate in order to finance their work. The country was divided into school districts, which were boroughs or civil parishes, and the principle of compulsory education from 5 to 13 was accepted. The success of the School Boards in supplementing the work of the

---

[3] J. S. Maclure, *Educational Documents, England and Wales*, 1816–1963, Chapman & Hall, 1965, p. 18.

voluntary schools pointed the need for a similar leaven in secondary education. This was done by the Education Act 1902, which made the counties and county boroughs education authorities. Under Part III of the Act borough councils with a population of 10,000 and urban districts with 20,000 population became authorities for elementary education only.

The Education Act 1918, strengthened local authorities, reformed the grant system so that not less than 50 per cent of the cost of education was met by central government, abolished elementary school fees and all exemptions from the leaving age of 14, and extended the local education authority's range of permissive services. The Act had laid the duty of establishing "a national system of public education" on the councils of counties and county boroughs, where it remained until 1944.

B. *The Education Act* 1944

The principal act which governs public education in England and Wales is the Education Act 1944.[4] Its main provisions were:

1. The Ministry of Education superseded the Board of Education and the Board's president became a Minister.

2. The Minister of Education was made responsible for the education of the people of England and Wales and the local education authorities were required to perform their part "under his control and direction".

3. The former division into "elementary" and "higher" education was replaced by primary, secondary and further education—"a continuous process conducted in three successive stages".

4. County and county borough councils were made responsible for all stages. Local education authorities were given the duty of ensuring "adequate provision of primary and secondary education" including nursery and special schools, and to prepare development plans showing how this was to be done. Tuition fees at maintained schools were forbidden. Part III authorities were abolished.

5. The dual system, i.e. the co-existence of local education authority schools and voluntary schools, was modified considerably. The financial settlement was made more generous to the voluntary bodies. Church schools could choose "Aided" status, with capital grants of 50 per cent (raised to 75 per cent in 1959) or "Controlled" status, where the local education authorities appoint a majority of the managers.

6. The leaving age was raised to 15 (came into effect in 1947) and provided for it to be raised to 16 by Order in Council "as soon as it

---

[4] As amended by various Education Acts from 1946 to 1968, the Local Government Act 1958 and the London Government Act 1963.

has become practical". A general principle was laid down concerning the right of the parent to have his wishes taken into consideration over the choice of school.

7. Part-time day attendance at County Colleges was to be required at some future date for those who had left school before the age of 18.

8. The obligation and powers of the local education authorities in connection with such ancillary services as medical, school meals, transport, provision of school clothing and the award of scholarships for higher education, was extended.

9. In all primary and secondary schools the day should begin with a corporate act of worship and religious instruction should be given in county schools according to a syllabus agreed by representatives of the religious denominations.

C. *Classification of Schools*

The three stages envisaged by the 1944 Act, which were to be the responsibility of the local education authorities, were:

1. *Primary Stage* (up to the age of 11 years) which includes Nursery (to age 5), Infant (from 5) and Junior Schools (age 8 to 11).

2. *Secondary Stage* (11–15 years, to be raised to 16 in 1973) which comprises Secondary Grammar, Secondary Technical and Secondary Modern Schools; all intended to be of equal status.

3. *Further Stage* which includes County Colleges, Technical Colleges and Colleges of Art and Commerce, Evening Institutes, Services for Youth, Adult Education and Community Centres.

Since 1959 a number of reports have detailed certain of the inadequacies of educational provision in the three stages. The *Crowther Report*, 1959, on the educational needs of youngsters between 15 and 18 years of age recommended: the raising of the school-leaving age to 16; compulsory part-time further education for those leaving school at 16; improvements in further education for technicians, craftsmen and operatives, including "sandwich courses"; the recruitment of more teachers; and the revision of syllabuses to prevent pre-specialisation. The *Albermarle Report*, 1960, advocated: the adoption of a ten-year programme for the youth service, with the service to be available for the 14 to 20 age group; priority for training professional youth leaders; a generous building programme; and the establishment of a Youth Service Development Council to advise the Minister of Education in refashioning the service.

The Newsom Report, 1963, entitled "Half our Future", considered the education of pupils aged 13 to 16 of average and below-average ability. It recommended: raising the school-leaving age for secondary modern pupils from 1965; longer school hours, some of which were to be spent on "extra-curricular" activities; a curb on examinations and the provision of a school-leaving certificate for 16 year olds; the replacement of inadequate buildings; the relief of overcrowding; the arrangement of an experimental building programme to try different forms of school organisation and teaching methods in purpose-designed schools; specific attention for schools in slum areas; and an emphasis on spiritual and moral development.[5]

In 1967, the *Plowden Report*, "Children and their Primary Schools", recommended: special assistance ("positive discrimination") for schools in slum areas in the form of more teachers, additional finance for school buildings, and more generous supplies of equipment; the recruitment of over 50,000 "teachers' aides" by 1973–74; a large expansion of nursery schools; smaller classes; the abolition of corporal punishment; regular parent-teacher contacts; more teaching aids; and special attention to the teaching of English to immigrant children.

In July 1968 the Report of the Public Schools Commission, under the chairmanship of Sir John Newsom, recommended *inter alia* that: independent boarding schools should take at least 50 per cent assisted pupils from maintained schools after a period of about seven years; the cost of assisted places, subject to parental contribution, should be met by L.E.A.s on a pooled basis; the only justification for public expenditure on boarding education should be the need for boarding, for either social or academic reasons; independent schools should take pupils of a wider range of ability; they should be encouraged to work closely with each other and with maintained schools; there should be more co-educational boarding schools; and schools that are charities but which serve no truly charitable purpose should lose any financial reliefs.

D. *Comprehensive Secondary Education*

In July, 1965, the Department of Education and Science, which replaced the Ministry of Education in 1964, issued its now-famous Circular 10/65 which stated:

> "It is the Government's declared objective to end selection at eleven-plus and to eliminate separatism in secondary education. ... The Secretary of State accordingly requests local authorities, if they have not already done so, to prepare and submit to him plans for reorganising secondary education in their areas on comprehensive lines".

The plans were to be prepared within a year.

The Labour Party defined the comprehensive school in the following manner:

"It is a secondary school which is intended for all normal children in a district without dividing them into grammar, technical or modern departments".[5]

Circular 10/65 described the main forms of comprehensive organisation. These were (i) the orthodox comprehensive schools with an age range of 11–18; (ii) "two-tier" systems of various kinds, under which pupils transfer at the age of 11 to a junior comprehensive school, and thence at 13 or 14 some or all transfer to a senior school; (iii) comprehensive schools with an age range of 11–16, combined with sixth form colleges for those over 16; and (iv) a system of "middle schools" under which pupils transfer at 8 or 9 to a comprehensive school with an age range of 8 or 9 to 12 or 13, and thence to another comprehensive school for older pupils.

All children leaving primary school would enter the comprehensive school for their area without taking a streaming or selection test (11 + being abolished). The first year or two would entail diagnosis of abilities and aptitudes, and by the age of 13 (believed to be a better age than 11 to assess abilities) would be allocated to their "sets", i.e. the classes for which they are best suited in the appropriate subjects. Children would be transferred to higher or lower streamed classes on the basis of teachers' assessments.

Since 1965 comprehensive education has been the centre of controversy in a number of L.E.A.s, with public protests in Liverpool, Bristol, Luton, Sunderland, Cardiff, Newport, Westmorland, Surrey, Bournemouth and the inner London Boroughs culminating in "the triumph of the village Hampdens"[6] in the case of *Bradbury and others v. London Borough of Enfield* in 1967. As a result the Education Act 1968 clarified and amended the law relating to changes in the character and premises of county and voluntary schools so as to prevent the Court of Appeal's decision in the above case invalidating changes effected since 1945 by L.E.A.s.

The editorial in the Comprehensive Schools Committee's bulletin (Spring 1968) showed how the Government's request to L.E.A.s to submit reorganisation plans was being thwarted in a number of ways and how as a result, it was alleged, at least half of the 103 schemes approved by the D.E.S. were unsatisfactory. A Parliamentary reply in November 1968 showed that 116 plans had been implemented or

---

[5] *Fair Deal for Kids*, Labour Party, April, 1965.
[6] "Enfield and the law", *The Times Educational Supplement*, 1 September, 1967.

approved, and of the remaining forty-seven, sixteen were under consideration by the D.E.S., the proposals of seven had been rejected and revised schemes were awaited, seventeen had not submitted schemes, and seven—Bournmouth, Bury, Kingston upon Thames, Richmond, Rutland, Westmorland and Worcester—had refused to submit schemes. To deal with the "recalcitrant" authorities, the Queen's Speech in October 1969 referred to the Government's intention to introduce legislation to compel L.E.A.s to submit schemes for comprehensive organisation.

E. *The Current Debate*

The supporters of the comprehensive school system claim the following advantages:

1. The comprehensive school will rescue those children who have been misjudged on the eleven plus examination. It is an examination which some claim is not scientifically valid or discriminating, and is taken on one day when a child may perform below par; additionally, 11 is too early an age for such an important decision to be made.

2. The comprehensive school will make for fluid movement within and among streams.

3. It will equalise and extend educational opportunity for all children. The grammar system is unfair in that the availability of places varies from area to area, e.g. in 1963 33 per cent of all Welsh secondary scholars were in grammar schools, 22·6 per cent in the eastern counties. Even more important, "parity of esteem" is a myth because differences in class, parental attitudes and home conditions affect a child's progress and middle class children have a better chance of getting into a grammar school (research in 1946 showed 54 per cent of upper middle class children got grammar school places, 11 per cent of lower manual class). Therefore, parental affluence is a determining factor.

4. It will allow good students to move ahead as well as they would in a grammar school and at the same time encourage the less able by their example.

5. It will develop everybody's capacity for intelligence and make the most of the nation's "pool of ability".

6. It will allow economies of scale in buildings, schools and teaching staff.

7. It will make the services of the best teachers available to all instead of to a narrow band of top students in the grammar school, where the best qualified teachers generally gravitate.

8. Most of all, the protagonists allege, the comprehensive school will overcome social barriers, snobbery and inequality and put an end to the social divisiveness of the present system.

The opponents of the comprehensive schools put forward the following counter-arguments:

i. All the above claims seem attractive on paper, but are based on little more than theoretical assumptions, e.g. Dr. J. D. Koerner, an American educationist, wrote:

> "The comprehensive school will not necessarily do any of these things, certainly will not do all of them and probably can never do some of them. Moreover, none of them really has much to do with how schools are organised and administered. Most of the things that need doing in British education could be done through the existing school system".[7]

ii. The grammar schools and the direct grant schools, many of which are the admiration of the Western world, will be swept away on the basis of unsubstantiated theory. In America and Russia, where almost all schools until recently have been comprehensive:

> "Separate schools for the children at the very top of the ability range seem to be an inevitable consequence eventually of all otherwise fully comprehensive systems".[8] (K. Ollerenshaw).

Why not use the experience of these countries and keep our "proved" schools? The fate of these schools, their traditions, their effectiveness are in the balance, and fears of their abandonment have led one public school headmaster to comment: "Nowadays there are only two types of secondary school—comprehensive and apprehensive!" Britain should preserve her unique and in many cases unrivalled educational establishments, "avoid massive standardisation and leave room for heterodoxy and choice and dissent". In addition, what happens to the denominational schools in this standardisation?

iii. The secondary modern schools and their students have not been given a fair chance; they have been allowed to become "custodial institutes" which contain "the submerged three-quarters". Greater research needs to be undertaken and greater efforts need to be made to develop these children by orientating the teaching to more positive practical, realistic and vocational subjects. Where academic ability is shown, the children can be prepared for the appropriate examinations and the high incidence of "O" and "A" level successes is proof of what can be achieved by enlightened teaching in these schools.

iv. The argument that social distinctions would be eradicated is more theoretical than realistic. In any case, school is primarily a place for education and not social reform. Putting all children in a comprehensive school is no more valuable than in three schools, and may positively serve to emphasise social distinctions: "The social effect of such schools is to reinforce rather than combat class con-

---

[7] *Daily Telegraph*, 25 February 1966.
[8] *Sunday Times*, 6 March 1966.

sciousness" (Koerner). "There is no easy way in a free society to achieve a true social *and* intellectual mix in each school" (Ollerenshaw). Social distinctions would also be emphasised by the fact that "grammar" stream students would take the leadership posts.

v. The cost of conversion is prohibitive. There is no mention of cost in Mr. Crosland's Circular and the change has never been worked out in terms of finance, buildings or manpower. Existing buildings (including the Newsom "slums") and the existing short supply of teachers will have to be pressed into service. Said the *Sunday Times* (18 July, 1965):

> ". . . to spend money on reorganisation when about £1,250 million is needed to bring school buildings up to standard and when the school population is growing fast . . . is wrong. Obviously existing school buildings cannot be discarded. There are now about 6,000 secondary schools with an average of 500 pupils".

The raising of the school-leaving age in 1972–73 will aggravate teaching and accommodation difficulties, but in order to offset the necessary extra building costs the D.E.S. announced that £36 million would be allocated for each year from 1968 to 1971 to local authorities.

vi. Comprehensive schools, to stand a chance of success, require purpose-built buildings. These are not generally available, and any scheme thus necessiates patched compromises. Yet even if such buildings were available, size becomes a major problem and serves to destroy the pupil/teacher relationship which is so essential in the education process. The children become members of a vast impersonal and anonymous empire, and the teachers, perhaps confined to the lowest streams, may become disillusioned and inclined to neglect the backward pupils. The best teachers (particularly the science graduates) may leave and so aggravate the teacher shortage.

vii. The lowest streams may tend to drag down the better.

> "The greatest problem of the American comprehensive school has been to escape mediocrity—to avoid having the standards and the ethos of the school established by the average instead of the best" (Koerner).

viii. Many parents are worried by the lack of choice and the feeling that education is being subordinated to political expediency. Their fears are not lessened by the complexity of the prototype schemes and the failure of local education authorities to prepare acceptable schemes. It is, as Lord James of Rusholme has said,

> "an area characterised by prejudice and misconceptions, by inconsistencies and an enormous amount of sheer ignorance".[9]

---

[9] Quoted in *Daily Express*, 21 January 1966.

ix. There is no surety that comprehensive schools are educationally better. What if theory does not work out in practice—a generation of student guinea-pigs will have been sacrificed. Why not have purpose-built comprehensive schools in new towns and not tamper with the existing system? Allow them to run side by side for a decade, compare results and then decide.

2. Housing

Nineteenth-century industrialisation left Britain with a heritage of speculatively built dwellings grouped in squalid and dilapidated ranks around the mines and factories which originally attracted the workmen and their families. Problems of sanitation, water supply and drainage were all tackled before any attempt was made to improve housing conditions, and not until the Labouring Classes Lodging Houses Act 1851, was there legislation empowering borough councils and local boards of health to provide tenement houses for the working classes and to regulate and control common lodging houses. In 1868 local authorities were enabled to compel landlords to repair their property, and Manchester in 1867 procured a local act which permitted the closure, without compensation, of houses unfit for human habitation. The Artizans' and Labourers' Dwellings Improvement Acts of 1875 and 1879 introduced slum clearance by authorising local authorities to condemn, demolish and reconstruct areas, and in 1884 the Government appointed a Royal Commission on Housing. The Housing of the Working Classes Act followed in 1890 which consolidated and amplified previous legislation and gave local authorities the permissive power to purchase land and raise loans for housing the working classes. Nevertheless, only 5 per cent of working class houses built between 1890 and 1914 were built by local authorities.

Slum clearance aggravated overcrowding and slum conditions in other areas, while the First World War worsened the housing problem. Drastic remedial action was required and the government responded with the Housing and Town Planning Act 1919, whereby the entire loss of local authorities' housing schemes in excess of a penny rate was met by the Exchequer. Approximately 176,000 houses were then built, but the cost to the Exchequer led to the Act's discontinuance in 1921 and subsequent Housing Acts in 1923 and 1924 gave less extravagant financial assistance to encourage building by local authorities and private builders. Between 1919 and 1930, one and a half million new houses were built, amounting to a 20 per cent increase in the nation's housing.

The Housing Act 1936, consolidated all previous housing legislation and became the principal Act. It defined the powers and duties of local housing authorities—the repair, maintenance and sanitary condition of houses, the clearance of unfit houses and the redevelopment of the area, the abatement of overcrowding, and the provision of new houses. The local housing authorities were to be the councils of county boroughs and county districts.

During the 1939-45 war one-third of Britain's houses were destroyed or damaged, and the population increased by $2\frac{1}{4}$ million. The housing situation was critical, and building during the war (only 220,000 houses) had fallen behind the 1934-39 average of 360,000 houses per year. The Housing (Financial and Miscellaneous Provisions) Act 1946, brought housing within the scope of the Minister of Health (Aneurin Bevan) and he placed the responsibility for meeting the demand squarely on the local authorities. A ratio of four local authority houses for one private dwelling was established, and local authority rentals were to be subsidised. At first a subsidy of £22 per annum for sixty years was specified, but increasing building costs necessitated a revision of the subsidy and rents rose above the 10s. level.

The Housing Act 1949, empowered local authorities to make improvement grants to private owners to improve and convert existing property, to advance loans for the improvement and purchase of freehold property, and encourage local authorities to build houses for all sections of the community and not only, as formerly, for the working classes. The Housing Act 1952, increased subsidies to local housing authorities for every house built and readvocated the sale of council houses; this latter matter was further clarified in 1960 with the minister's circular 5/60 encouraging local housing authorities to assist council house tenants to become owner-occupiers. The Housing and Repairs Act 1954, stimulated the improvement and conversion of old houses by emphasising the existence of grants, brought into prominence the slum clearance powers of the local housing authorities and required them to make five-year plans for slum clearance, and facilitated the acquisition of slum areas for clearance and redevelopment. Under the Housing Subsidies Act 1956, the Minister repealed all subsidies for the building of houses for general purposes, and retained only those for dwellings to rehouse households from slums, for houses for overspill population from congested areas, and for one-bedroomed houses.

The Housing Act 1957, consolidated the law relating to housing, excepting financial provisions which were consolidated in separate legislation in 1958, and defined Local Housing Authorities in England

and Wales as the councils of county boroughs, boroughs, urban districts and rural districts. The Act makes provisions for securing the repair, maintenance and sanitary condition of houses, clearance and redevelopment, the abatement of overcrowding, and details their general powers and duties in providing housing and for its management. Part VII deals with a number of general matters including the Central Housing Advisory Committee, building byelaws, acquisition of land, joint action, etc.

The Housing Act 1961, proposed to redistribute housing subsidies in such a way as to encourage the introduction by local housing authorities of differential rent schemes based on "realistic" rent policies towards council house tenants able to pay. This remains, however, one of the most controversial aspects of housing finance. It also made provision for £25 million to be paid in advances to non-profit making housing associations for the construction of small houses to rent. The modernisation of older homes was also encouraged by permitting the landlord to receive a greater return on his share of modernisation expenditure.

The Parker Morris Committee recommended housing improvement standards in its report *Homes for Today and Tomorrow*, published in 1961. Local authorities are expected to incorporate the recommended standards, which were subsequently more precisely defined, in new designs, and schemes submitted to the minister after 31 December, 1968, would qualify for subsidy or loan sanction only if they complied with the standards.

The 1963 White Paper *Housing* (Cmd. 2050) made particular reference to these older dwellings which were becoming obsolescent although not yet unfit for habitation. Towns already faced the twin tasks of slum clearance and building for current need, but plans for the redevelopment of the older areas, for "twilight area renewal", were also necessary.

From 1953 about 300,000 new houses were built each year, increasing to 382,000 in 1964. In the 20 years since the war nearly five million houses or flats have been built or renovated, (2·9 million by local authorities and 1·9 million by private builders) and by 1965 about 45 per cent of the population either owned or were buying their homes. In 1961, however, it was calculated that four million houses were over 80 years old and in 1964 500,000 houses were classified as slums.

The Housing Act 1964, established a Housing Corporation to stimulate, through non-profit-making housing societies, the building of new houses and flats either for letting at cost rents or on the basis of group ownership in order to meet the demand of persons who did

12

not wish, or are unable, to rent or buy in the ordinary way and cannot expect help from local authorities. Other parts of the act were framed to accelerate the modernisation of older houses, in some cases compulsorily, and to give local authorities greater powers to combat squalid conditions in houses in multiple occupation.

The Housing Subsidies Act 1966, gave effect to the Government's proposals in its White Paper *The Housing Programme* 1965 *to* 1970. Part I of the Bill provided for the payment of housing subsidies to public authorities in England and Wales. These comprised (a) A *basic subsidy* which took the place of the £24 per house normally payable under existing legislation and calculated in respect of all approved dwellings completed in a financial year. It took the form of a contribution towards the loan charges incurred in financing their capital costs and broadly had the same effect as if the local authority had been able to raise a loan at 4 per cent per annum; and (b) *Supplementary subsidies* where appropriate for expensive sites high flats, building in special materials, town development, extra cost of precautions against subsidence and special needs. Part II provided for assistance to owner-occupiers on mortgage payments on houses, and was designed to help those in lower income groups by providing for a new type of loan—an option mortgage—at a reduced rate of interest.

The Government aimed to redress a long-felt grievance of occupying leaseholders with the passing of the Leasehold Reform Act 1967, which was based on the principle "that the freeholder owns the land and the occupying leaseholder is morally entitled to the ownership of the building which has been put on and maintained on the land." Consequently the Act stipulated that tenants (with five years tenancy) of houses held on long leases (twenty-one years or more) at low rents were enabled to enfranchise the property by purchasing the freehold, or alternatively to obtain a fifty years' extension of the lease. Part I implemented substantially the proposals of the White Paper *Leasehold Reform in England and Wales* (Cmnd. 2916), and Part II amended previous legislation by extending the protection of the Rent Acts to long tenancies.

A housing survey in 1967 showed that there were more unfit houses and substandard houses, with 3·7 million needing repairs and 2·3 million lacking one or more of the basic amenities. It was considered that this housing was worth saving and a White Paper *Old Houses into New Homes* (Cmnd. 3602), published in April 1968, made proposals for general improvement areas and for the raising of the discretionary grant and the standard grant.

These proposals were put into effect by the Housing Act 1969, which increased the discretionary limits of the improvement grant to private owners from £400 to £1,000 and the conversion grant from £500 to £1,200, with a minimum cost of works of £100. The standard grant limit was raised from £155 to £200, and basic amenities were not all required to be provided at the same time. In addition, a special grant of one half of the cost (up to a maximum of £200) could be paid by a local authority for the provision of standard amenities in a house in multiple occupation. Part II enabled authorities to declare general improvement areas where "living conditions . . . ought to be improved by the improvement of the amenities of the area or of dwellings therein or both" (s. 28). Thus authorities became responsible for the improvement of whole areas and not just individual houses. The authority must inform residents and property owners of the action they propose to take and the assistance available for the improvement of amenities. The local authority has powers to carry out works, to acquire and to let land, and may be authorised by the minister to acquire compulsorily any land.

Part III provided a procedure whereby houses let on controlled rents and satisfying certain conditions became regulated tenancies on the issue of a qualification certificate. Such a certificate may be issued provisionally, before the dwelling is provided with the standard amenities, and the landlord can obtain a certificate of fair rent in advance.

Compensation, supplementary to the existing site value payments, may be claimed by an owner-occupier whose house is dealt with under slum-clearance powers, provided the house has been occupied by an owner (whether or not it is the same owner) throughout the qualifying period of two years. The payment brings the compensation payable for the house up to market value. Other provisions extend the availability of this compensation to certain exceptional cases which do not fall into the normal category. In the case of tenanted houses, the well-maintained payments will be doubled to four times the rateable value, and this rate of payment will continue for owner-occupiers who do not qualify for the supplementary payments.

There is a new definition of a house in multiple occupation (s. 58), and in certain areas the authorities have the power to regulate, prevent, or impose conditions on, new multiple occupation. Provisions are also introduced to register houses in multiple occupation.

Rent Control

Since the Rent and Mortgage Interest Restrictions Act 1939, the majority of house rents in Britain had been frozen at the pre-war level. Their tenants, often paying a lower rental than the market value of the property, were obviously disinclined to move out of accommodation which they perhaps no longer fully utilised, while others found it almost impossible to rent accommodation. The landlords of rent-controlled property were losing from the low rentals, and, with the increased costs of maintenance, were allowing their property to deteriorate.

The Minister of Housing and Local Government consequently introduced the Rent Bill which was enacted in 1957. Houses let unfurnished, with a rateable value above £30 (£40 in London and Scotland), were decontrolled (totalling about 390,000 houses in England and Wales), while the rents of the remaining 4½ million rent-controlled properties could be increased to a maximum of generally twice the 1956 gross value,[10] exclusive of rates and services, and would also become decontrolled when the sitting tenants left. All houses which were let after the Act were free from control. The Labour Party opposed the Bill because it feared that many tenants would experience hardship, and they kept up their attack whenever housing was subsequently debated. In 1963 an opposition motion deplored "the intolerable extortion, evictions, and property profiteering which have resulted from the Rent Act 1957", and Mr. Harold Wilson referred to the "disease of Rachmanism" and to instances of alleged intimidation. The persecution of tenants by unscrupulous landlords was not unknown in London, but there was little evidence of such pressure being applied in the provinces, or for that matter of the increased rentals being used to improve properties or of tenants moving to more suitable accommodation.

The Milner Holland Committee's Report on *Housing in Greater London* (Cmd. 2605), published in 1965, commented upon the acute housing shortage in London and the abuse of tenants by bad landlords. It observed that fifty years of rent restriction had hidden the real cost of housing provision and maintenance and that neither rigid rent restriction nor random decontrol would alleviate the situation. The Report also referred to the lack of security of tenure as one of the main problems facing tenants. Three months earlier some protection had been afforded by the enactment of the Protection from Eviction Act 1964, restricting the right of the landlords of furnished or unfurnished property to regain vacant possession without a court order.

The Rent Act 1965, restored rent control, in the form of rent "regulation", over most unfurnished lettings which were not controlled on 8 December, 1965. A new system for reviewing and register-

---

[10] This could vary from 1⅓ times to 2⅓ times the 1956 gross value dependent upon the liability for repairs.

ing rents was introduced and principles for determining "fair" rents were laid down. Severe penalties were imposed for harassing, or evicting without a court order, the residential occupier of any premises. The law relating to furnished dwellings, mortgages, and premiums was also amended.

Thus tenants in decontrolled unfurnished dwellings who feel their rent is too high[11] can approach a rent officer who will investigate and fix a "fair" rent. If this rent is unacceptable to either tenant or property owner the case will go before a rent assessment committee of three independent persons who will review all relevant factors and fix a "fair" rent. This will then be entered on a register and remain fixed for three years. The act also froze immediately all rents for unfurnished property of a rateable value of up to £200 in the provinces and £400 in London, subject only to the landlords' and tenants' rights of application for the fixing of fair rents.

From October 1966 rent tribunals were integrated with rent assessment panels, and rent officers, whose duties under the Rent Act 1965 had previously concerned only unfurnished lettings, were authorised to answer queries about furnished lettings as well and also to issue forms of application to Rent Tribunals. Owing to pressure of work, the integration did not take place in the Greater London area until April 1969. The Rent Act 1968 consolidated previous rent legislation, except for certain provisions affecting tenancies under rent control and other tenancies. These exceptions still comprise ss. 30–36 of the Rent Act 1965, and refer to protection against harassment and unlawful eviction, and s. 16 of the Rent Act 1957, which requires the minimum length of a notice to quit to be four weeks.

In the politically controversial area of council house rents, the Prime Minister announced in November 1967 that rent increases in twenty-two local housing authorities would be referred to the National Board for Prices and Incomes. Having examined fifteen of the schemes, the Board required a larger sample to determine broad trends and the result of their inquiries was published in Report No. 62 (Cmnd. 3604) in April 1968. It referred to the great variation in standard rents and rent increases between authorities, stemming partly from increasing costs. The Report therefore proposed "a set of uniform principles for the determination of rents which could conduce to a greater uniformity in rents for comparable dwellings". The Board favoured raising local authority rents, but that it should be effected gradually and not exceeding 7s. 6d. per

---

[11] Or landlords who feel the rents to be too low.

dwelling in a twelve-month period; when this amount was inadequate equalisation account funds should be used for the benefit of the housing revenue account. The Board also advocated local authorities to adopt rent rebates for low income tenants and to extend rebate schemes to tenants in the private sector.

There were protests against the Government's approval of the N.B.P.I.'s findings from, for example, the local authority associations, the G.L.C. and the London Boroughs Association and those authorities which were trying to bring rents "up to a more realistic level" (e.g. the G.L.C. scheme was based on the "fair" rents for private tenancies assessed under the 1965 Act). Nevertheless the Prices and Incomes Act 1968 introduced certain restrictions on the freedom of housing authorities to fix rents by imposing a degree of central control up to the end of 1969 and for a further year for rents registered during its currency. Ministerial approval had to be sought to increase the rents of local authority houses, while the minister could require local authorities to reduce rents if they were increased after 31 March and before 10 July, 1968, when the Act came into force.

Housing Needs

In February 1969 it was suggested that "it is now generally accepted that within a few years there will be a 'statistical' surplus of houses",[12] and in the same month the House of Commons was informed by a minister that: "By 1973 we should have a margin of a million more houses than householders." In contrast, *Shelter*, the National Campaign for the Homeless, viewed the situation through a different frame of reference and referred to the housing problem as "a national crisis". Its report *Face the Facts* in September 1969 called for emergency action on behalf of at least one million homeless families and the eradication of the worst overcrowding and squalor. The report condemns official statistics which, it says, do not reveal the true nature and extent of homelessness. The report of the Cullingworth Committee into council housing similarly stressed the importance of giving more attention to social need and commented that there is not just one national housing problem but a large number of local housing problems of great variety.[13] Local authorities "should be looking for hidden needs which are not being met elsewhere, and for needs which may arise in the future". The committee also expressed surprise at the moralistic attitude of housing authorities

---

[12] *Barclays Bank Review*, February, 1969.

[13] *Council Housing—Purposes, Procedures and Priorities*, Report of Housing Management Sub-Committee of the Central Housing Advisory Committee under the chairmanship of Professor J. B. Cullingworth (H.M.S.O.) December, 1969.

towards tenants: "The underlying philosophy seemed to be that council tenancies were to be given only to those who 'deserved' them. Thus, unmarried mothers, cohabitees, 'dirty' families and transients tended to be grouped as 'undesirable'. Moral rectitude, social conformity, clean living and a 'clean' rent book sometimes seemed to be essential qualifications for eligibility—at least for new houses." The highest priority should be given "to those householders in bad conditions with which they are unable to cope and where the potential ability to improve the situation themselves is low".

3. Town and Country Planning

The towns of industrial revolution Britain were, with few exceptions, unplanned and haphazardly constructed. Some "good" employers attempted to develop planned communities, e.g. Robert Owen at New Lanark, but the majority of entrepreneurs and local authorities were not concerned with land usage. Dwellings were jerry-built and speculators scorned the ideas which were being put into practice at Bourneville in 1879 and Port Sunlight in 1888. The late nineteenth-century town planner, Ebenezer Howard, inspired garden cities at Letchworth (1903) and Welwyn (1920), but such instances are exceptional and most local authorities,

> "still cringing to private enterprise and clinging to the creed of non-interference with business, remained apathetic".[14]

Eventually, in 1909 a Town Planning Act empowered local authorities to prepare schemes for new and undeveloped areas, but despite further legislation the old built-over areas were not cleared and progress, because of heavy compensation costs to landowners, was slow. Moreover, the emphasis was on the control of land use and the prevention of unsuitable development rather than the promotion of beneficial schemes or concern for the wider problems of regional or national planning.

The Barlow Commission (1937) studied "The Location of Industry and the Distribution of the Industrial Population" and reported in 1940. It recommended the redevelopment of congested urban areas and the dispersal of population and industry in order to balance employment throughout the kingdom. The Scott Commission of 1941 reported on "Land utilisation in rural areas" and emphasised the necessity of maintaining good agricultural land, of preserving natural amenities and of reinvigorating certain declining towns by transferring industry to their vacant sites. Also in 1941 the Uthwatt Committee was appointed to make an objective analysis of payment

---

[14] H. Hamilton, *History of the Homeland*, Allen & Unwin, 1946, p. 136.

of compensation and recovery of betterment in respect of public control of the use of land. One of its recommendations was the establishment of a co-ordinating body to bring together the work of existing departments dealing with national development. This was achieved in 1943 with the creation of the Ministry of Town and Country Planning, and in 1944 the Town and Country Planning Act permitted the purchase of land by local authorities for planning purposes.

The Town and Country Planning Act 1947, the principal Act for the next fifteen years, reduced the number of local planning authorities from 1,441 to the 145 county and county borough councils. All changes in the use of land had to be approved by the local planning authorities. They were also required to produce development plans every five years and were given wider powers of compulsory acquisition. County local planning authorities were authorised to delegate to county districts any functions relating to the control of development, while a regulation made in 1959 enabled county districts with a population of over 60,000 (or under if authorised by the Minister) to claim delegation of certain planning functions, which included applications for planning permission. The Act also introduced a general development charge, which was abolished in 1952.

Subsequent Acts from 1951 to 1959 did not change the principles of the 1947 Act, but were concerned mainly with drafting changes and financial provisions. The development charge of 1947 was abolished, and in 1959 market value was fully restored as the basis for compensation on compulsory purchases. The Town and Country Planning Act 1962, consolidated previous legislation and is now the principal act for planning.

In order to increase the amount of land available for dwellings and to prevent its development by speculators, the Land Commission Act was passed in February, 1967. Its main features are: the establishment of a Land Commission with wide powers of compulsory purchase; the imposition of a betterment levy on the development value of land at an initial rate of 40 per cent; the introduction of a new "Crownhold" lease system; and improved arrangements for financial assistance to local authorities.

From its inception the Land Commission came under attack from the Conservative opposition and from certain newspapers; for example, *The Financial Times* commented that it "was born by expediency out of muddle" (10 January, 1967), and the *Daily Express* compiled a "Black File of Injustice" which outlined cases of hardship caused by the contentious betterment levy. The pressure upon the government to introduce measures to alleviate some of the worst features of the levy intensified during the early part of 1969 and in

April a White Paper *Modifications in Betterment Levy* (Cmnd. 4001) recommended the following changes which were incorporated in the Finance Act, 1969: (i) exemption from levy for chargeable acts or events with market value up to £1,500 subject to conditions; (ii) relief for people who build single houses on plots given or bequeathed to them or sold to them at a low price; (iii) partial relief, by an increase in the base value, on the sale or lease of an owner-occupied house of up to £10,000 in value and a quarter-acre in extent; (iv) allowances of professional fees levy; and (v) waiver of interest on unpaid levy for assessments up to £1,000.

The Commission's second report, published in October 1969, showed that it had increased the total number of assessments from 3,449 in 1967–69 to 15,390 in 1968–69, the gross amount of levy assessed from £1·65 m. to £15·27 m., and the amount of levy collected from £0·46 m. to £8·10 m. On the other hand, its first priority to make key sites available for private development and to make land available for housing associations and for schemes of comprehensive development had progressed slowly, with only 159·6 acres having been sold for development up to 30 September, 1969. Of the 946 acres purchased for development in 1968–69, 274 were bought for resale to builders. In the same year, nine compulsory purchase orders came into force covering 172 acres with an estimated value of £541,000, and twenty-nine draft orders were published relating to 1,140 acres with an estimated value of £6·9 million. There were five public local inquiries, four being concluded in favour of the Commission.

The Civic Amenities Act 1967 required local planning authorities to designate as conservation areas those parts of their areas which it was desirable, for architectural or historic reasons, to preserve or enhance. Once designated as a conservation area it becomes the duty of the planning authority to pay special attention to the character and appearance of the area, and any application for planning permission for the development of land which would affect the character or appearance of the area must be published in the local press and twenty-one days must be given for the proposal to be inspected by the public. The authority must take into account any representations relating to the application. The penalty for contravening a building preservation order, in summary proceedings before the magistrates, is raised from a fine of £100 to a maximum of £250 or three months' imprisonment or both; if the proceedings are on indictment before a jury, the fine has no limit (and will have regard to the financial benefit which the offender received) and imprisonment may be for as long as twelve months. The Act also gives increased powers and duties to authorities to encourage the planting and preservation of trees (maximum fine for felling increased from £100 to £250); to disposal of abandoned cars and other refuse; to repair an uninhabited building on the Ministry's list of historic buildings; to purchase compulsorily (subject to Ministerial confirmation) any listed building or other building subject to a preservation order if reasonable steps are not being taken for its proper preservation; and to provide off-street parking and playgrounds.

Major changes in planning procedures were effected by the Town and Country Planning Act 1968 which amended the law relating to town and country planning, the compulsory acquisition of land and the disposal of land by public authorities; made provision for grants for research relating to, and education with respect to, the planning and design of the physical environment; extended the purposes for which Exchequer contributions may be made under the Town Development Act 1952; and dealt with connected purposes.

Local planning authorities are to survey their areas and keep under review those matters which might affect development. They are instructed to prepare and submit for the Minister's approval a *structure plan* which will be a written statement with diagrams setting out the broad policy for land use, including proposals for the improvement of the physical environment and the management of traffic. It will also set out in general terms proposals for "action areas" where comprehensive change by development, redevelopment, or improvement is expected to begin within a prescribed period. Local planning authorities are also required to prepare a *local plan* formulating their proposals for the development and other use of land in the light of the structure plan. The proposals must be publicised and public enquiries into objections raised to a structure plan will be conducted by a Ministry inspector, and in the case of a local plan, by an inspector appointed by the Minister.

Part II strengthened the power of enforcement of planning control available to local planning authorities, provided for the grant of established use certificates and gave them power to stop further development pending proceedings on an enforcement notice. Planning appeals (Part III) will be speeded up by empowering inspectors to make decisions on such matters as appeals against a refusal of planning permission to develop land, advertisement control, enforcement notices, or the refusal of planning permission to alter or demolish buildings of architectural or historic interest.

Sections 67 and 69 of the 1962 Act relating to the compulsory acquisition of land were repealed and permitted the minister to authorise a local authority to acquire land compulsorily for development, redevelopment or improvement and other planning purposes.

Any minister or local or public authority duly authorised to acquire land by compulsory purchase may vest such land in themselves by a general vesting declaration. The provisions were extended whereby an owner occupier of property whose property becomes virtually unsaleable on account of a development proposed by a public authority (planning blight) may require that authority to buy it.

New powers of control over the demolition or alteration of "listed buildings" of special architectural and historic interest were substituted for those which were exercised by means of building preservation orders. Local authorities may, after giving the owner an opportunity to repair a listed building, acquire any such building compulsorily if it is in need of repair and, if it has been deliberately neglected, compensation need only be paid on site value.

The minister is empowered to set up Planning Inquiry Commissions to look into certain matters, including applications for planning permission, appeals, and development by a government department. Their main concern will be matters of national or regional importance requiring special consideration. Local planning authorities are required to keep a register of planning applications for public inspection, and are empowered to delegate certain planning decisions to a special officer.

These wide-ranging changes were regarded as a major devolution of responsibility and initiative to local planning authorities, and "a charter for citizen participation".[15] This aspect of public participation was given further emphasis by the appointment in March, 1968, of a committee under the chairmanship of Mr. A. Skeffington "to consider and report on the best methods, including publicity, of securing the participation of the public at a formative stage in the making of development plans for their area". Reporting in July, 1969, the committee proposed "guidelines for constructive action" rather than "a deadening book of rules".[16] Among their main recommendations to encourage co-operation between planners and the public were: the establishment of community forums to represent a wide range of local bodies ("the yeast of the community"), which would discuss information from the planning authority and present the views of the constituent organisations during the preparation of structure and local plans; the appointment of community development officers to stimulate the "non-joiners" and to provide them with information, to link with existing groups and to promote new ones, and, particularly at the local plan stage, to put the proposals

[15] *The Observer*, 5 *January*, 1969.
[16] *People and Planning*, H.M.S.O.

to the "non-joiners" and act as their advocate both to the forum and to the authority; societies and individuals should be brought in more to advise the planners, with people being able to put their names on a "participation register" to ensure they are notified about the preparation of plans; people could apply some parts of a local plan before the main proposals were passed (e.g. tree planting); and authorities should involve the local press, radio and T.V. in the formative stages of a plan, in committee and open council, and facilities should be provided for broadcasting council debates on big planning decisions. Four points during preparation are defined as the right moments to secure participation: the initial announcement that the plan is to be prepared; the report of survey; the identification of the choices available; and the statement of proposals favoured by the local planning authority. The Minister, and the Secretaries of State for Wales and Scotland, accepted the recommendations in principle.

New Towns

"The creation of new towns has been perhaps the greatest achievement of post-war town and country planning."[17] Towns such as Coventry and Plymouth were devastated by aerial bombardment in the Second World War and were rebuilt as fine modern cities, incorporating advanced planning ideas. Densely populated London, having borne the brunt of the bombing, was the subject of Sir Patrick Abercrombie's Greater London Plan which was published in 1944. It conceived of London as four concentric circles and proposed that a million people would be moved out of Inner London (the London County Council area), that the second circle of pre-war suburbs would remain as it was, but that the communities in the Green Belt circle and the outer circle of existing towns and of new towns which were to be built would receive the overspill from Inner London.

The Reith Committee was appointed to consider the problems of establishing new towns and to suggest guiding principles. Three reports were quickly submitted and the New Towns Act, 1946, was passed embodying many of the Committee's recommendations. The Minister was given the power to designate sites for new towns and to appoint development corporations to develop and administer the estates until their assets and liabilities could be transferred to the local authorities within whose areas they were built.

The twelve new towns which were initially envisaged were built

---

[17] R. H. Best "New Towns in the London Region", in *Greater London* (ed. Coppock & Prince), p. 313.

with the assistance of Exchequer loans, and eight were to be satellites of London. All were to be self-contained communities with their own shops, recreational facilities and industries, so that people would be able to work within the community and avoid travelling long distances to work. Their population growth has been rapid, increasing during the intercensal years from a total of 134,974 in 1951 to 426,150 in 1961.

The twelve new towns originally planned were at Basildon, Bracknell, Crawley, Harlow, Hatfield, Hemel Hempstead, Stevenage and Welwyn Garden City (all within a radius of 30 miles of London), Newton Aycliffe, Peterlee, Corby and Cwmbran, accommodating the manpower requirements for neighbouring industry. By 1965 the number had increased to twenty-one with the addition of Cumbernauld, East Kilbride, Glenrothes and Livingstone, to relieve overcrowding in Glasgow; Skelmersdale and Runcorn, absorbing families from Merseyside; Dawley and Redditch, taking families from Birmingham and the Black Country, and Washington, taking the overspill from the Tyneside-Wearside area.

The New Towns Act 1959, amended the 1946 Act by providing that when the development corporations were wound up, their assets and liabilities would be transferred to a new body, the Commission for New Towns, and not to the local authorities. The Commission of fifteen paid members would be responsible for the properties and welfare of the townspeople, but the local authorities would be responsible for schools, roads, lighting and refuse disposal. The Commission could assist in providing amenities, water supplies and sewerage. The Commission was required to set up local committees, after consulting with the district councils, to manage their rented houses and it was intended that other local committees would be set up to which the Commission might delegate part of its business. The New Towns Act 1965, now consolidates existing legislation. The New Towns Act 1966 increased to £800 million the limit on advances to be made to meet capital expenditure on new towns and also amended the Land Compensation Acts, and the New Towns Act 1969 further raised the limit on advances to £1,100 million.

In addition to the new towns, further relief for congested towns was attempted by the Town Development Act 1952, which enabled a congested town to negotiate overspill agreements with towns which would provide accommodation for the former's surplus population. Financial inducements were to be offered by the exporting town, the county council and the Exchequer. A 50 per cent grant is available for the provision of major services for town development, and the Housing Act 1961, increased the subsidy payable in England and

Wales from £24 to £28 for every house let to relieve urban congestion.

The Buchanan Report *Traffic in Towns* (1963) highlighted another dimension of the urban planning problem—that of the necessity of integrating the needs of the motorist ($2\frac{1}{2}$ million cars in 1953 growing to $7\frac{1}{2}$ million in 1963), of industrial traffic and of the pedestrian into future urban development schemes or having to pay the social and economic price which would result from an increasing chaos of congested roadways.

The most recent stage in planning development began in 1963 with its regional orientation in the publication of a government White Paper, *The North East: A Programme for Regional Development and Growth* (Cmd. 2206). Its emphasis was placed on a "growth zone" from Tyneside to Teeside and an increase in public service investment from £55 million in 1963 to £90 million in 1964–65. Similar proposals were made for the development of central Scotland. In March, 1964 the South-East study was published relating to the area from the Wash to Dorset and containing nearly 40 per cent of the United Kingdom population. An increase of $3\frac{1}{2}$ million people in the South-East was anticipated by 1981, and the study proposed that the increase should be accommodated outside the London conurbation. The Green Belt area around London was to be doubled to prevent the continued expansion of the metropolitan area, and three new cities were recommended at Southampton–Portsmouth, Newbury and Bletchley. Other towns would be greatly expanded and others would be listed for expansion.

In 1965 regional studies of the West Midlands and the North-West were issued, the former recommending the redevelopment of the Birmingham conurbation, the completion of new towns at Dawley (to be known as Telford) and Redditch, certain town expansions and development, house-building around the green belt, and a regional road programme. The North-West study analysed basic data and commented on such matters as housing improvement, the adaptation of the economic structure, and provisions for planned overspill. The whole area needed to be planned as a unity, with a balanced employment structure and ease of access to the countryside and coasts. In 1965 also a comprehensive plan for the urban develop-ment of mid-Wales was under active consideration, culminating in the formation of the Mid-Wales New Town Development Corpora-tion in 1968.

4. Police

The maintenance of order is one of the primary functions of a state. In eleventh-century Britain the system of frankpledge existed whereby most men over the age of twelve were grouped into tithings (ten) whose members were mutually responsible for the good behaviour of each other and their families. An Ordinance of 1252 decreed that in every township one or two constables were to be appointed to ensure the due execution of the Assize of Arms, which required every man to furnish himself with arms and armour suitable to his station. This was an essentially military duty for the constables, but they were also conservators of the peace and had right of arrest. With the introduction of J.Ps., the constables were put under their control, and later the J.Ps. became responsible for their appointment and removal. By a statute of 1662 the constable became a parochial officer, still under the J.Ps.' control.

By the eighteenth and early nineteenth centuries the growth of industrial towns strained an already inefficient constabulary, while unemployment and bad harvests after 1815 helped to create a revolutionary social ferment. Various law enforcement expedients were tried until, in 1829, a full-time police force for the metropolitan area was established and put in the charge of the Home Office. The City of London followed suit in 1831, the municipal boroughs in 1835, and counties had the optional power in 1839 to establish a full-time force, but were compulsorily required to do so in 1856.

In 1840 county J.Ps. and borough councils were statutorily empowered to consolidate small police establishments and in 1856 legislation stopped the police grant to any borough with a population of under 5,000 where it had not amalgamated its force with that of the county. By the Municipal Corporations Act, 1882, new boroughs with a population of under 20,000 were not to be authorised to establish a separate police force, while the Local Government Act, 1888, transferred the police powers of boroughs with a population of under 10,000 to the counties.

The Police Act 1946, abolished the separate police forces of all non-county boroughs, unless their population (on 30 June, 1939) had been at least half of that of their administrative county, and transferred them to the county. The Home Secretary had possessed powers since the 1939–45 war to amalgamate forces and the 1946 Act provided for their voluntary or compulsory amalgamation. The former required the Home Secretary's approval, while compulsory amalgamation was a matter of expediency decided by the Home Secretary with one limitation only—no county or borough with a population of over 100,000 could be compulsorily amalgamated, without its consent, with any other police area(s) whose population exceeded its own. Examples of compulsory amalgamation include Cheshire and Chester (1949), Leicestershire and Rutland (1951) and Carmarthenshire and Cardiganshire (1958).

At this stage the main types of police authority were:

(a) *County Police*—the Local Government Act, 1888, transferred the powers and duties of J.Ps. relating to police to a standing joint committee comprising equal numbers of representatives of the county council and of quarter sessions. The standing joint committee was an executive body with powers of compulsion over the county council.

(b) *Borough Police*—by the Municipal Corporations Acts of 1835 and 1882, watch committees were to be appointed by the municipal council and were to consist of the mayor and not more than one-third of the council members. The watch committees were not under the control of their councils, except in financial matters and any extra-police functions which may have been delegated piecemeal to them, e.g. fire services, licensing of street hawkers or pawnbrokers, cinema hours, etc.

(c) *Combined Police Forces*—created by amalgamation under the Police Act 1946, are bodies corporate and consist of representatives of their constituent authorities. Where amalgamation involves the combination of county and borough, the authority with the greater population decides whether the county or borough constitution of a standing joint committee or a watch committee will apply.

(d) *Metropolitan Police*—created 1829 and comes directly under the Home Secretary's control. He recommends to the Crown a Commissioner and five Assistant Commissioners.

(e) *City of London Police*—created 1831 and is organised independently by a Commissioner of the City police force who is responsible to the Court of Common Council and the Home Secretary.

In December, 1959, a Royal Commission on the Police was appointed under the chairmanship of Sir Henry Willink, Q.C. Its Interim Report (Cmd. 1222) was produced in November 1960 and recommended substantial pay increases, the biggest for forty years, which were implemented retrospectively to 1 September, 1960. The Royal Commission produced its Final Report (Cmd. 1728) in May, 1962 and its main recommendations were:

1. Police constables should receive pay increases ranging from 18 per cent on joining to 40 per cent after 22 years' service.
2. Separate local police forces should be retained and not brought under the direct control of the Government. (There was one dissentient who advocated the establishment of a centrally-controlled force administered by regional commissioners. The other members

rejected the creation of a national force, seeing considerable value in the local associations and in the local knowledge of forces).[18]

3. Certain responsibilities, including those for the efficient policing of each area, should be centralised under the Home Secretary.

4. The number of police forces should be reduced.

5. A Chief Inspector of Constabulary should be appointed for the whole of Great Britain.

A Home Office Circular commending many of the Royal Commission's recommendations was issued in the same month to police authorities and chief officers of police. In 1963 the Home Secretary (Mr. Henry Brooke) introduced a Police Bill which gave effect to the Final Report's recommendations and consolidated a large body of legislation dealing with the control and administration of police forces in England and Wales, outside London.

The Police Act 1964 is based largely on the recommendations of the Royal Commission and is a consolidating and rationalising measure whose main provisions are:

1. The constitution of police authorities was altered. The watch committees and the standing joint committees are to consist of two-thirds council members and one-third magistrates. The standing joint committee is to be renamed "Police Committee".

2. The powers of a watch committee to appoint, promote and dismiss police officers are to be transferred to the Chief Constable, as is the practice in counties.

3. The police authority will continue to appoint the chief constable and also, in future, the deputy chief constable and any assistant chief constable (in each case subject to the approval of the Home Secretary).

4. The police authority will have power to require the chief constable or any such officer to retire in the interests of efficiency subject to the Home Secretary's approval.

5. The police authority may now call upon the Chief Constable to provide a report on local police matters, but if he is of the opinion that a matter is contrary to public interest he can refer it to the Home Office for adjudication.

6. The Chief Constable becomes vicariously responsible for the torts of the constables under his command (the Royal Commission recommended that the police authority should be made liable) and the police authority is empowered to make payments in respect of damages against, and costs incurred by, police officers who have had legal action taken against them. Complaints against constables are to be investigated immediately and a report sent to the Director of Public Prosecutions unless no criminal offence has been committed.

---

[18] See *Public Law*, Spring 1967, for an appraisal of the advantages and disadvantages of a national force.

13

7. The Home Secretary is given a greater measure of control over provincial police forces. His powers to amalgamate forces in the interests of efficiency are increased and there is to be no prohibition against the compulsory amalgamation of a police area with a population of over 100,000. He has also a new duty to promote police efficiency by requiring an authority to retire its chief constable, to call for reports from chief constables, to set up a local enquiry into the policing of areas, and to lay down minimum standards of equipment.

8. Increased penalties are laid down for assaulting a police officer.

One commentary upon the Act stated:

> "Although these changes leave unaltered the basic structure of local police forces controlled by virtually autonomous chief constables, the beginnings of a movement towards centralisation is clearly discernible."[19]

The parish constable disappears at long last, but certain anomalies still remain. One of the largest forces in the country, the Transport Police, is untouched by the Act; Bristol still maintains two police forces, one in Bristol itself and a separate force for Avonmouth Docks; and the Manchester Dock Police is maintained by a limited liability company in the Manchester Ship Canal Company.

The Final Report of the Royal Commission had been critical of keeping relatively small forces, and mergers had reduced the separate forces in England and Wales from 126 to 117 by 1 April, 1966. In May, the Home Secretary (Mr. Roy Jenkins) announced that the 105 forces in England and the twelve in Wales would be further reduced by amalgamation to forty-five and four respectively. Tyneside reorganisation would reduce the English figure to forty-two. The Home Secretary said that amalgamations would produce: (a) a better career structure and promotion prospects; (b) a more effective deployment of men; (c) better, more advanced and more sophisticated equipment, both in communications and in other fields; (d) the avoidance of wasteful duplication of effort; (e) economies of administration; and (f) the opportunity to deal with problems on a wider scale (*C.C.A. Evidence to Royal Commission on Local Government in England*, p. 7). He hoped the local authorities would recognise the need for rationalisation and enter into voluntary schemes.

> "If they do not I must use my powers under the Police Act, 1964, to promote compulsory amalgamations."

---

[19] *Modern Law Review*, Vol. 27, p. 682.

Both praise and condemnation followed the announcement of such a radical reduction in the numbers of forces. Some forces felt there would be an increase in efficiency, and economies of scale would be achieved in transport and equipment; conversely, many policemen feared that they would be transferred, that promotion would be more difficult in a larger authority, that there would be an increase in administration and that existing good services would be weakened by having to cover wider areas.

The amalgamations represented a clear threat to the job security of chief constables, of whom an estimated seventy-nine would be displaced. Some would get jobs as assistant chief constables but this would not always be possible, for example in Lancashire twelve chief constables would be displaced and in the West Riding another seven.

Several police authorities (e.g. Blackpool, Reading, Southend, Cardiff, and Coventry) objected to amalgamation but lost their appeals, and by November 1969 there were forty-seven police forces in operation. Meanwhile the "unit policing" system, introduced in 1966–67 to integrate the foot-patrol constables resident in the area of their beat with twenty-four hour coverage by motorized beat patrols, was extended throughout the country.

5. Health and Welfare Services

The National Health Service Act 1946, created a tripartite structure comprising (i) hospital and specialist services, (ii) general medical, dental, pharmaceutical and ophthalmic services, and (iii) personal health services provided by local health authorities which were to be the county and county borough councils.

Local health authorities are responsible for the provision of the following services under the terms of the National Health Service Acts 1946 to 1966, the National Assistance Act 1946 and the Health Services and Public Health Act 1968:

A. Health Centres—their provision, equipment, maintenance, and staffing (except for doctors and dentists) for general medical, dental, pharmaceutical, specialist and health education purposes. Their capital cost is high and by 1964 only twenty-one had been set up, almost wholly in new towns or housing estates. From 1964 to 1967 an additional twenty-four were built, and at December 1967 forty were under construction. The Guillebaud Committee on the Cost of the National Health Service, 1953–56, emphasised their experimental nature and acknowleged that equivalent benefits might be achieved in other ways, such as the co-ordination of group practices with local health authority clinics. Nevertheless, it is envisaged that there will be 300 health centres by March 1976.

B. Maternity and Child Welfare—the provision of medical and dental care for expectant and nursing mothers and children under five years of age. Services include ante-natal and child welfare clinics and centres, day nurseries, child minders, houses and hostels for ante-natal and post-natal care for unmarried mothers, and the care of premature infants. Midwives and health visitors play a prominent part in these services, and local health authorities must ensure that adequate numbers are employed.

C. Home Nursing—for the care of those who require nursing in their own homes, and nurses may be employed by the local health authority or by a voluntary body acting as its agent.

D. Vaccination and Immunisation—local health authorities must make their own arrangements, either through general practitioners or their own clinics to provide free immunisation against diphtheria and tetanus and vaccination against poliomyelitis, smallpox, tuberculosis and whooping cough.

E. Services for the Handicapped—the local health authorities must provide services for the blind, deaf, and dumb, those permanently and substantially handicapped by illness, injury or congenital deformity, and also for the mentally disordered. Voluntary bodies may be utilised as their agents and the local authorities contribute to their funds.

F. Mental Health Services—local health authorities must make provision for the care of the mentally ill and subnormal, the prevention of mental illness, the care of those who suffer from mental disorders, and their after-care. Arrangements will include separate residential premises for different groups, centres for occupational training and general rehabilitation. These services catered for almost 156,000 in 1964.

G. Ambulances—local health authorities directly or by arrangement with voluntary bodies provide a free ambulance service between the home and hospital or clinic. Patient journeys have risen rapidly from 7 million in 1949 to 22½ million in 1968. In 1967 the Minister of Health decided to transfer the administration of the service to the regional hospital boards; there was a storm of protest and the Royal Commission said there were "insufficient grounds" for the transfer, and eventually the Minister announced that the transfer would be delayed.

H. Services for the Elderly—include home assistance for the housebound and residential accommodation. Also provided, but not as a health and welfare responsibility, will be specially-designed single-bed, roomed houses and flatlets with residential wardens.

I. Nursing Homes—must be registered with the local authority who are empowered to ensure the maintenance of proper standards.

J. Home Help Services—may be provided by local health authorities to householders where there is illness, maternity, mental defectiveness, old age, or children below school age, and a charge may be made according to the recipient's means.

K. Family Planning—under the National Health Service (Family Planning) Act 1967 local health authorities may provide family planning services for all who want them. The L.H.A.s have a general approval to charge for prescriptions and contraceptive supplies in non-medical cases, but the scale of charges is at the discretion of the authority. All but six L.H.A.s have implemented the Act, and in 1968 paid about £92,000 to the Family Planning Association, as their agent.

Total expenditure by local authorities on these services rose from £34·1 million in 1949–50 to £153·5 million in 1964–65 and to £216 million in 1967–68. The first report of the amalgamated Department of Health and Social Security announced in July 1969 that total expenditure was estimated to exceed £238 million in 1969–70. In 1962 all local health authorities were required to review their services and plan developments to 1972–73. The results were published in a White Paper, *Health and Welfare: The Development of Community Care* (Cmnd. 1973) where plans for capital expenditure amounting to nearly £223·5 million and revenue expenditure of £163 million by the 146 local health authorities are detailed. The National Plan (1965) "takes a more expansive view", forecasting an increase of 34 per cent in net revenue expenditure in the first five years as opposed to a 30 per cent growth rate in a decade forecast by local authorities.[20]

In addition to the personal health services, local authorities fulfil a broader public health function which includes the following environmental health services: water supply and sewerage; the control of air pollution; securing the repair, maintenance and sanitary condition of houses; clearance and redevelopment of unhealthy and congested areas; the abatement of overcrowding; the control of infectious diseases; disinfection; health control at seaports and airports; the composition, description, hygiene and fitness of food for sale for human consumption; street cleansing and refuse disposal;

---

[20] *The Local Health Services*, Office of Health Economics, 1965, p. 39.

the provision of burial grounds, baths, wash-houses, disinfestation and rodent control; the abatement of noise and vibration nuisances; and the regulation of the provision of sanitary conveniences in places of work, and the health and comfort of workers in Offices, Shops and Railway Premises.

In December 1965 a committee under the chairmanship of Mr. Frederick Seebohm had been appointed "to review the organisation and responsibilities of the local authority personal social services in England and Wales, and to consider what changes are desirable to ensure an effective service". Its report on 23 July, 1968, called for fundamental changes in the administration of health and social welfare.[21] At local level all major local authorities should set up a unified social service department with its own principal officer, who would report to a separate social service committee. At national level there would be one central department responsible for the relationship between central government and the new social service department and for the overall national planning of the service's intelligence and social research.

The new local authority would cover the work of the children's department, welfare services under the National Assistance Act 1948, education welfare, child guidance, home help services, mental health social work, adult training centres, other social work services and day nurseries, as well as certain social welfare work undertaken by some housing departments. It should also become the focal point for voluntary workers. The new department should work through area officers with teams of not less than ten to twelve social workers serving populations of 50,000 to 100,000 and its head should not be subordinate to any other departmental head.

Published on the same day as the Seebohm Report was a Green Paper[22] containing the proposals of the Ministry of Health for the restructuring of the National Health Service. The main proposals which had a significance for local authorities were: the unification of the administration of medical and related services in an area by one authority, an Area Board, which would replace the existing Executive Councils, Regional Hospital Boards, Boards of Governors and Management Committees; these authorities would also take over the functions of the present local health authorities and links would be established between medical and environmental services (refuse disposal, sewerage, clean air, housing, etc). About forty to

[21] *Report of the Committee on Local Authority and Allied Personal Social Services*, H.M.S.O., Cmnd. 3703, July, 1968.
[22] *National Health Service: the administrative structure of medical and related services in England and Wales*, H.M.S.O., July, 1968.

fifty Area Boards were envisaged, comprising "professional members with direct broad experience of practical problems of the service".

The Green Paper "sparked off a vigorous discussion" which led to the proposal for Area Boards being superseded in a second Green Paper,[23] published on 11 February 1970. It related only to England and proposed about ninety Area Health Authorities whose boundaries would generally match those of the unitary and metropolitan districts. The main provisions of the second Green Paper as they affect local health services are summarised in Chapter 10. At the same time the Local Authority Social Services Bill was published incorporating the main proposals of the Seebohm Committee. The Bill proposed that in each local authority nearly all the personal social services should come under the control of a social services committee. It would replace the existing statutory children's and welfare committees and would also assume responsibility for social services assigned by existing law to the health committee. A principal officer called the Director of Social Services would be responsible for unifying in each local authority the administration of personal social services, and his functions would include those of the present statutory post of children's officer which would be abolished. In moving the second reading of the Bill, the Secretary of State for Social Services stated that if the Bill reached the statute book in its existing form the Directors could be in their posts not later than 1 April 1971.

---

23 *The Future Structure of the National Health Service*, H.M.S.O., February 1970.

CHAPTER 8

Finance of Local Government

The services provided by local authorities entail large expenditure on both current and capital accounts. In 1967–68, local authorities in England and Wales spent £3,988·5 million on revenue account and £1,563·3 million on capital account. The increase in expenditure has been in the region of 9¼ per cent a year, and to meet part of this rates have been raised to give an annual increase of between 9 and 10 per cent a year. The factors which have contributed to the increase in expenditure have been: (a) central demands for the development of local services; (b) increasing public demand for higher standards; (c) rising population and its greater mobility; (d) a proportionately higher increase in the dependent age groups of young and old, who make special demands on the social services; and (e) the intensification of these pressures by inflation and rising costs. According to the Redcliffe–Maud Report, these factors are "likely to persist" and "local expenditure will continue to expand both absolutely and as a percentage of the G.N.P.". The proportion of the gross national product accounted for by local authorities has grown from 5·1 per cent in 1900 to 15 per cent in 1966–67. Regarding the scale of local government finance, the Royal Commission's report added pessimistically: "Local authorities are in sight of a solution to scarcely any of their problems".

The allocation of expenditure on local government services has been detailed in the previous chapter. The table on page 189 shows the composition of revenue income, and shows also that central government grants contribute more than do rates and that a further substantial amount is contributed by a variety of miscellaneous sources.

1. Central Government Grants

The industrial revolution, the population explosion after 1750, the extension of communities with inadequate public utilities and the ever-present threat of unemployment and destitution on a scale which could not be relieved by the Elizabethan poor law, created an urgent need for remedial services. The main source of wealth before industrialisation was land, and its owners could not be expected on their own, to meet the costs of services. It was their complaints about the burden of rates, however, which led to the appointment of a

TABLE 7. LOCAL GOVERNMENT INCOME—REVENUE ACCOUNT
(£ million)

Year	Total revenue income	Rates		Grants		Miscellaneous sources		% of grants to rates
		Amount	%	Amount	%	Amount	%	
1923–24	341·3	143·3	42·0	75·2	22·0	122·8	36·0	52
1933–34	446·6	148·6	33·3	121·6	27·2	176·4	39·5	82
1943–44	739·0	204·1	27·6	228·4	30·9	306·5	41·5	112
1947–48	963·2	283·3	29·4	269·7	28·0	410·2	42·6	95
1950–51	899·3	304·9	33·9	304·6	33·9	289·8	32·2	100
1955–56	1352·3	421·0	31·2	500·4	37·0	430·9	31·8	119
1960–61	2091·0	696·7	33·3	756·0	36·2	638·3	30·5	108
1961–62	2268·2	747·4	32·9	830·6	36·7	690·2	30·4	111
1962–63	2491·9	831·3	33·4	907·0	36·4	753·6	30·2	109
1963–64	2772·2	923·1	33·3	1022·4	36·9	826·7	29·8	111
1964–65	2994·3	991·2	33·1	1103·0	36·8	900·1	30·1	111
1965–66	3394·1	1131·5	33·4	1260·0	37·1	1002·6	29·5	111
1966–67	3742·9	1266·1	33·8	1389·1	37·1	1087·7	29·1	110
1967–68	4100·4	1323·3	32·3	1591·0	38·8	1186·1	28·9	120

Royal Commission in 1835 which advocated a re-assessment which would include the new mills and factories. The outcome was the introduction of grants in aid of rates which were first paid to all local authorities on a uniform basis in 1835 to meet half the cost of administering criminal justice. Social reform measures involved local authorities in increased expenditure and in order to maintain a national standard services were subsidised by further grants. The reformed poor law unions of 1845 received 50 per cent of the salaries of their medical officers and all the salaries of teachers and industrial instructors in the workhouses from grants, and with the repeal of the Corn Laws of 1846 the agricultural interests were further protected by grants from the national exchequer.

Between 1870 and 1880 grants were made for elementary education, public health services, police, prison maintenance, registration of births and deaths, and highways. Since that time grants have been extended in proportion and amount, and have become, since 1950–51, the major source of revenue income. Increased financial dependence has meant the diminution of local authorities' independence and the increased subordination of local authorities to central government control.

Grants are made to local authorities for a number of reasons:

(a) as local authorities are required by the State to establish new services, the State should meet part of the cost by grants;

(b) the extension in the number of services and their increasing cost have drained rate resources and the State has felt compelled to shoulder some of the burden;

(c) local authorities lose rate income when State legislation derates fully or partially certain classes of hereditament and grants help to make good this loss;

(d) the disparity in income between local authorities and the necessity to maintain national standards require State aid for the poorer local authorities to help equalise the costs.

Various types of grants have been tried since 1835:

A. *Percentage grants*

These were the main type of Exchequer grant until 1887, and they were so called because the amount of grant was based on a percentage of "approved" expenditure by a local authority on a particular service. The expansion of social services in the early twentieth century was accompanied by percentage grants. The process began with a grant for education in 1902, and followed with grants for roads, small-holdings and allotments, sanatoria, dispensaries, police pensions, housing, etc. The amount of the grant varied according to the service, e.g. class I roads, 75 per cent; class II roads, 60 per cent; individual health, police and the protection of children, 50 per cent; fire service, 25 per cent.

Criticisms have been made of percentage grants because the local authority might have been inclined to have undertaken more grandiose and extravagant provisions than it could have done if supporting the service without grant aid. Moreover, the control exercised over spending by the government has been thought by local authorities to be too detailed, but the government has felt it to be inadequate. Additionally, the grant is tied to one service and any surplus cannot be allocated to other needs.

B. *Assigned Revenues*

By the Local Government Act 1888, many of the direct percentage grants were discontinued and the proceeds of licences issued for the sale of liquors, dealing in game, taxes on dealers in beer, wines, spirits, sweets and tobacco, licences on dogs, game and guns and a proportion of probate duties were assigned to local authorities. Goschen's theory of separating national and local finances as much as possible led to much controversy and complaints about the narrow basis of local taxation, and the inadequacy of the state's contribution led to the appointment in 1896 of a Royal Commission on local taxation. The system was ultimately abolished by the Local Government Act 1929, and to-day, only vestiges remain in the revenue from dog licences which is paid to local authorities, while fines and fees in magistrates courts are retained in proportion to their net expenditure on magistrates courts.

C. *General Exchequer or "Block" Grants*

Local authority expenditure more than doubled after the First World War, and government demands for economy, prompted by the nation's economic position, led to the appointment in 1922 of a Treasury committee to investigate the feasibility of an alternative system to the percentage grant. For various reasons its report was never published, but the Government and the Chancellor, Mr. Winston Churchill, was intent upon replacing the percentage grant by a block grant which would be paid over a limited number of years. There was much hostility to the proposed change and the block grant proposal was withdrawn, but in 1926 Mr. Churchill referred in debate to the percentage grant system, stating:

> ". . . the expenditure, apart from legislation to alter the scale of grants, is uncontrollable. The local authorities call the tune, and it only remains to calculate the percentage upon which the Exchequer pays the piper . . . it is a very unsatisfactory field".

He continued by stating the government's intention to convert the percentage grant system to block grants,

> "that is to say, to pay definite sums instead of percentages to the local authorities, to give those authorities increased discretionary powers, to make them responsible for any extravagance or any unduly bold enterprise to which they may commit themselves, and to give them 100 per cent of any economies they may themselves be able to effect".[1]

In 1929 agriculture was derated, industry was partially derated and the losses of the local authorities in rate income needed to be compensated. Thus by the Local Government Act, 1929, despite further opposition and only mild enthusiasm from the local authorities, many percentage grants and most of the assigned revenues were

---

[1] Maureen Schultz, "The Development of the Grant System" in *Essays on Local Government* (ed. C. H. Wilson), Blackwell, 1948, pp. 131–2.

discontinued, and block grants were introduced and apportioned to counties and county boroughs on the basis of a formula calculated "on general characteristics, independent of actual expenditure". These characteristics were: (a) the population of the area; (b) the number of children under 5 years of age; (c) the rateable value per head of the population; (d) the proportion of unemployed insured men to the total population; (e) the population per mile of public road.

Capitation grants were made to county districts at a flat rate per head of the population, with rural districts receiving one-fifth of the amount given to urban districts. The transistion to the new system was achieved over three periods of five years when 25 per cent, 50 per cent and 75 per cent of the block grant were allotted. By the 1929 Act the grants which were abolished were agricultural rates grants, health percentage grants for maternity, tuber-culosis, venereal disease and certain grants for mental deficiency and blindness, classification grants for Class I and Class II roads in Lon-don and county boroughs, and the maintenance grants for scheduled roads in county districts. The percentage grants which remained after 1929 were those for police, education, housing, roads and certain specialised health services.

D. *Exchequer Equalisation Grants*

The General Exchequer Grants of 1929 were replaced by Exchequ-er Equalisation Grants by the Local Government Act 1948. Post-war legislation effected changes in the relationship between local authorities and the government over the administration of certain services, e.g. education, where the major authorities were required to act as agents of the government; in addition, the 1944 Education Act removed the power of local authorities to charge fees for secondary education. Some services formerly controlled by local authorities, e.g. hospitals and public assistance services, were transferred from local authorities. Such changes relieved them of certain expenditures and necessitated a revision of the financial relationship between central and local government. The Exchequer Equalisation Grant was, like the block grant, a contribution to a local authority's general expenses and not to specific services.

It was based upon weighted population but calculated on the basis of a formula which was constructed to benefit the poorer areas and to equalise the resources of local authorities. The weighted population was calculated by adding to the actual population the number of children who were under 15 years of age, so that they were counted twice, and in county councils an additional weighting was added where the population per road mile was under seventy. The total rateable value of England and Wales was then divided by the weighted population of all the counties and county boroughs and the result was the average rateable value per head of weighted population. If the rateable value per head of weighted population in counties and county boroughs fell below the national average, the local authority was credited by the Exchequer with the deficiency in rateable value and rates were paid by the government to each county and county borough on the credited rateable value. County councils were to make grants on a capitation basis to county districts (with rural districts receiving half payments), calculations being made annually, as opposed to the five-yearly intervals of the previous block grants. Those counties and county boroughs whose rateable value per head of weighted population was above the national average received no equalisation grants, but county councils were still required to pay a capitation grant to their county districts.

Percentage grants still remained for certain specific services, which included police, education, roads, health services, and town and county planning.

E. *General Grants*

Dissatisfaction with the exchequer equalisation grant system and the percentage grants led the Conservative government to reconsider the "radical recasting of the system of grants", stating that the improvement needed was

> "one which secures that a substantially larger part of the grant aid is in the form of general assistance and is not tied . . . to specific services and expressed as a percentage of expenditure upon these services".

The percentage grant was seen as "an indiscriminate incentive to further expenditure and also carried with it an aggravating amount of central checking and control of detail".[2] These alleged disadvantages were eliminated by the controversial Local Government Act 1958, which substituted general grants for many of the percentage grants, and the rate deficiency grant for the exchequer equalisation grant. A large number of percentage grants were either absorbed in the general grant formula or discontinued. Excluded from the

---

[2] *Local Government Finance (England and Wales)*, 1957, Cmd. 209 p. 3.

Act, were the specific grants for housing on a unit cost basis, highways and the police.

The "recipient authorities" were the councils of counties and county boroughs and the grants would be assessed in advance for two or three years "grant periods". The amount of the grant payable for any year would be fixed by the Ministry of Housing and Local Government and would be the aggregate[3] of a basic grant and a number of supplementary grants. The aggregate could be reduced by the Minister on the basis of a rate in the pound. The basic grant would be determined by such factors as population and the number of children in that population under 15 years of age. There were seven supplementary grants which would take into account: (1) the number of children under 5 years of age; (2) the number of persons over 65 years of age; (3) a high ratio of pupils at maintained or assisted schools and at occupation centres to population; (4) a high population density per acre of the authority; (5) a low population per road mile; (6) a high percentage population decline over a prescribed period; and (7) whether the authority or part of it lay within the metropolitan police district.

F. *Rate Deficiency Grants*

These were to be paid to county district councils, metropolitan borough councils, the Common Council of the City of London, county and borough councils. The conditions for payment

> "shall be that the product of a rate of one penny in the pound for the area of the authority for that year is less than the standard penny rate product for the area".

Note that there is no reference here to rateable value. Capitation payments by county councils to county districts were abolished. Arrangements were also made for the "pooling" of expenditure on certain training and educational services.

G. *The Rate Support Grant*

Instituted from 1 April, 1967, by the Local Government Act 1966 the rate support grant (RSG) is now the principal grant and replaced both the general and the rate deficiency grants, and specific grants for school milk and meals, and Class II and III roads. The RSG was intended to be a short-term solution until the Royal Commission reported and the entire position of local government finance would be re-examined in the context of its conclusions. The RSG's pur-

---

[3] Virtually the expenditure on absorbed grants.

poses were to help reduce the rate burden and produce a fairer distribution of Exchquer assistance among local authorities.

In order to arrive at the aggregate amount of the grant in any year the minister determines the aggregate of Exchequer grants (other than housing subsidies) to local authorities in respect of their relevant revenue expenditure for that year. He will then deduct from this total the estimated amount of the specific grants for the year in aid of revenue expenditure and the balance will be the aggregate of the rate support grant.

In determining the annual aggregate of grants to local authorities and the specific grants portion of it, the minister is required to take the following considerations into account: (a) the current level of prices, costs and remuneration, any future variation in that level which can be foreseen and the latest information available to him as to the rate of relevant expenditure; (b) any probable fluctuation in the demand for services giving rise to relevant expenditure so far as the fluctuation is attributable to circumstances prevailing in England and Wales as a whole which are not under the control of local authorities; and (c) the need for developing those services and the extent to which, having regard to general economic conditions, it is reasonable to develop those services. In the White Paper *Public Expenditure*—1968–69 *and* 1969–70 (Cmnd. 3515) it was said that:

> "the Goverment expects that in 1969–70 local authorities as a whole will restrain the level of their expenditure so that it does not in total exceed a figure in the region of 3 per cent in real terms above what has already been agreed for purposes of the Exchequer contribution in 1968–69, and the Government will propose rate support grants for 1969–70 on this basis when the time comes."

The aggregate of the RSG is divided into three parts:

1. *Needs element*—is the largest part of the RSG and is similar to the former General Grant but wider in scope and payable to all councils except those of county districts; regulations under the Act may also provide for the payment to the G.L.C. of a proportion of the needs element which would otherwise be payable to the councils of the Inner London boroughs and the Common Council of the City. The Act provided for the distribution of the needs element on the basis of population and on numbers of pupils and students at different stages of education, road mileages and other objective factors. The weightings which were prescribed in the Rate Support Grant Order 1968, however, had to be revised owing to unforseen increases in

costs, and for 1969–70 and 1970–71 (the 1970–71 amounts in brackets) the weightings are:

(a) *Basic payements* £15·59 (£16·24) per head of population; plus £1·22 (£1·26) for each child under 15.

(b) *Supplementary payments*

(i) Young children and old people: £1·10 (£1·13) for each child under 5 and each person over 65.

(ii) Education units: £0·083 (£0·087) per head of population, multiplied by the number of units per 1,000 in excess of 200.

(iii) Roads: £277 (£289) per mile for all roads other than trunk roads. £1,354 (£1,414) per mile for principal roads reduced by £26·15 (£27·35) per mile for each 100 population per mile below 4,000 (subject to a minimum of £831 (£867) per mile) and increased by £34·14 (£35·63) for each 100 population per mile above 5,500.

The remaining supplementary payments—for high density, for low density, for declining population, and for high cost in the metropolitan district—are each percentages of the basic payment and are increased by virtue of increases in that payment.

2. *Resources element*—replaced the Rate Deficiency Grant, but differed only in being fixed in advance, and is payable to any local authority with rate resources per head of population below the national average.

3. *Domestic element*—an entirely new feature to relieve the burden of increasing rate poundages by permitting reductions on the rate levied on dwelling houses (domestic hereditaments) by 5d. in the £ for 1967–68 and 10d. for 1968–69, and on mixed hereditaments by 2d. and 5d. respectively; and 1s. 3d. in the £ for 1969–70 and 1s. 8d. for 1970–71, and on mixed hereditaments by 7d. and 10d. respectively.

The amounts of the three elements of the rate support grants, as revised, are thus:

		£ million
	1969–70	1970–71
Needs element	1,302	1,394
Resources element	237	250
Domestic element	73	100
	1,612	1,744

As explained earlier, the aggregate of the rate support grants for any year is arrived at by subtracting from the aggregate of Exchequer assistance to local authorities the estimated amounts of specific grants in aid of revenue expenditure. The minister estimated that these grants would amount to £141 million in 1969–70 and £154·1 million in 1970–71. The police grant accounts for over a half (£85·5 million in 1970–71) of all specific grants; the amount of the grant is based on one-third of the estimated expenditure of the City of London force and one-half of the expenditure of other police authorities. Of the remaining grants the largest are the housing improvement grants (£13·1 million in 1970–71) and the grants towards rate rebates (£11·5 million in 1970–71), the latter being equivalent to three-quarters of the rebates which are expected to arise. The grant to civil defence (£1·2 million in 1970–71) reflects the Government's decision to put that service on a care and maintenance basis. Other specific grants are made in connection with the administration of justice (magistrates courts, legal aid, approved schools, remand homes, probation and aftercare); the employment of staff owing to substantial numbers of Commonwealth immigrants; open space and derelict land; preserving and improving the countryside; urban redevelopment; clean air; sewerage; port health; small holdings; youth employment and sheltered workshops. Specific grants have also been paid since 1 April 1967 for the construction and improvement of the most important local authority roads which were classified "principal roads" and which were roughly equivalent in mileage to Class I roads; all other expenditure on highways by local authorities is assisted through the RSG.

In July 1968 a Government-initiated programme was introduced to provide financial aid for urban aras of severe social deprivation in housing, education, health, and welfare, owing to bad housing, over-crowding, persistent unemployment, large families and children in trouble or in need of care. The scheme envisaged Government-aided local authority expenditure amounting to £20 million to £25 million in the following four years. The Local Government Grants (Social Need) Act 1969 gave effect to this programme and provided for a new specific grant of 75 per cent of approved revenue expenditure, which included loan charges on capital projects financed by loans.

2. The Rating System

The General Rate Act 1967 repealed and re-enacted in consolidated form most of the statute law relating to rating and valuation in England and Wales. By s.1 of the Act, every rating authority (i.e.

14

the councils of county boroughs, non-county boroughs, London boroughs, urban districts, rural districts, the Common Council of the City of London and the Sub-Treasurer and Under-Treasurer of the Inner and Middle Temples) has the power to make and levy rates on the basis of an assessment in respect of the yearly value of property in their rating area.

With a few exceptions which will be considered later, rates are levied by rating authorities upon all hereditaments, that is, visible estate in the form of land or buildings. The greatest rate burden falls upon domestic hereditaments as the following figures of rateable values of all local authorities in England and Wales on 1 April, 1966 and 1968 show:

Types of Hereditament

	1966		1968	
	£m	%	£m	%
Domestic	1,049·0	47·8	1,113·5	48·0
Commercial	492·9	22·5	520·0	22·5
Industrial	325·1	14·8	334·4	14·5
Other undertakings (gas, water, electricity, etc)	100·0	4·6	103·3	4·5
Entertainment and recreational	21·6	0·9	23·1	1·0
Educational and cultural	72·3	3·3	79·3	3·5
Miscellaneous (Crown occupations, hospitals, municipal offices, etc.)	134·1	6·1	140·0	6·0
Totals	2,194·9*	100·0	2,313·7*	100·0

The domestic ratepayer thus pays the lion's share and he anticipates little hope of relief as the average rate levied increases yearly. Since 1956–57 the amount collected from rates has increased at an annual rate of between 9 per cent and 10 per cent and it would appear that "this process will continue and even accelerate".[4]

In 1966–67 householders were expected to pay out in rates an average of £36 8s. in comparison with £30 12s. in 1963–64 and

---

*"*Report of Commissioners of Inland Revenue*" for 1966 and 1968 (*Cmnd*. 3200 and 3879). *The apparent discrepancy results from the methods of the Inland Revenue Board which uses the sum of category totals of Tables 177–178 and 154 rather than totalling the "Converted" component parts of a category.*

[4] *Local Government Finance England and Wales*, 1966, Cmd. 2923, p. 3.

£18 13s. in 1956–57. The 1966 White Paper on local government finance states in respect of these figures:

"... averages conceal more than they reveal; many householders pay a lot more than the average, and others a lot less, and those who pay most are by no means always those who can best afford to do so."

In 1968–69 the average householder paid £44 13s. 2d.

AVERAGE RATES LEVIED, 1965–66 AND 1966–67[5]
(figures are arithmetic averages)

Year	County Boroughs	London Boroughs		Non-county Boroughs	Urban Districts	Rural Districts
		Inner London	Outer London			
	s. d.	s. d.	s. d.	s. d.	s. d.	s. d.
1965–66	11 2	9 10	10 6	11 6	11 2	9 10
1966–67	12 3	10 8	11 9	12 5	12 3	10 9

Since 1601 when a poor rate was imposed upon parish inhabitants to relieve local poverty, the practice has developed of financing current expenditure on services from rates levied locally. Originally, in 1601, the rate was assessed on the basis of a parishioner's visible estate, "both real and personal", but difficulties encountered in its true assessment led to rates being based upon real property. Later, a tangled variety of different rates emerged to finance different services, but attempts to create a simplified and consolidated system in a general rate were fruitless until the passing of the Rating and Valuation Act of 1925. This act abolished the overseers of the poor and transferred their powers for making and levying rates to rating authorities, i.e. the councils of county boroughs, municipal boroughs, urban and rural districts. County councils are not rating authorities, but issue precepts to those county districts and boroughs over which they have jurisdiction; these, being rating authorities, then levy a general rate which includes not only their own financial requirements but also takes into account that proportion which is required by the percepting authority. Parishes are not rating authorities either and issue precepts on the rural district councils to defray their expenses.

---

[5] *Return of Rates*, I.M.T.A., 1966, p. 6.

Rating authorities continued to value their property for rates until the introduction of Exchequer equalisation grants, by the Local Government Act of 1948, which were designed to help those rating authorities with a low rateable value. The danger that rating authorities would undervalue local property in order to increase their equalisation grant was foreseen, and the act consequently transferred the valuation function to the Board of Inland Revenue where it has since remained.

The Board's valuation officers assess the rateable value of all hereditaments on the basis of their annual gross value, i.e. the amount which a tenant might reasonably be expected to pay in rent to his landlord, with the latter being assumed to include repairs and insurance costs in his estimate of a rent. The valuation officers make certain deductions[6] to arrive at a "net annual value" which is, in effect, the rateable value. Valuation lists are required to be prepared by valuation officers every five years for each rating authority, showing the rateable value of every rateable hereditament within the authority. Objections to a valuation or the inclusion of a hereditament on the valuation list will be heard before the local valuation court, or the case may be referred by agreement to arbitration.

Post-war valuation lists had been based on 1934 letting values, the 1939 revaluation having been postponed by the outbreak of war. By the Valuation for Rating Act 1953, houses were revalued on the basis of 1939 rents, and by the Rating and Valuation Act 1959, the 1961 revaluation was postponed to 1963 when new lists came into force. The 1968 revaluation has been postponed to 1973 by the Local Government Act, 1966, and until then new properties will be rated on 1963 valuations.

Some hereditaments are not required to pay full rates but are "derated" either partially or wholly. By the Local Government Act 1929, total relief from rate payment was granted to all agricultural land and buildings (not, however, farm dwellings) while 75 per cent relief was granted to industrial hereditaments, i.e. mines, mineral railways, factories and workshops, and to freight transport hereditaments i.e. railways, canal transport and docks. Subsequently, the Local Government Act 1958, derated industrial and freight transport hereditaments to the extent of 50 per cent, and by the Rating and Valuation Act 1961, the derating of industrial and freight transport hereditaments was ended completely.

In addition to agriculture, the main exemptions from rate liability are: undeveloped land; sewers and water courses maintained by

---

[6] Deductions are for carrying out repairs in accordance with a formula.

river-boards and drainage authorities; places of religious worship; almshouses and charities will have 50 per cent relief, but rating authorities may reduce or completely remit their rates, and those of non-profit charitable, educational or recreational organisations. Ex-gratia payments are made in lieu of rates by the Crown. By the Local Government Act, 1966, office premises of nationalised boards are rated where they are not situated on operational land and the Minister can change the formulae for distributing the cumulo rateable values of, and payments made in lieu of rates by, the boards.

A. *Fixing the Rate*

The local authority's financial year extends from 1 April to 31 March, and every year, around January, each spending committee of a local authority meets to consider its financial requirements for the next year. Estimates are prepared which are then submitted to the scrutiny of the finance committee who will propose their acceptance or amendment to the council. From the estimates of all the committees the Treasurer is able to calculate the council's expenditure for the year, and after deducting income from grants, trading undertakings, etc., he will be able to determine the required rate in the pound. This is calculated by totalling all the rateable values of hereditaments within the area,[7] to arrive at the authority's rateable value, and by finding what income the authority would receive if a rate of one penny were levied on every pound of the total rateable value. For example, if the total net rate income were £720,000, the product of a penny rate would be 720,000 pennies or £3,000. The rate in the pound is then fixed by dividing the amount of money required by the product of the penny rate, e.g. if the approved estimates (minus other sources of income) total £423,000, the rate in the pound will be 423,000 ÷ 3,000 or 141 pence. Each ratepayer will then pay 11s. 9d. for every pound of the annual rateable value of his property.

A demand note is then issued to the occupier, and in order to encourage early payment, a local authority may allow a small discount, which must not exceed $2\frac{1}{2}$ per cent, for payment before a stipulated date. Should a ratepayer default upon his payment the local authority cannot sue for rates, but a warrant for distress and seizure of his goods may be issued. The local authority may then sell the ratepayer's goods, but if insufficient money is raised in this way, the ratepayer may also be imprisoned. If the rating authority finds

---

[7] After making due allowance for void properties, rate rebates, costs of collection, owners' allowances, empty properties, charitable organisations, write-offs, etc.

that default is caused by poverty the authority may reduce or remit the rate.

B. *Appraisal of the Rating System*

The rating system as a form of taxation has many merits:

1. It is a simple tax which is easily understood by the ratepayer. As a national assessment all authorities are treated according to the same standards and it generally works well. Decisions are subject to appeal, so no householder should pay more than the net annual value of the property.

2. It is the only major independent source of a local authority's income, although the local authority's freedom to use this money is greatly limited by the high cost of the services which it is statutorily required to provide. Nevertheless, the rate poundage is a locally-determined matter which, so long as it is lawful, cannot be changed by central government and allows the local authority some discretion in its spending.

3. It is a stable source of income for a local authority. As rates are assessed on visible property which is immovable the ratepayer cannot avoid paying and the local authority knows precisely how much it will collect.

4. It is reasonably convenient to pay, particularly since payment by instalments has been introduced. The collection costs are low, amounting to about 1·2 per cent of rate revenue, in comparison with 1·37 per cent on the gross Inland Revenue receipt.[8]

5. Whereas income tax is minimal for a married couple with four children and a reasonable wage, rates do require such families to contribute to the cost of local services.

6. As rates are based upon property, they encourage people to occupy only accommodation which is needed. Thus, in areas where housing is scarce and accommodation is limited, it may be essential that individuals do not occupy properties which could be better utilised by larger families.

7. There is no intrusion into the home, nor any requirement to disclose domestic income unless applying for rate rebates.

The rating system's various disadvantages have been the subject not only of much popular criticism, but also of parliamentary enquiries dating from 1836 to 1965. The disadvantages are:

i. Rates are a regressive tax because assessments are not based upon a person's ability to pay.[9] Thus the lower a ratepayer's income

---

[8] County Councils Association, Local Government Finance Committee: "Report of a Working Party on the Rating System and Local Revenues", 1963, p. 3.

[9] Although Rate rebates make it less regressive.

the higher the proportion of his income paid out in rates. This was confirmed by the Allen Committee's findings:

	Household Income Group					
	Under £312	£312– £519	£520– £779	£780– £1,039	£1040– £1559	£1560 and over
Rates as a percentage of house-hold income	8·1	6·0	3·8	2·9	2·4	1·8
Rates as a percentage of dispos-able income	8·2	6·2	4·1	3·2	2·7	2·2

Rates fall particularly heavily on domestic ratepayers[10] who cannot claim any tax-relief, whereas those who pay rates for shops, commercial or industrial properties are able to class their payment as an expense to be charged against income in computing profits chargeable to income tax or corporation tax. This could have the effect of relieving them of about half their rate burden. It has been argued that similar relief could be given to householders by a tax allowance equivalent to the standard rate of income tax on the rate payment through their P.A.Y.E. coding.

ii. Since rate increases have not kept pace with income increases local authorities between quinquennial revaluations have had to put up rate poundages. Comparisons of anomalies both within and between local authorities attract much criticism and bring the entire system into disrepute.

iii. They are unjust in that they bear no relation to a man's use of a local authority's services. Many local income earners pay no rates directly although they make extensive use of local services. Moreover, many industrial and commercial enterprises are ratepayers but receive no local vote—taxation without representation.

iv. It has been said that occupiers have been deterred from improving their property because this would automatically increase the rateable value of the property.

v. Taking rental value as the basis for rateable value is unsatisfactory. The method for determining rental value is unscientific,

---

[10] Although eased somewhat by rate rebates and the domestic element provision of the Local Government Act, 1966.

arbitrary, and based upon spurious subjective criteria. Moreover, free market conditions do not obtain at present, nor is it likely that the supply of accommodation will match demand and allow free choice for many years to come. Capital values would probably be a better basis for assessment.

vi. They are inflexible and do not grow to meet increases in the costs of local authority services. There was no revaluation between 1934 and 1956, the 1961 revaluation did not come into effect until 1963 and the 1968 revaluation has been postponed to 1973.

vii. There is a great disparity in the resources of different local authorities owing to size, density and composition of the population. Even with the former rate deficiency grants the basis of their calculation

"is inadequate to measure need, and . . . no account is taken of the differing resources of those local authorities which do not qualify for it".[11]

viii. Agricultural land should not be treated exceptionally and should be re-rated. The poorer rural districts would thus receive a financial boost which would minimise their heavy dependence upon the resources element, and a hidden agricultural subsidy could be replaced by an increased direct subsidy.

C. *The Impact of Rates on Householders*

The rate burden upon the householder shows no sign of diminishing or even of stabilising while standards of services are improving and their scope widens. The average annual increase in total rates levied by all local authorities for the five years up to 1962–63 was 11 per cent and the 1963 revaluation was followed by widespread concern. Although rates are increasing at a slower rate than incomes, other taxes or local expenditure, and represent a smaller proportion of the gross national product than before the war (4·4 per cent in 1938 to 3·8 per cent in 1961) and a smaller proportion of personal expenditure on housing costs (11·8 per cent in 1938 to 9·1 per cent in 1961), many people faced real hardship by having to pay large rate increases after revaluation. Therefore, in May, 1963, the Government appointed a committee of enquiry under the chairmanship of Professor R. G. D. Allen:

"To assess the impact of rates on householders in different income groups and in different parts of Great Britain, with special regard to any circumstances likely to give rise to hardship."

Before the committee's report was produced, however, the Government had passed the Rating (Interim Relief) Act 1964[12] which

---

[11] *New Sources of Local Revenue*, R.I.P.A., 1956, p. 36.
[12] Lapsed in 1968.

gave local authorities the power to grant some remission of rates to domestic ratepayers if the 1964–65 rates exceeded those for 1962–63 by a quarter or £5, whichever was the greater, and if local authorities felt that the increase caused hardship. The amount to be remitted was not to be greater than the excess of one quarter or £5 over the 1962–63 rates. The act was primarily designed to help retired people and those living on small incomes above the national assistance level. Those people drawing national assistance were already protected against rate increases by special allowances. The cost of relief given would be met by an Exchequer grant for one half of the remission given, plus one-sixth of any remission in excess of 3 per cent of a local authority's gross rate income for the year. In addition, local authorities received a special Exchequer grant of £5 for each person over 65 in excess of one-tenth[13] of the population in their areas. This second factor would help places such as seaside resorts, where the proportion of retired people was high, and where there was unlikely to be any industry to benefit the area after its re-rating.

The Allen Committee's 400 page report (Cmd. 2582) appeared in February, 1965 and showed that revaluation had meant an average rate increase of £2 with one-tenth paying an extra £9 or more. The largest increases affected London's householders and those living in modern houses, flats and bungalows. Whilst revaluation introduced consistency, some householders gained and some lost. It has already been noted that an average of 8 per cent of the lowest incomes (£312 or less per annum) was allocated to rates in comparison with less than 2 per cent of high incomes (£1,560 +) but poor householders contributed a relatively small proportion of total rates. The average domestic ratepayer in England and Wales paid nearly £31 in rates in 1963–64; with owner-occupiers paying on average £37, council house tenants £28, and private tenants £21. Generally, the higher the income, the higher the rate payments, but as income increased the rate payments grew slowly and an extra £1,000 of income added only about £10 to rates. On the other hand, rates increased considerably with income in one- and two-person retired households and there were about 500,000 retired householders who should have received National Assistance but did not. Over 40 per cent of retired householders spent more than a quarter of their income on housing while 5 per cent of the retired spent over half their income on housing costs. There was resentment and hardship caused by having to pay rates once or twice a year, and the committee thought that instalment schemes should be extended.

---

[13] Changed to one-fifth by the Local Government Act, 1966.

The report caused much discussion and the whole system of local government finance became the centre of emotional criticism and informed comment. In August, 1965, the rating committee of the Association of Municipal Corporations rallied to the defence of the system but also made recommendations for its improvement. They stated that many of its present defects are the result of

> "erosion caused by past governments granting social or economic relief by means of sectional derating and postponement of revaluations" (*The Times*, 12 August, 1965).

Organisations excused from paying rates should be rerated. This would include Crown property; 30 million acres of agricultural land and buildings; nurseries on potential building-land in urban areas with buildings used for the "factory production" of eggs, livestock, vegetables, and flowers. Pig and calf breeders, many societies and charities "whose financial circumstances are such that relief is not justified", and nationalised boards should make a proper contribution to the cost of local services. With reference to domestic rates, the assessment of rented values was based on insufficient evidence and the A.M.C. committee recommended the alternative basis of capital values. Yet even if all the proposals in the report were carried out, the committee stated, the reforms could amount to an additional rate increase of only 9 per cent which would be barely enough to meet increased expenditure for one year. Major relief to the ratepayer could not, therefore, come from modifications to the rating system.

It appeared by the end of 1965 as if the Minister of Housing and Local Government might grasp the nettle of local government financial reform. In November, the Rating Bill was published and during its second reading on 6 December, the Minister committed himself to a radical overhaul of local finances "including the abolition of rates"; without this he could see "no future for local democracy" (*Guardian*, 7 December).

D. The Rating Act 1966

The Act had two main objects: to enable certain domestic ratepayers with low incomes to obtain rate rebates, and to provide for rates to be payable by monthly instalments. An estimated two million domestic ratepayers in England and Wales and Scotland would be eligible for rebates, while ratepayers already in receipt of National Assistance were excluded, except where a wage stop was in operation. Every applicant would have to meet in full the first £7 10s. of his rates for the year. After that, rebate would be payable at the rate of two-thirds of the remainder of the rate bill for married ratepayers whose joint income did not exceed £520 a year (£10 a week), and single people earning £416 a year (£8 a week). These amounts would be increased by £78 (30s. a week) for each child. If the rate-payer's income exceeded the figure laid down, the amount of full rebate is cut by 5s. for every pound above the limit. The payment by instalment provision was restricted to ratepayers in private dwellings, and local councils would be obliged to allow not fewer than ten payments in respect of a full year's rates. It was estimated that rebates in the first year would total about £29 million, including an exchequer grant of about £22 million, all of which would be payable in the financial year 1966–67. The cost to local authorities—£7 million—would be paid for by other ratepayers in each district.

The Rate Rebates (Limits of Income) Order 1968, coming into operation on 1 August, 1968, raised the income limits affecting rate rebate entitlement from £8 to £9 per week for single householders, from £10 to £11 for married couples, and from £1 10s. to £2 for each child. As a substantial number of people eligible for the rebate had not claimed it, rating authorities were urged in circular 39/68 to arrange effective publicity to complement that provided by central government.

The 1966 Act entailed a means test, a greater burden on the majority of ratepayers and further central control over the local authorities' financial affairs. The act must be regarded as a temporary expedient, "a patching-up operation", as Mr. Crossman later called it, pending a root and branch reform of local government finance. Moreover, the decision to postpone the 1968 quinquennial revaluation may be viewed as part of the same process, in that revaluation would be unable to remove the system's "intrinsic iniquities" and only a new fiscal method could eradicate the defects. It is difficult, however, to see what alternative sources may be utilised which will bring in as much revenue as do rates and which would not increase local government's dependence upon central finance.

3. Alternative Local Sources of Revenue

A number of alternative sources of income have been proposed but none, considered singly, would ever match the income obtained from rates. As supplementary sources some might be worthy of consideration by local authorities but others bristle with difficulties.

A. *Increased charges for services*

It has been stated that:

> "Little more than one-fifth of the cost of local government services is recovered by charging users of the services" (p. 3 C.C.A. op. cit.)

Such services include trading undertakings, private street works, smallholdings and, the largest single item, council house rents. The expense of the social and protective services are, on the other hand, mainly met from rates and grants, and if rates are to be diminished charges must be made within this sector. What has been suggested, therefore, is that where a service is required by all inhabitants, e.g. fire brigade, police, preventive health, no charges should be made, but where services are not equally used charges should be levied on the users. Thus, childless couples or older people whose children are in employment should not be charged for education services; also suggested are flat rate charges, with relief for lower income groups, of 10s. per week per child in primary and secondary schools (producing £140 million), £1 per week for sixth-form students (£5 million) and loans instead of grants for university students (saving £20 million). It has been further suggested that charges might be increased for libraries, local health services and for the fire service where there is usually insurance cover. One can anticipate the outcry if such charges were introduced and the C.C.A., commenting on charges for education, stated that

> "it would be totally unrealistic to expect such a fundamental reversal of political thought in the foreseeable future".

B. *Assigned Revenues*

The suggestion that local authorities should retain part of the taxes it collects, that is the motor vehicle and driving licences taxes, is attractive and the Minister in a debate on 5 May, 1965, stated that he had considered such a scheme but that it could only be a partial solution. According to A. H. Marshall, motor vehicle licences and driving licences could give local authorities £133 million and £4 million respectively,[14] and the Royal Institute of Public Administration Study Group recommended the transfer of these fees to local authorities.[15] A further R.I.P.A. enquiry, published in 1968, estimated that the amounts would be £230 million and £5 million respectively, and suggested also a motor fuel tax which would bring in an additional £830 million.

---

[14] A. H. Marshall, "Rates: Are they Overworked?" in *New Society*, 30 May 1963.
[15] *New Sources of Local Revenue*, R.I.P.A., 1956, and S. H. H. Hildersley and R. Nottage *Sources of Local Revenue*, R.I.P.A., 1968.

C. *Adjust rating law relating to derated hereditaments*

If agricultural land and buildings were re-rated the yield would amount to approximately £100 million.[16] The Redcliffe–Maud Report regarded this as an "important reform", the present exemption being "even more anomalous when authorities uniting town and country are set up". The Local Government Act 1966 made property owners liable for half rates on property unoccupied for three months (six months for newly erected dwellings), but fewer than 50 of the 1,460 rating authorities in England and Wales had used this permissive power by March 1967. It appeared that collection costs would not make it worthwhile.

D. *Site value rating*

The possibility of raising revenue by this form of taxation has been examined since the nineteenth century and was thoroughly studied by the Simes Committee in the 1950's. The Committee failed to agree because of the technical difficulties of valuation but concluded that between £100 million and £300 million might be added to the country's total rateable value. Site value rating has been adopted in the U.S.A., New Zealand, Australia and South Africa and very successfully in Denmark as a land value tax. In Britain its main advocate has been the Liberal Party and in one of its publications[17] the author substantiates his case by reference to a survey undertaken by the Rating and Valuation Association in Whitstable. The survey showed that it is quicker and cheaper to make rate assessments on site values and that the yield is higher than has generally been predicted. It was alleged that it would reduce substantially the liability of domestic ratepayers, but some doubt has been expressed about this.

E. *Local Income Tax*

This would be levied in addition to the national tax and has been adopted in Scandinavia and parts of the U.S.A., and advocated by many bodies in Britain. The Royal Institute of Public Administration examined the scheme and confined its assessment to the personal incomes of the inhabitants of county councils and county boroughs. On the basis of a maximum rate of 3*d.* in the £ the estimated yield in 1956 would have been about £150 million and, in 1964, £240 million. There might, however, be great difficulties in the administration of the tax. Would it be levied at the place of work or in the area of

---

[16] *New Society, ibid.*
[17] R. Lamb, *Make Rates Fair*, Liberal Publications Dept. 1965.

residence? Would it include income from dividends, rents and distributed profits? What assessment machinery would be required to prevent tax evasion? What procedure would be required to assess tax and its distribution to a number of authorities when a professional man earns his income in a number of places (e.g. architects or doctors)? How would undistributed profits be taxed? The R.I.P.A. Study Group recommended the tax on personal incomes with "an equivalent charge on companies".

The Redcliffe–Maud Report, in pointing out how the financial position of English local authorities compared unfavourably with their counterparts abroad, referred (para. 529) to Swedish local authorities which "are relatively rich because of the highly productive local income tax", and added "not surprisingly they enjoy a large measure of freedom". The Report also referred to the R.I.P.A. enquiry of 1968 which found that a local income tax "has now become even more feasible because of the introduction of corporation tax, and will become still more so when the transfer of the Inland Revenue records to the computer has been completed".

F. Local Sales Tax

This system is in operation in the U.S.A. and Canada but in Britain there may be great difficulties in its application. Would each local authority fix its own schedule of commodities to be taxed and the level of the tax? Would it not have the effect of benefiting the urban areas, where there were more shops, than the rural areas? The retailer, as unpaid tax collector, might not be particularly scrupulous, and the cost of administration and financial control might make the scheme uneconomic.

G. Local Entertainments Tax

Since 1916 central government has imposed an entertainments duty and its yield to the Exchequer in 1954–55 was £41 million. The Royal Institute for Public Administration, having conducted a survey of twelve countries, concluded that local authorities should be given the powers to levy such a tax, subject to certain statutory qualifications regarding the maximum rate of duty and the relationship between the scales of duty for different entertainments.

H. Municipal Trading Enterprises

Most local authorities, with the exception of county councils, have obtained the right under general or private acts to run trading services. These usually include water-supply, passenger transport services, cemeteries and crematoria, harbours, docks, piers, putting-greens, markets and car-parks. Before nationalisation, gas and electricity undertakings were also run by many local authorities. Local authorities could exercise their initiative and establish profitable trading services and some of the more unusual which are currently being operated include: a municipal bank (Birmingham), a bonded warehouse (York), an oyster fishery (Colchester), plant for the recovery of wool grease from fleeces and its conversion into industrial soaps (Bradford), piggeries (Gateshead), an aerodrome (Bristol), the manufacture and sale of ice (Burnley), hiring out plants for floral decoration (Stockport), a cinema (Oundle), and a race-course and hop-market (Worcester). Such enterprises have separate accounts from those of the rate fund services, but under the Local Government Act, 1933, profits may be transferred to aid rates. Profits may accrue to individual enterprises, but national figures would indicate a net deficit, e.g. in 1953–54 profits of £1·6 million were transferred to rate funds from trading enterprises run by local authorities in England and Wales, but £7·5 million were transferred in the same year from rates to meet trading deficits.[18] For this reason trading enterprises are severely criticised by the ratepayers where they do not show profits, while within the council there may be political groups who will find difficulty in reconciling the profit motive and community interest. Moreover, in the community, the likelihood of competition from a cut-price local authority will not be welcomed by local commercial groups.

Some such schemes as these might be attempted with beneficial results by local authorities. Perhaps the most effective methods, however, would be either to increase the grants-in-aid, despite the extra limitations which might be imposed, or to transfer all the major cost services to central government. In the first case, local authorities would undoubtedly object violently to any suggestion that central government control should be further extended in financial matters, and the second solution would equally be rebuffed by the larger authorities who have seen many of their major functions and powers whittled away since the Second World War. Yet it appears remarkable to many that local authorities should cling to such high costs as the payment of teachers' salaries and university grants, when they have little control over the amounts to be paid and when they form such a substantial proportion of the revenue expenditure.

---

[18] *New Sources of Local Revenue*, R.I.P.A., 1956, p. 76.

Although it has been said that "to transfer services . . . for financial reasons" would be "a sorry confession of failure" [19] the problem of finding one alternative source to replace rates entirely appears to be insoluble for the moment, and local authorities may have to persevere with the rating system, warts and all, and experiment with additional supplementary sources. The alternative of abandoning the attempt to maintain a burdensome financial partnership with central government in the high cost services and the concentration of local resources upon the lower cost services is unlikely, and would seriously diminish the status and the remaining powers of local authorities.

The Government White Paper, *Local Government Finance England and Wales* (Cmd. 2923) issued in February, 1966, commented on the fact that "rates as at present constituted are ill-adapted to carry the strain now placed on them", and further stated that the Government was "driven to the conclusion that within the present structure of local government there is no prospect of any major reform of local government finance". The Government consequently looked to the Royal Commission's review, "and the new structure which emerges from their deliberations should provide a more promising context for drastic reform of local government finance". For this reason it was felt impracticable to change fundamentally the grants system but that the severity of rates could be moderated in the short term until the Royal Commission reported. This was subsequently attempted by the rebate and instalment provisions of the Rating Act 1966 and by the new rate support grant introduced by the Local Government Act 1966.

Unfortunately, finance was not specifically included in the Royal Commission's terms of reference, an omission which led *The Accountant* (21 June, 1969) to comment that "a discussion of local government reorganisation without a detailed consideration of its financial basis is rather like staging *Hamlet* without the Prince of Denmark". Nevertheless, a brief chapter of nine pages was devoted to local government finance and indicated that the proposed restructuring would require the "financial map of local government" to be "drastically altered". An adequate local taxation system was seen to be essential and the Commission urged "that the opportunity offered by reorganisation be taken to examine fundamentally the short-comings of the present local taxation system and remove them". It commented how grants were expected to reach 57 per cent of expenditure by 1970–71, with some authorities already receiving

---

[19] A. H. Marshall, *op. cit.*, p. 14.

70 per cent or more of their revenue from grants. The Commission had few suggestions, however, which could provide local authorities with the desired "reasonable measure of financial independence".

Thus although aware of the need for a new source of income and the need for a "wider tax base, and in particular for a more buoyant and elastic tax which grows with the advance of incomes" (a local income tax?), the Commission believed that the old standby, "the rate, modernised from time to time, will remain the chief local tax". There was no further appraisal of the rating system beyond pointing out that it "is reasonably productive, well established, simple to operate and is, in fact, the principal local government tax in many countries". Reference was made to its drawbacks, but they were not analysed, although "various modifications" which were suggested in evidence were felt to merit "serious consideration". One of these was that capital values might be substituted for rental values, with valuations in bands rather than in precise figures, and the other was the re-rating of agricultural land and buildings.

It was anticipated that the fifty-eight unitary authorities proposed by the Royal Commission would be large enough for efficient management and would have more resources of their own. Financial responsibility would rest squarely on the unitary authorities and would not be shared with provincial or local councils. In the three metropolitan areas, the metropolitan district councils would be the rating authorities and would be responsible for the bulk of expenditure in metropolitan areas. Disparities in resources would be reduced by equalisation schemes which would be worked out and agreed between district councils and metropolitan authorities, but there was no indication if such equalisation schemes would operate on the same basis as that formulated by Professor Ilersic for Greater London.

4. Miscellaneous Sources

Table 7 showed that nearly 29 per cent of local authority revenue is received from miscellaneous sources. These sources are so diverse that they are virtually impossible to classify, but they would include:

(a) charges for personal services such as the maintenance of old people in homes, where the charge is based on income, or the provision of police at public functions or entertainments;

(b) charges for work done, e.g. making up private streets, cleaning drains on private property; and

(c) charges for facilities provided including council house rents, putting or bowls fees in parks, etc.

15

5. Borrowing

In discharging statutory duties and powers, the capital costs of tangible and permanent assets in the form of buildings, roads, bridges and land are not met from grants, rates or other local sources but by raising loans which are repaid over a number of years. Under the provisions of Section 195 of the Local Government Act 1933, loans may be raised by any local authority providing the consent of the sanctioning authority has been given. For sums not exceeding the product of a 2d. rate or £5,000, whichever is the greater, loan

TABLE 8. COMPOSITION OF LOCAL AUTHORITY DEBT IN
ENGLAND AND WALES, 1955–68

Type of Debt	Percentage of Total Loan Debt at 31 March				
	1955	1958	1960	1965	1968
Stock	10·5	9·0	9·3	11·4	12·1
P.W.L.B. Mortgages	65·5	57·3	49·2	33·3	32·6
Mortgages (other than P.W.L.B.)	14·2	18·0	21·9	28·4	23·2
Bonds	0·4	0·6	0·8	0·6	6·1
Other Loans	0·1	0·1	0·2	—	1·6
Internal Funds	6·1	6·2	6·2	4·7	8·5
Temporary Money	3·2	8·8	12·4	21·6	15·9

consent has not been required since 1 April, 1969. Control is thus exercised over capital schemes by the sanctioning authority which will be the Ministry of Transport for public service vehicles and the Ministry of Housing and Local Government for most other purposes. The ministerial sanction, whether it is for a specific scheme or is a "block sanction" covering a programme of capital expenditure, will specify the maximum amount to be borrowed and the period of repayment of the loan. This period will be based on the functional life of the asset and must not in any event exceed sixty years, except in the case of land for housing and other purposes when a maximum of eighty years is specified. Local authorities may decide to repay the loan over a shorter period or they may, even though the loan sanction may have been given, resort to meeting their capital expenditure, or a proportion of it, out of revenue income or internal funds. These latter include sinking funds, reserve funds, insurance funds, trust and charity funds, superannuation funds and special funds. By the Local Authority Loans Act 1945, local authorities are authorised to use any surplus moneys in "any fund established for the repayment of debt, or as a reserve, or for the maintenance, renewal or repair of property, or for the superannuation of staff, or for insurance, or otherwise for meeting future expenditure of a capital or non-recurring nature or for any like purpose". [20]

The sources available to a local authority for external borrowing are briefly described below and the extent of their borrowing is shown on the accompanying Table 8.

A. *The Public Works Loan Board*

This is an independent statutory body of twelve unpaid Commissioners appointed by the Crown for four years, with three Commissioners retiring each year. Their functions, derived mainly from the Public Works Loans Act 1875 and the Local Authorities Loans Act 1945,

> "are to consider loan applications from local authorities and other prescribed bodies, and where loans are made, to collect the repayments".

The Board is financed by government loans and the rates of interest are fixed by the Treasury. The amounts borrowed by local authorities have varied considerably within the last twenty years from 64 per cent of the total loans raised by local authorities in 1946–47, building up to 85 per cent in 1951–52 and thereafter declining.

The variations have reflected different phases in the Board's lending policy. Up to 1945 local authorities with a rateable value of more than £200,000 were deterred from borrowing, and its loans were available only to the smaller local authorities. The 1945 Act restricted local authorities from borrowing from any other sources and this policy prevailed until 1952 when they were permitted to borrow from the open market or from the Board. After 1956 there was restriction of access to the Board and only £39·9 million was advanced by the Board in 1959–60. The Radcliffe Committee of 1957–59 recommended that full access to the Board should be restored but this was rejected by the Government.

By 1963 local authorities were able to get 20 per cent of their long-term borrowing from the Board, and the White Paper of that year, *Local Authority Borrowing* (Cmd. 2164) commented that the Board would

---

[20] The general power to maintain capital funds and repairs and renewals funds was not available until the Local Government (Miscellaneous Provisions) Act, 1953.

"continue to act as a lender of last resort" and would "make additional loans if it is satisfied that an authority cannot raise the money on the market". To help smaller authorities, each would be allowed to borrow £50,000 a year from the Board and later possibly £100,000. The 7 years' maximum period for loans would be extended to 10 years, with 40 years for maturity loans and 80 years for annuity loans.

The Public Works Loan Board Act 1964 put the new arrangements into operation, placing up to £750 million at the Board's disposal, and the 20 per cent limitation on long-term borrowing was raised to 30 per cent. In his April, 1965 Budget speech, the Chancellor stated that authorities in selected areas would be allowed up to 50 per cent and a further £40 million would be allowed for the purpose. By July, 1965 he commented that drawings on the Public Works Loan Board during the financial year had been "exceptionally heavy" and in the existing economic circumstances a "more regular phasing of issues" was necessary. P.W.L.B. Circular No. 11, dated 12 April, 1967, stated that the percentage limitation could be based upon the net capital expenditure instead of on long term borrowing. Currently these are 43 per cent for development areas and 33 per cent for other areas. During 1968–69 the P.W.L.B. approved applications for advances totalling nearly £602 million.

B. Stock

Under the Local Government Act, 1933, all local authorities, with the exception of parishes, have the general power to issue stock. The consent of the Minister of Housing and Local Government is required unless powers have been granted by local acts, as is the case with some larger authorities, but all will also require Treasury consent. The merits of stock issue are its attraction to lenders because of its ready negotiability and the large amount which can be raised[21] but it is an expensive method of borrowing if high interest rates have to be paid. This would to some extent account for the small number of issues, totalling sixty-one from 1955–61, with only five issues in 1961, up to November, involving £41 million.[22]

C. Mortgages

Both before 1939 and after 1955 mortgage loans have provided local authorities with a major and regular source of capital. They will be repayable either by instalments or in lump sum at the end of a specified period and the sources, now that inter-authority lending on

---

[21] Minimum of £3 million, thus effectively excluding most smaller local authorities.

[22] *Local Authority Borrowing*, I.M.T.A., 1962, p. 93.

mortgage has declined, are mainly the mortgage market and individual investors. The latter are generally the smaller, but for the investor with a little capital they are attractive, safe and had, in 1966, a yield of 7 per cent for investments of £500 and 7⅜ per cent for £2,000 plus.

D. Bonds

These are trustee securities, requiring local act powers for their issue and, like mortgages, are secured on the issuing authorities' revenues.[23] They are attractive to small investors being issued in multiples of £5, may be issued below par and on housing bonds have a yield which is paid gross up to £100. Housing bonds have a high popularity, they must be issued at par and the proceeds have to be allocated to housing purposes.

E. Temporary Borrowing

Local authorities are empowered to raise temporary loans or bank overdrafts and if such loans can be raised for periods of less than one year the low rate of interest, "the call rate", makes it a cheap source of capital. The Radcliffe Committee was concerned about the increase in large-scale temporary borrowing after the Government's curtailment of access to the Treasury through the P.W.L.B. in 1955, but the proportion of local authority debt met from this source has increased. By the end of the first quarter of 1969 the outstanding temporary debt reached £2,023 million, compared with only £933 million eight years earlier.

F. Loans Bureaux

Local authorities with temporary surpluses of funds may indicate, through the agency of a loans bureau set up by a regional branch of I.M.T.A., that they have temporary funds to lend. The borrowing authority is put in touch with the lending authority by the liaison officer of the Loans Bureau and the terms of the loan are negotiated between the lender and borrower. By 31 March 1967, there were six Loans Bureaux in existence with a membership of 1,043 local authorities, and loans negotiated in 1966–67 amounted to £238,232,000.

G. Borrowing Abroad

A precedent was established by Derbyshire County Council in July 1969 when it arranged to borrow 50 million marks (the equivalent of over £5 million) for six years at 8¼ per cent from a Frankfurt

---

[23] General Act power granted by Local Government (Financial Provisions) Act, 1963.

bank. The rate was cheaper than the rate at which comparable accommodation could be obtained in the British capital market, even allowing for the ⅝ per cent charge which the council had to pay the Treasury to guarantee against the effect of a change in the mark-sterling rate of exchange. Even with this addition the cost was still ¼ per cent below the rate which would have to be paid for a comparable loan from the P.W.L.B. By December 1969 over fifty local authorities had presented Private Bills containing powers to borrow money abroad.

At 31 March, 1968, the gross loan debt of local authorities amounted to £9,795 million, with 32·6 per cent of the loan debt in direct loans from the Government through the P.W.L.B. It has already been noted that central government controls the capital expenditure of local authorities by the necessity to obtain loan sanctions, and in this manner local development can be integrated with the social and economic strategy of central government. Once loan sanctions have been obtained, however, the method of obtaining capital rests with the local authority. In 1955 the restriction of access to the Treasury through the P.W.L.B. stimulated local authorities to seek their capital requirements from the market, but in 1964 the government envisaged local authorities borrowing 50 per cent of their capital needs from the P.W.L.B. by 1968, and set a limit on temporary borrowing from the market. This ceiling was to come into force on 31 March, 1969, and although an I.M.T.A. survey found that £300 million of temporary borrowing required to be funded if local authorities were to comply with the Treasury's ceiling, the target was nevertheless achieved. It has been suggested that this broad pattern of 40 per cent from the Board, 20 per cent short-term borrowing and 40 per cent long-term borrowing may remain the basis of local authority borrowing for the next few years.[24]

A further dimension has been suggested by the Royal Commission's report which stated that the rigid mechanism of the loan sanction sometimes led to authorities suffering from the lack of co-ordination between central government departments. The Commission suggested an alternative system of investment control by which each main authority should be given a comprehensive rolling programme for all its capital expenditure, stretching five years ahead. Each authority should have an unallocated margin within the total of its investment programme for use at its own discretion, to provide a new public park or to spend extra on a major service. Capital expenditure by local councils should be authorised by the main authorities, with the

---

[24] *The Times*, 30 September, 1968.

unitary authority's total investment programme containing an amount for capital expenditure by its local councils. The same should apply for district councils in a metropolitan area, where there should also be arrangements for the metropolitan authority and district councils to prepare in co-operation an agreed programme of major capital projects. The authority should have the right to comment to the provincial council and to central government on the investment plans of district councils. Lastly, the procedure applying to the borrowing of money should be simplified:

> "Central government will continue to have a major interest in the manner and timing of local authority borrowing for investment purposes. At present this is subject to detailed statutory rules. The drastic reduction in the number of borrowers, and the distinction now to be made between investment control and access to the money market, combine to offer a new opportunity to simplify procedure. We assume it will be taken".

CHAPTER 9

Central Control over Local Authorities

The power exercised by central government departments over the affairs of local authorities is extensive. It is deemed necessary to ensure a high national standard of service which otherwise might vary greatly from one authority to another. Any restraint must to some extent limit local autonomy, but the degree of control and its many forms perturb those who feel that local democratic participation in decisions which determine the conduct of local services is being, and in some cases has been, superseded by the remote dictates of a White-hall juggernaut. Whether the choice is as simple as that between local but democratic inefficiency and centralised competence, as is sometimes suggested, is highly debatable, but we have already seen how local authorities have lost functions to a number of governmental and *ad hoc* bodies and it now remains to see how the services which local authorities retain are subject to central government controls.

1. Legislative Control

Local authorities are administrative and not legislative bodies and require statutory powers to carry out functions which they are required to perform by Parliament. The supremacy of Parliament as the law-making body in the Kingdom implies that it may confer upon or deny to a local authority any powers or services. Moreover, since county councils, district councils and parish councils are directly incorporated by Acts of Parliament they are themselves statutory corporations and are subject to the doctrine of *ultra vires*; boroughs, on the other hand, if incorporated by royal charter before 1835 are common law corporations and are not in theory limited by the *ultra vires* rule, but in practice are so limited in some activities by statutory regulation. No other local authority, however, may engage in activities which are not specifically permitted by the appropriate statutory powers, and these are conferred in the following ways:

A. Public General Acts

These establish or regulate certain services for all inhabitants in local authorities throughout the country. Such acts may be (i) obligatory—local authorities are compelled to administer the particular service, or (ii) permissive—powers are conferred but the local authorities need not exercise them.

B. Adoptive Acts

These permit local authorities to exercise certain powers if the local authorities themselves formally adopt the Acts. They were first introduced in the early nineteenth century for the provision of lighting, baths, washhouses and public libraries, by enterprising local authorities who wished to take advantage of the enabling provisions before such services were applied nationally. The Public Health legislation of 1890, 1907 and 1925 was adoptive. The Local Government and Public Health Consolidation Committee reported in 1936 that the method had been "overdone" with some "cases of patent absurdity".

C. Local Acts

Individual local authorities seek powers which are not contained in general legislation by promoting private bills in Parliament. Extensively used during the industrial revolution to create such *ad hoc* bodies as turnpike trusts, gas undertakings and improvement commissioners the procedure is now utilized to obtain powers to operate trading services, to obtain special borrowing powers or to provide additional welfare facilities, etc. The power to promote or oppose such bills is granted to all local authorities, excepting parishes, by Part XIII of the Local Government Act 1933. It is a flexible device but the preliminary formalities before it is deposited in Parliament are complicated. The resolution to promote a private bill must be passed by a majority of the council members at a meeting. This meeting cannot be held until ten clear days' notice in the local press has been given of the meeting and of its purpose. In addition to publication of the resolution it must be submitted to the Minister of Housing and Local Government for approval and the local authority may not proceed with the Bill's promotion if the Minister disapproves of the resolution. The Minister shall not give approval of a resolution until seven days after its publication and in the meantime any of the electors of that area may give written notice of their objections to the Minister. In the case of the bill's promotion a meeting of the local authority must be held after fourteen days from the time when the bill is deposited in Parliament. The action of depositing the bill must first be confirmed by a majority of the council at a further meeting called after ten days' notice has been given.

This completes the formalities in county and rural districts but if the bill is being presented by a borough or urban district council a public meeting of local electors must be held and the resolution is put for their approval. The bill may be analysed in detail at this meeting and the decision of the meeting is final unless a poll of electors is demanded by 100 electors, or one-twentieth of the electors, whichever is the less. A poll may also be demanded by the council if the meeting is against the bill's promotion and the result of the poll shall be decisive; should the poll result in a tie this will be deemed to be against the resolution.

The private bill procedure is expensive and the cost is met out of local authorities' general rate fund. The need for a cheaper and less complex alternative led in 1848 to the introduction and subsequent development of Provisional Orders.

D. *Provisional Orders*

These are made by the Minister. The Minister will investigate the local authority's application for an order and may either reject it or, more usually, will give interested parties an opportunity to object before a Ministry inspector at a local inquiry. The inspector will make a confidential report on the basis of the evidence he has heard, and will submit it to the Minister for his decision. If he decides in favour of the application he will make the necessary order which must then await confirmation by Parliament before it comes into force. Should the provisional order be opposed by Parliament it will be referred to a Select Committee and dealt with as if it were a separate private bill.

This procedure is less costly and far simpler than that for promoting a private bill, and its passage through Parliament in the Provisional Orders Confirmation Bill ensures government support. The passing of the Statutory Orders (Special Procedure) Act 1945, has greatly reduced the need for provisional orders and substituted a simpler procedure, whereby uncontested orders come into effect automatically after the order has been laid before Parliament for a prescribed period.

2. Administrative Control

Central administrative control over local government was conspicuously absent until the nineteenth century and is not observed until the Benthamite concern for centralised control was put into effect with the appointment of Poor Law Commissioners to manage the system established by the 1834 Act. Yet the centralist idea was not adopted when the municipalities were reformed in the following year, and when public health legislation was introduced in 1848, an attempt was made to emulate the central supervision and control of the then unpopular Poor Law Commissioners. The matter became an issue of principle and the General Board of Health was opposed both within and without Parliament. The result was that subsequent control grew unsystematically, varying in extent according to the particular service and generally on the basis of the authorities' dependence on grant aid. As grants have become an increasing proportion of a local authority's revenue the control has become more sure, and ministerial discretion to reduce grant aid for inadequate standards has developed since 1929 to give the central government great powers.

The forms of administrative control exercised by government departments over local authorities may be summarised as follows:

A. *General Supervision*

Legislation since the 1940s has emphasised the national importance of services administered locally and has charged the appropriate minister with the duty of co-ordinating all local endeavours and bringing them into line with national standards. The Minister of Housing and Local Government is required to secure

> "consistency and continuity in the framing and execution of a national policy with respect to the use and development of land throughout England and Wales".

The Minister of Education has the duty

> "to promote the education of the people of England and Wales and the progressive development of institutions devoted to that purpose, and to secure the operative execution by local authorities, under his control and direction, of the national policy for providing a varied and comprehensive educational service in every area".

Similar phraseology in recent statutes emphasises the controlling executive influence of the central department and the subordinate administrative function and limited discretion of the local authorities. This is further reinforced by the requirement of certain acts, e.g. the Education Act 1944 and the National Health Service Act 1946, for local authorities to submit their plans or proposals for approval by the appropriate department and also to submit reports and various returns such as the annual returns of income and expenditure.

B. *The Issue of Orders, Regulations, Directions and Circulars*

Much contemporary legislation is confined to broad principles
of policy and confers upon the responsible Minister and his department powers to make orders, regulations, directions, generally
referred to as statutory instruments which fill in the detail of such
legislation. Thus the Secretary of State for Education will make
regulations which prescribe standards to which local education
authorities have to conform, regarding school premises, or attach
conditions to the receipt of a grant. Similarly, the Minister may issue
general or specific directions to local authorities as to the way they
are to exercise their statutory powers or duties, and if the local authorities are given discretionary powers and are deemed by the Department to have acted unreasonably the Minister may exercise the powers
himself, or in the words of the Education Act 1944:

> "give such directions as to the exercise of the power or the
> performance of the duty as appears to him to be expedient".

In this respect, Sir W. O. Hart has written,

> "Powers which thus permit local discretion to be overruled by
> the Central Departments go a long way to destroy the idea of
> local self-government and reduce local authorities to little more
> than agents of the Central Government".

Departmental circulars amplify, explain and give guidance to local
authorities on the provisions of various acts and also explain changes
in governmental financial policy and communicate the particular
department's attitude towards economic and financial measures and
the department's likely response in the light of such measures to local
authority proposals.

C. *Central Inspection and Inquiries*

Since assistant commissioners were appointed after 1834 to inspect
the manner in which the poor law was administered, subsequent
legislation has made provision for the inspection of services by
departmental officers to ensure adherence to national standards.
Thus Her Majesty's Inspectors of Schools visit all educational
establishments and Inspectors of Constabulary visit police authorities,
and their grant in aid is dependent upon a satisfactory certificate of
efficiency from the inspectorate.

Under various acts Ministers are empowered to hold inquiries and
section 290 of the Local Government Act 1933, stipulates the powers
to direct such inquiries and the procedure to be followed. Any person
may be required to attend and may give evidence on oath and
produce any documents in his possession. The costs of the inquiry

will be paid by the local authority "or party to the inquiry as the department may direct", but the practice of awarding costs is not generally adopted. Where permitted by the appropriate act, the simplified procedure of an "informal hearing" may be adopted, and since the Franks Committee recommendations of 1957 the Minister now gives his reasons for a decision and makes available a copy of the inspector's report and findings. Examples of local inquiries would include planning appeals or objections to proposals to acquire land by compulsory purchase order. In 1965 the Ministry of Housing and Local Government alone held 5,490 inquiries.

D. Financial Control is exercised in three ways:

1. *Control over Grants.* The receipt of grant aid has always been conditional upon the right of central government to supervise the way it is spent. In theory, a local authority does not have to accept a grant in aid but where the cost of a service can be reduced by a proffered grant the council is unlikely to refuse it unless it is prepared to face the aggrieved ratepayers' wrath. The receipt of grants has thus been accompanied by departmental control: the Home Office exercising considerable control over the police, the Department of Education and Science over educational provisions, the Ministry of Housing and Local Government over housing. Unreasonable expenditure by a local authority or inefficiency in the maintenance of standards may result in the grant being reduced or withheld, and the threat of such action is invariably sufficient to keep local authorities vigilant. In such a manner does the government call the tune, and it may reasonably be argued that central control over grants is at once the most direct and debilitating control over local authorities.

2. *The Audit.* With the exception of borough councils, the accounts of all local authorities, their committees and their officers must be audited by district auditors who are civil servants appointed by the Minister of Housing and Local Government and assigned to prescribed districts. The Municipal Corporations Act 1835, did not make provision for audit by central government, and since that time a borough is not subject to district audit but its council may resolve to adopt a district audit or a professional one. If the council decides on the latter, the auditors must be qualified. Alternatively, the borough may have its accounts audited by three borough auditors, two elected by the local government electors, and called elective auditors, and one appointed by the mayor and called the mayor's auditor. None need be qualified and they are not allowed to be members or officers of the council, but they must be qualified to stand as councillors. Their term of office is one year and they do not have the power of

disallowance or surcharge. There will, of course, be an internal audit conducted by the borough's chief finance officer.

The accounts must be made up yearly to 31 March and will be audited as soon as possible thereafter. The auditor's report must be sent to the local authority within fourteen days of the audit's completion. The accounts must, however, be available for inspection and copying by any interested person for seven clear days before the audit, and notice of the deposit of accounts must be made in the local newspapers at least fourteen days beforehand. Any elector for the area may object to the accounts before the auditor and if aggrieved by the auditor's decision may appeal to the High Court.

The district auditor's duties are: (i) to disallow every item of account which is contrary to law; (ii) to surcharge the amount of any expenditure disallowed upon the person responsible for incurring or authorising the expenditure; (iii) to surcharge any sum which has not been duly brought into account upon the person by whom that sum ought to have been brought into account; (iv) to surcharge the amount of any loss or deficiency upon any person by whose negligence or misconduct the loss or deficiency has been incurred; (v) to certify the amount due from any person upon whom he has made a surcharge; (vi) to certify at the conclusion of the audit his allowance of the accounts, subject to any disallowances and surcharges which he may have made. The Maud Report regarded the fear of surcharge as an inhibiting influence on the attitudes of members and officers and consequently recommended (para. 290) its abolition.

No expenses paid by an authority shall be disallowed by the auditor if they have been sanctioned by the Minister of Housing and Local Government, whether legal or not. Any person who is aggrieved by a disallowance or surcharge made by the local authority may, where they relate to an amount exceeding £500, appeal to the High Court; and in any other case may appeal to the High Court or the Minister. The Court and the Minister are then empowered to confirm, vary or quash the auditor's decision. In the case of surcharge the person surcharged may apply for a declaration that he acted reasonably or in the belief that his action was authorised by law, and if the Court or Minister thinks he should be excused from personal liability a declaration to that effect may be made.

The district auditor is not completely excluded from boroughs for he audits the rate fund, the accounts of any joint committee which has representatives from any authority subject to district audit, the housing and road accounts of boroughs and the accounts of sub-committees who exercise functions under the Education, National Health Service, National Assistance, Children, and Coast Protection Acts.

3. *Control over Borrowing*. This has already been considered in the section on the capital account of local authorities. Their borrowing powers require in almost every case the consent of the Minister of Housing and Local Government whose decision will be influenced by many factors, including the local authority's financial situation, the advice of his experts, the results of a local inquiry if one is held and the prevailing national economic policy.

E. *Control over Officers*

It has previously been noted that local authorities are statutorily obliged to employ certain officers and that some government departments exercise control over their appointment, dismissal and payment. The original justification was to ensure the availability of properly qualified functionaries to administer services where high national standards of efficiency had to be maintained and where a degree of independence from the control of the local authority would ensure that no local pressure should affect the quality of the service or the incumbent's security of tenure. Every council, apart from a parish council, must appoint a clerk whose remuneration in a county is a matter for ministerial approval and his dismissal requires the prior consent of the Minister of Housing and Local Government. Central control may be reinforced by making the grant conditional upon the appointment of an officer, for example, the Chief Constable, and his appointment is subject to the Home Secretary's approval. Similarly, no Local Education Authority may appoint a chief education officer without first consulting the Secretary of State for Education who has the right to veto the appointment. Even where services are not grant-aided similar controls exist—for example, the Minister of Health will prescribe the duties of all Medical Officers of Health and their qualifications, and they may not be dismissed without the prior consent of the Minister.

F. *Power to act in Default*

Government departments are empowered by various statutes to deal with local authorities who fail to discharge their appropriate functions. Under the Public Health Act 1936, the Minister may make an order declaring a particular local authority to be in default and direct it to perform its duty within a specified time; if the local authority refuses to comply with the order, the Minister may enforce it in the courts. In the case of a defaulting county district he may make an order to transfer the function to the county council, and where the defaulting authority is a county or county borough he may make an order transferring the function to himself. The cost of performing the transferred function will in either case remain with the defaulting authority. Similar powers are exercisable by the Minister in respect of housing, with the one difference that the county council makes the enquiry into the default of a rural district council and is empowered by order to transfer the function to itself. Under the Education Act 1944, the Minister of Education may make an order declaring a Local Education Authority or the managers or governors of a county or voluntary school who have not discharged a duty, to be in default, and give "such directions for the purpose of enforcing the execution thereof as appear to the Minister to be expedient". Such directions will be enforceable in the courts.

Default powers are nowadays included in all legislation relating to local government and constitute a last-resort check upon local authorities who fail to exercise their proper duties. Local authorities do not generally ignore their obligations, and the Minister is rarely called upon to exercise his powers. The knowledge that the powers exist is an adequate deterrent.

G. Confirmation of Bye-Laws

County and borough councils may make bye-laws for "good rule and government" and "for the prevention and suppression of nuisances". Additionally, almost every local government statute confers the power on different authorities to make bye-laws for a variety of services and may establish new offences and fines, but in every case there must be a "confirming authority" to whom bye-laws must be submitted for confirmation or rejection. The confirming authority for bye-laws relating to "good rule and government" will be the Home Secretary, and for public health matters, the Minister of Housing and Local Government and, where appropriate, the Minister of Health and of Agriculture, Fisheries and Food. The appropriate person or authority will be specified in the Act. Moreover, local authorities, in framing bye-laws, are advised to follow the uniform pattern of "Model Bye-Laws" issued by the Ministry of Housing and Local Government, and should they deviate from the model, government departments will invariably reject the bye-law unless there is some local justification.

H. Powers of Adjudication

The Minister will be required to exercise a judicial role in the following cases:

1. Disputes between authorities over responsibility for the provision of a service or the division of expenses payable to a joint committee.

2. Disputes between a local authority and its officers will in certain cases be referred to the appropriate Minister, e.g. a dismissed constable, a public health inspector or a medical officer of health.

3. Disputes between a local authority and private individuals—where public and private interests conflict over such a matter as a compulsory purchase order for private property required by a local authority the Minister will hold a public inquiry or private hearing to decide whether the order is to be confirmed.

3. Judicial Control

Until the nineteenth century the administrative powers to deal with local government matters were vested in the J.Ps. who exercised them in the Courts of Petty and Quarter Sessions. Though dealing with administrative matters, in the eyes of the law these were primarily courts of justice subject to the judicial control of the King's Bench so that J.Ps. could be restrained from exceeding their legal administrative powers and be compelled to do their duty. When the J.Ps. were stripped of their administrative functions this judicial control continued and the Queen's Bench Division of the High Court still exercises supervisory jurisdiction over the activities of the local authorities by means of the Orders of mandamus, certiorari and prohibition.

A. *Order of Mandamus*

This is a High Court Order which compels any local authority to discharge its statutory, though not discretionary, duties where no other remedy is convenient, e.g. to require the election of a mayor, alderman or Town Clerk or the levying of a rate. Non-compliance with an order of mandamus may lead to imprisonment for contempt of those members of a local authority refusing to comply with its terms, e.g. *R.* v. *Poplar Borough Council*, [1922] 1 K.B. 72. In *R.* v. *Bedwellty Urban District Council*, [1934] 1 K.B. 333 mandamus was obtained by a ratepayer to compel production of the local authority's accounts, but in those cases where the statute itself provides a remedy when there is non-compliance mandamus will not lie.

B. *Certiorari*

This is an order which removes a case from an inferior court into the Queen's Bench Division of the High Court. So far as local authorities are concerned it extends to those acts which are quasi-judicial e.g. where the local authority can impose a liability or make decisions which determine the rights or property of the parties concerned.

In *R.* v. *Hendon Rural District Council*, [1933] 2 K.B. 696 the order of certiorari was used to quash a decision granting development permission because a council member interested in the use of the land had voted on the resolution.

16

C. *Prohibition*

This order restrains an inferior court or tribunal from proceeding when it has no jurisdiction. It is frequently sought along with certiorari so that the act complained of may be reviewed to determine its validity and at the same time prevent its operation, e.g. *R.* v. *Paddington and St. Marylebone Rent Tribunal*, [1949] 1 K.B. 666 and *R.* v. *Northumberland Appeal Tribunal*, [1951] 1 K.B. 711.

In a wider sense the term "judicial control" includes all matters concerning local government which may come before the Courts. Local authorities, being incorporated bodies, can be sued in the courts for wrongs deemed to have been committed by them, hence they are vicariously liable for damages in respect of torts committed by their servants in the course of their employment. Since the decision in *Cassidy* v. *Ministry of Health*, [1951] 2 K.B. 343 the term "servant" has been extended to include even professional persons over whom the authority concerned has the ultimate power of dismissal. On the other hand it must be remembered that an official appointed by a local authority who in his official capacity exercises an independent public duty placed on him directly by law is not a servant of the authority, e.g., a police officer.

Apart from boroughs incorporated by Royal Charter, local authorities are statutory corporations incorporated by Act of Parliament and therefore subject to all implications of the *ultra vires* doctrine. This means that the ambit and extent of the powers and duties conferred on local authorities are contained in Statutes and that nothing shall be done beyond that ambit. Should the powers and duties laid down be exceeded the action is *ultra vires* and void, e.g. *Prescott* v. *Birmingham Corporation*, [1955] Ch 210. A resolution of the Birmingham City Council to allow old age pensioners to travel free on its trains and buses was *ultra vires* as the private acts of Parliament under which the City of Birmingham operated a transport system required it to charge such fares as it thought fit.

Borough Councils are prima facie not subject to the *ultra vires* rule as common law corporations, yet they are not permitted to infringe statutory limitations imposed on them and, in this respect, like other local authorities are subject to the *ultra vires* doctrine.

Any aggrieved person wishing to question the validity of a decision of a local authority alleged to be *ultra vires* may appeal to the court for an injunction or a declaration.

D. *Injunction and Declaration*

An injunction is an order of the High Court which prevents a specific act from being carried out, whilst a declaration is simply a statement made by the court concerning the rights of the plaintiff but of itself provides no method of enforcing them. For example, a rate-payer who wishes to contest his liability to pay rates may bring an action for a declaration against the rating authority—*Waterson* v. *Hendon Borough Council*, [1959] 2 All E.R. 760.

Apart from the two exceptional cases[1] laid down in *Boyce* v. *Paddington Borough Council*, [1906] A.C. 1; 75, an action for an injunction or declaration in respect of public rights or interests has to be brought at the suit of the Attorney General to avoid unnecessary litigation, e.g. where a local authority is accused of failing to prevent its sewers from polluting rivers as laid down in Public Health legislation.

A private individual may sue either when the interference with the public right also amounts to an interference with a private right of the plaintiff or, though no private right is infringed, the plaintiff suffers some special damage peculiar to himself. For example, where an obstruction of the highway is also an interference with a private right of access to the highway or where as a result of a public nuisance a person's premises have been made unfit for habitation.

E. *Statutory Appeals*

The statutory powers conferred on local authorities sometimes conflict with the interests of private persons. In order that individuals may avoid the necessity of having to resort to an injunction or any of the Orders specified above, he is allowed right of appeal. This may take the following forms:

1. Appeals to Justices. The J.Ps. sitting in local courts of summary jurisdiction or in Quarter Sessions may hear appeals under the provisions of various statutes against local authority decisions e.g. the refusal to grant a licence to carry on a particular business.

2. Appeals to the County Court. Housing legislation since 1930 allows appeals to the County Court by a person whose local authority has issued an order in respect of insanitary housing requiring its repair, its demolition or the closure of part of the house.

3. Appeals to the High Court. An aggrieved party may have right of statutory appeal against, for example, a clearance or compulsory purchase order where these are made by the local authority supported by the Ministry of Housing and Local Government. The High Court can quash the order only if it were made *ultra vires* or if there were a failure to comply with a statutory requirement.

The controls established during the war and the transfer of gas, electricity and hospitals from local authorities led to the appointment

---

[1] W. O. Hart, *Introduction to Local Government*, (6th Ed.), Butterworths, p. 362.

of the Local Government Manpower Committee, and one of its terms of reference was

> "to examine in particular the distribution of functions between central and local government and the possibility of relaxing departmental supervision of local authority activities and delegating more responsibility to local authorities".[2]

The Memorandum of Guidance to its five sub-committees outlined its "General Approach" as follows:

> "To recognise that the local authorities are responsible bodies competent to discharge their own functions and that, though they may be the statutory bodies through which Government policy is given effect and operate to a large extent with Government money, they exercise their responsibilities in their own right, not ordinarily as agents of Government Departments. It follows that the objective should be to leave as much as possible of the detailed management of a scheme or service to the local authority and to concentrate the Department's control at the key points where it can most effectively discharge its responsibilities for Government policy and financial administration".

This was the desired working relationship, and the sub-committees, appointed to examine the services supervised by the Home Office, Ministry of Health, Ministry of Education, Ministry of Town and Country Planning and Ministry of Transport, presented their reports containing revised procedures and arrangements. However, as Sir Francis Hill has observed, "not much came of it at last".[3] The controls remained and their application depends very much upon the differing attitude of the various central departments and their civil servants.[4] The formal controls outlined are reinforced by such developing practices as ministries dealing directly with chief officers and by-passing the council or its clerk, or the appointment of informal advisory groups which are made up of members of local authorities who do not specifically represent them nor the associations.

In *Central Departments and Local Authorities* J. A. G. Griffith underlines four major defects in the central-local relationship: policy is insufficiently defined to give local authorities the freedom to make their own decisions within that policy; there are too many small

---

[2] "First Report of the Local Government Manpower Committee", 1950, (Cmd. 7870).

[3] "The Partnership in Theory and Practice", *The Political Quarterly* Vol. 37, No. 2, April–June, 1966, p. 175. See also *Redcliffe–Maud Report*, Vol. 1, p. 30.

[4] J. A. G. Griffith comments in *Central Departments and Local Authorities*, Allen & Unwin, 1966, on the *laissez-faire* approach of the Ministry of Health, the regulatory attitude of the Home Office and the promotional attitude of the Department of Education and Science.

authorities both for present and future tasks; local authorities are financially too dependent on the central departments; and the departments are failing to collect and disseminate necessary information.

The fears of local authorities, grasping at their straws of autonomy, are made articulate at various annual conferences and by individuals who perceive the eclipse of local self-government and condemn the state's centralising tendencies. Professor Robson writes of "Local Government in Crisis" and diagnoses its malaise, while others criticise individual controls particularly the financial dependence of local authorities and the restrictive influence of the doctrine of *ultra vires*.

"It is one of those unfortunate historical anomalies—one of the archaic bits of machinery which we must sweep away",

said Sir John Maud to the Society of Town Clerks,[5] and his opinion re-echoes that of many who sense the underlying frustration of enterprising local authorities against the more pettifogging restrictions of *ultra vires*.[6] The Maud Report on Management in 1967 condemned the "deleterious effect" of *ultra vires* "because of the narrowness of the legislation governing local authorities' activities. The specific nature of legislation discourages enterprise, handicaps development, robs the community of services which the local authority might render, and encourages too rigorous oversight by the central government. It contributes to the excessive concern over legalities and fosters the idea that the Clerk should be a lawyer.... The evidence clearly points to the desirability of softening the rigours of the *ulta vires* doctrine".

The Report commented on the relative freedom enjoyed by local authorities abroad from statutory restrictions, and recommended not so much the abolition of *ultra vires* but the granting of a "general competence" to enable local authorities "to do (in addition to what legislation already requires or permits them to do) whatever in their opinion is in the interests of their areas or their inhabitants subject to their not encroaching on the duties of other governmental bodies and to appropriate safeguards for the protection of public and private interests". Additionally, it was recommended that the government should consult with the associations to examine what provisions might be repealed in order to provide authorities with maximum freedom to carry out their work.

---

[5] *The Local Government Chronicle*, 9 July, 1966.
[6] See "The Too-Narrow Powers of Council", by Brian Keith-Lucas in *Local Government To-day and Tomorrow* (ed. D. Lofts), Municipal Journal Ltd., pp. 27–32, and the *Maud Report*, Vol. 1, paras. 266–269, 283–286.

In conclusion, it might be added that any unsatisfactory dependency relationship, particularly one between major and powerful bodies like government departments and local authorities, will contain frustrating elements which could create in the subordinate partner hostility and the desire for independence and autonomy. The defects which have been mentioned go beyond hostility, however, and relate to matters which appear to be seriously undermining local self-government. It is obviously essential for Government departments to ensure that services are uniformly provided, and a measure of supervision and inspection will naturally follow. Does this necessitate, however, the almost complete negation of local discretion and the extension of central control well beyond the "key points" and into the detailed day-to-day management of services?

CHAPTER 10

The Future System
of Local Government

In presenting the Government's White Paper *Reform of Local Government in England* (Cmnd. 4276) on 4th February, 1970, the Secretary of State for Local Government and Regional Planning stated that there was widespread agreement that major structural reform was required and that the proposals of the Redcliffe-Maud Commission, with certain changes, provided the best basis for reorganisation.

The main conclusions set out in the White Paper were:

1. The Government retained 51 of the 58 unitary areas proposed by the Royal Commission. Of the remaining 7 unitary areas, the 5 in West Yorkshire (Bradford, Leeds, Halifax, Huddersfield, and Mid-Yorkshire) would form a new metropolitan area with each of the 5 becoming a metropolitan district; and the 2 unitary areas in South Hampshire (Southampton-South Hampshire and Portsmouth-South East Hampshire-Isle of Wight) would be combined to form another new metropolitan area with 3 metropolitan districts. The West Yorkshire changes were made because of interlocking problems of housing, pressure on land, particularly between towns, and a changing pattern of employment. In South Hampshire rapid and accelerating expansion of the two major towns towards each other, and the exceptional circumstances of the Isle of Wight, justified 3 districts.

2. Five metropolitan areas should be created comprising the 3 recommended by the Redcliffe-Maud Report (viz. Merseyside, Selnec and the West Midlands) plus the two new areas of West Yorkshire and South Hampshire, as detailed above.[1]

3. The Royal Commission's proposal for eight provincial councils was deferred until the Commission on the Constitution (the Crowther Commission) reported. The work of the Regional Economic Planning

---

[1] Thus 42% of England's population would live under a two-tier rather than a unitary system.

Councils would therefore continue and enter a new phase of co-operation with local government for planning purposes.

4. The Government adopted the Commission's recommendations for local councils throughout unitary areas and where people wanted them in the metropolitan areas. The Government believed "the basic concept to be of profound importance" but that it should be developed further if the councils were to be fully effective. Whereas the Government agreed that local councils should have power, at their own expense, to make their areas more attractive, convenient and agreeable to live in, it did not accept the Commission's suggestion that the larger local councils should play a part in the provision of major services. The right of local councils to be consulted by the main authorities about decisions which affected their areas was emphasised, as was the right of the members of local councils to serve on district committees to which unitary authorities would decentralise some of their administration. Local councils would have the right to appoint members of school governing bodies, management and house committees of old people's and children's homes respectively, and of "as wide a variety as possible of other bodies". Local councils would be based initially on the areas of existing authorities, but new areas would be worked out as soon as the main reorganisation had been completed. There should be no attempt to impose a uniform pattern, and voluntary amalgamations of small authorities would be considered. In unitary areas, the existing council of a town or city with a population of over 100,000 could decide whether to continue in being or whether it should be divided into a number of neighbourhood or community councils.

5. Councillors are to remain unpaid, but the Government intended to work out substantial improvements in allowances. There would be further discussions about the size of councils, the timing of elections, whether the term of service should be extended to 4 years and whether there should be single-member divisions. Councils should no longer include aldermen, and their future in Greater London would be the subject of consultation. The Government also wished to liberalise the law which disqualified local government employees from sitting on the council which employed them.

6. The Government agreed that councillors should concern themselves primarily with policy, that there should be fewer committees, and that more detail should be delegated to officers. "These and other matters of internal business should . . . be left to the authorities concerned; there should be a minimum of general rules and plenty of experiment".

7. The Government generally agreed with the Royal Commission's

division of functions between the two tiers in metropolitan areas, with the major exception of education. In spite of the arguments of the Commission and the Seebohm Committee, it was felt that education should be made the responsibility of the upper-tier authority which could command large resources.

8. The Government rejected the Royal Commission's proposal that the national health service should be managed within the new local government system, but endorsed the Commission's view that the unified health service and the local authority personal social services must be closely co-ordinated. A Green Paper on the revision of health service administration was subsequently published on 11th February, 1970, and announced that the N.H.S. would be administered not by local government but by about ninety area health authorities which would be closely associated with local authorities and would serve the same areas for which the new unitary areas and metropolitan districts would be providing personal social services. Among the services which would be administered by the area health authorities would be the following which are presently provided by local health authorities: ambulances; epidemiological work; family planning; health centres; health visiting; home nursing and midwifery; maternity and child health care; prevention of illness, care and after care, through medical, nursing and allied services; residential accommodation for those needing continuing medical supervision and not ready to live in the community; and vaccination and immunisation. The various services making up the school health service will also be administered by the area health authorities.

9. Appendix D related to services for which special arrangements might be needed and these included:

(i) *Police:* there should be one police force for the whole of each metropolitan area and for single or combined unitary areas.

(ii) *Fire:* arrangements would be considered when the Holroyd Committee reported.

(iii) *Passenger transport authorities:* the areas of P.T.A.s established under the Transport Act 1968 would be expanded to coincide with those of the metropolitan areas of Merseyside, Selnec and the West Midlands, and the unitary authority for Tyneside. In the rest of the country the main authorities would assume control of any existing municipal transport.

(iv) *Water:* the Central Advisory Water Committee would report on a special study in time for legislation.

(v) *National Parks in England:* each national park would be administered by an ad hoc authority, but country parks, serving a more local purpose, should be administered by the unitary and metropolitan authorities within which they lie.

17

(vi) *Youth Employment Service:* the future of this service is under
consideration.

10. A Green Paper was proposed which would discuss local government finance in depth. The Government shared the Commission's
view that "rates must remain the principal local tax", but that the
rating system needed modernisation. Detailed governmental control
over borrowing would be replaced by control through programmes
in respect of the more important sectors of the major services, and by
allowing "a significant freedom of decision" by way of an unallocated
margin of expenditure for the remaining services.

11. The Government would undertake a review of non-financial
controls which are obsolete and those which will be inappropriate
with large authorities, and have asked the local authority associations
to say which controls should be removed. The Government also
accepted the Commission's recommendation for a reduction in statutory control over the internal administration of local authorities, and
were sympathetic in principle to the proposal that the new main
authorities should have a revised and extended general power to
spend money for the benefit of their areas and inhabitants.

12. Ten or more "Local Commissioners for Administration"
should be appointed, each working independently in a particular
part of the country and reporting to local authorities and local
electorates. Complaints would be routed to them through the councillors.

13. No change in the structure or functions of the Greater London
authorities was proposed.

14. A White Paper on the future structure of local government in
Scotland was to be laid before Parliament in the Spring of 1970. Conclusions on a further review of Glamorgan and Monmouthshire were
also to be reported to Parliament shortly. Owing to the geographical
and historical differences of England, Wales and Scotland it would be
"inappropriate to try to force the structure of local government into
the same mould for each". Nevertheless, the unitary system was
suggested for Glamorgan and Monmouthshire in a White Paper,[2]
published in March 1970, which recommended three unitary
authorities for the area of the two counties.

15. A Bill to introduce the new system should be brought before
Parliament in the 1971–72 session. The new authorities should be

---

[2] *Local Government Reorganisation in Glamorgan and Monmouthshire*, Cmnd. 4310,
March, 1970. The unitary authorities are Swansea and West Glamorgan, Cardiff
and East Glamorgan, and Newport and Monmouthshire.

elected in 1973 and should take over from the existing authorities as soon as possible thereafter. To safeguard the interests of local government officers, and to help the new authorities in staffing themselves, a Local Government Staff Commission would be set up.

"The organisation of local government must always be contentious. Many people will differ from the conclusions revealed in this White Paper. The same would be true of any other set of conclusions. But all must be impressed by the general agreement that, not withstanding, the great achievements of the existing authorities, radical change is overdue. And only if such change occurs, and local government is organised in strong units with power to take major decisions, will present trends towards centralisation be reversed, and local democracy resume its place as a major part of our democratic system".

Index